VISIONS OF HEAVEN AND HELL BEFORE DANTE

To Nancy
With best wishes

VISIONS OF HEAVEN AND HELL BEFORE DANTE

*

EDITED BY
EILEEN GARDINER

ILLUSTRATIONS BY
ALEXANDRA ELDRIDGE

ITALICA PRESS
NEW YORK
1989

ITALICA PRESS, INC.
595 Main Street
New York, New York 10044

Library of Congress Cataloging-in-Publication Data

Visions of heaven and hell before Dante.

     Bibliography: p.
     Includes index.
     Contents: St. Peter's apocalypse — St. Paul's apocalypse — Furseus' vision — [etc.]
     1. Heaven —Early works to 1800. 2. Hell—Early works to 1800. 3. Visions—Early works to 1800.
I. Gardiner, Eileen.
BT844.V57   1988   236'.24   88-45731
ISBN 0-934977-14-3

Printed in the United States of America
5 4 3 2 1

Cover Art: Alexandra Eldridge

ABOUT THE EDITOR

Eileen Gardiner is an editor and publisher and lifetime resident of New York City. She received her Ph.D. in English Literature and Medieval Studies from Fordham University and has published previously on the *Vision of Tundale* and other medieval topics.

ABOUT THE ARTIST

Alexandra Eldridge has been painting and illustrating for the last twenty years. She now resides in Santa Fe, New Mexico with her two sons.

CONTENTS

Preface   ix
Introduction   xi

St. Peter's Apocalypse   1
St. Paul's Apocalypse   13
Three Visions from Gregory the Great   47
Furseus' Vision   51
Drythelm's Vision   57
Wetti's Vision   65
St. Brendan's Voyage   81
Charles the Fat's Vision   129
St. Patrick's Purgatory   135
Tundale's Vision   149
The Monk of Evesham's Vision   197
Thurkill's Vision   219

Notes & Primary Sources   237
Glossary   265
Abbreviations   276
Bibliography of Secondary Sources   277
Index   279

PREFACE

The following volume presents a collection of twelve of the most important, best known, and most influential medieval visions of heaven and hell written before Dante's *Divine Comedy*. They are arranged chronologically from the apocalyptic books of the second and fourth centuries to the literary visions of northern Europe dating from the late thirteenth century.

Many of the visions collected here were most recently translated in the nineteenth and early twentieth centuries and are now difficult to obtain. These have been edited to present readable versions of the texts for a contemporary audience. The translations from Latin of *Tundale's Vision* and *Wetti's Vision* are new; as with the other visions, however, the emphasis was on creating a readable text for a contemporary audience. Scholars wishing to refer to these visions should, of course, consult the original-language editions. Any extensive introductory material that was not part of the actual vision has been omitted. This material may often provide details about the composition of the vision but not about the vision itself.

The Notes provided for each vision present background information on the individual works. Entries in the Notes includes references to the primary sources for each vision. At the end of the Notes is an alphabetical list of many of the less-known visions that have been omitted from this collection. The Bibliography includes important secondary works on vision literature. This volume also includes a Glossary of Terms, particularly religious terms that may not be familiar to a general reader. In addition to proper names, the Index includes selected iconographic details from the otherworld descriptions.

*

INTRODUCTION

THE CONTEXT

Perhaps it is the state of the world, perhaps the state of the individual in contemporary mass society, but whatever it is, something is engendering a great interest in literature of the imagination – literature presenting speculations on realms beyond our daily physical existence. Science Fiction is the most obvious and most popular manifestation of this trend, but the genre of imaginary travel literature, which has included works like *Mandeville's Travels* and *Robinson Crusoe*, is being regenerated with works like Jan Morris' *Last Letters from Hav* and Italo Calvino's *Invisible Cities*.

If we examine further we find that each year many new scholarly books appear on out-of-body experiences, the concepts of heaven and hell, the devil, and mysticism.[1] Scholars are examining these concepts and the function they serve as symbols and archetypes for the individual psyche and for society. As fascinating as all these subjects are, it is our purpose here to look more closely at only one manifestation of this type of literature – medieval visions of heaven and hell. We conclude our study at Dante because *The Divine Comedy* was the culmination of the entire body of medieval imaginative literature on the subject of the otherworld. His systematization of the cosmology of the otherworld seems to have ended the speculation of the medieval mind on the topic.

THE GENRE

Visions of heaven and hell are narratives that attempt to describe the afterlife in terms of an otherworld, a world beyond this life. The subject of this collection, medieval Christian visions of heaven and hell, reflect the belief that at death the soul is separated from the body. It is then judged according to the life it has lived on earth and assigned a place in the otherworld until the Last Judgment, when it will be assigned its final place for all eternity.

The otherworld was certainly not an idea unique to Christianity. Otherworlds were constructed at earlier times and in other cultures, such as the Buddhist, Brahman, Persian, Egyptian, Jewish and Western Classical cultures. These cultures influenced Christianity's understanding[2] of exactly what the otherworld was – whether a place for only the gods, whether a place to which people travelled after death, a place where they might be punished and rewarded, or just a place of continued existence. Christianity also drew from these cultures a vocabulary for describing the physical appearance and geography of the otherworld – whether it would contain rivers and bridges, pits and fires, flowers and fields, music, dancing and food. Such descriptions drew on a large body of sources, such as the Buddhist descriptions of hell, the Persian bridge of judgment, the visits to the underworld in Virgil and Homer, and the apocryphal *Book of Enoch*.

These visions also seem to have been influenced by the penitential literature that was of great importance especially in the early Irish tradition, with which many of these visions are associated.[3] These penitentials were actual handbooks for confessors who regulated the repentance process in their communities. They were used from about the fifth century to the eleventh century, when they were incorporated into the emerging canon-law collections sanctioned by the church.

Until the mid-twelfth century there was no distinct place known as purgatory.[4] The Christian otherworld included only heaven and hell. Purgation was, however, a part of the afterlife, and the place of purgation occupied the outer reaches of either hell or heaven, depending on whether the soul was "good but not totally good" or "bad but not totally bad." The former might spend some time waiting outside the walls of heaven in wind and rain, while the latter might spend some time wading through fire and ice above the pit of hell. In the mid-twelfth century the concept of purgatory as a separate and distinct place was formalized, but the visions included here, those written after the *Book of Revelation* of John and before *The Divine Comedy* of Dante, concern themselves with only heaven and hell.

These visions were extremely popular literary works. They were often initially written as records of the vision itself. Later they might be modified or expanded. Because these visions were believed to be factual and not fictional, they were often also incorporated into chronicles of the period.[5] They were obviously used as didactic pieces in the church and were therefore actively preserved and disseminated. Generally a vision would be translated into many different languages and spread in manuscript throughout Europe.

A good example of this process is evident in the literary life of *Tundale's Vision*. The vision itself dates from 1149 and is said to have occurred in Ireland. During the following year an Irish monk who was travelling through Europe stopped at Regensburg in Bavaria and wrote down this vision in Latin at the request of the Abbess G. of a convent there. It was translated into German shortly thereafter. By the end of the fourteenth century it had been translated into at least thirteen languages, including Serbo-Croatian. Many of the manuscripts of *Tundale's Vision* also include pious tracts, such as works on the nature of the Holy Eucharist. As late as 1400 there was a verse translation into Middle English. It preserves and elaborates the most fantastic details of this vision but minimizes the more theological issues. The vision had made its way back to the British Isles after a long and impressive career, but was now included in manuscripts with romances and other fictional works.[6] Today there is hardly a medieval manuscript collection of any importance in Europe that does not contain at least one copy of this vision.

The incredible vitality of this genre is evident in the many different ways that monks and nuns, poets and popes, mystics and theologians were able to use the material of these visions to create unique works. In general, however, these visions share a great deal of common material and ideas. In order to provide a guide to the reader for travelling through this body of literature, we can point out these similarities. The collection of texts that follows will allow the reader to observe the changing nature of these works.

Introduction

THE ELEMENTS OF VISION LITERATURE

Generally these visions involve one individual visionary, in all cases here a man. On the extreme ends the visionary might be a saintly figure, like St. Paul or St. Peter, or a sinner like the knight Owen in *St. Patrick's Purgatory* or the Irish knight Tundale, who was notorious among his contemporaries for his boisterous life. There are medieval visions in which the visionary is a woman, but these tended to be mystical tracts and never entered the canon of the popular literature or had the influence of those works that have been included here. Much new work is being done to reintroduce these neglected works. Although it is not within the scope of this book to examine these works and why they have been omitted from the canon, it will be important for the reader to bear in mind that we are dealing solely with works by men and that their imagery is, therefore, essentially masculine.

After a short introduction the vision begins when the soul of the visionary is separated from his body. *St. Peter's Apocalypse* is what might strictly be called a vision in that there is no separation of body and soul, and the vision comes to him. In others there might actually be a journey involved, as in *St. Brendan's Voyage,* and no separation of the body from the soul. But in most cases the soul leaves the body, and the visionary appears to be dead. But because he also appears to be not quite fully dead – a slight breath or a little bodily warmth might remain – his friends and family do not bury him immediately. He usually lies as if dead for three days, while his soul views heaven and hell.

The soul is usually accompanied by a guide. This might be the guardian angel who was responsible for this soul on earth, or it might be a saint who either was a family patron or who had some other special interest in the soul. The guide is responsible for enlightening the soul about the meaning of the places he sees and, indeed, the meaning of the journey itself. The guide also serves as a protector. He either prevents the soul from being hurt by the demons encountered in hell, or he heals the soul after he is wounded. The guide acts as a charm against the demons; or he might carry a charm, like the ball of light that the angel carries in *Charles the Fat's Vision*. In the darkness of hell the countenance of the guide is often the only source of light, since the fires of hell produce heat but no light. The knight Owen in *St. Patrick's Purgatory* has no guide, but he has counsel beforehand and has the name of "Jesus Christ" as a charm against the devils.

In most cases the visionary is led to hell first, descending toward the pit of hell. The descriptions of hell vary considerably. Many merely mention one or two places where the soul sees other souls in fire, tortured by demons. In some visions all the souls are grouped together no matter what sins they are guilty of. In others the souls are in the same place, but the degree of their punishment differs depending on the nature of their specific sins. The more highly developed works, like *Tundale's Vision,* have separate places and torments for each type of sin.

In visions where the types of sins are delineated, it is clear that different visions are preoccupied with different types of sins. The earlier works seem to follow more strictly all of the standard categories of sin as found in, for instance, the Ten Commandments or the early penitential literature described above. Later we find works that might be totally obsessed with one type of sin. Some concentrate on sins of a sexual nature, or even with a particular sexual sin, such as Wetti's obsession with homosexuality. If the modern reader finds the obsession with sexual sin, such as adultery, fornication, promiscuity and sodomy distasteful, he or she might take heart to note that in other visions an almost equal zeal is applied to punishing the wealthy, the powerful, and the corrupt.

If the visionary was a monk, and the vision was written down within a religious community for the edification of that community, the sins emphasized would most likely be those that violated a monastic rule. Other visions might concentrate on lack of charity, disloyalty to the church, and murder, especially in war. Focusing on a specific type of sin might arise because of the preoccupation of the visionary himself or the author who initially recorded the vision, the social, political or religious milieu in which the vision is recounted, or the literary life that the text of the vision had after the original experience has been documented. Although it is certainly not within our scope, these visions might be examined to determine whether a larger agenda, such as monastic reform or political struggle, might lurk beneath the surface of the text.

Like the penitentials mentioned above, which established a punishment for a specified length of time, the souls that the visionary encounters in hell are sometimes performing penance for a limited time as they proceed on their way to heaven. They are often in movement and are described as passing through a series of torments. These souls are undergoing the purgation that later would have occurred in purgatory itself. Finally the visionary is often led to see the pit of hell, the place from which no one escapes. Here with Lucifer, or Satan, the souls will suffer for all eternity. The mouth of hell, which is often used in

Last Judgment scenes in medieval sculpture and painting, is described in gruesome detail in several of these visions.

Punishment in hell almost universally involves fire. Often cold is added, and souls are tossed back and forth from one to the other. Pitchforks and other sharp implements are popular among the demons for moving the crowds of souls through the infernal regions. Awful smells and horrendous noise are often associated with hell, along with the assaults on the tactile and visual senses. The images invoked for the descriptions of hell are very often related to the masculine images of work provided by the nascent industrial economy. Forges, furnaces, hammers, smoke and burning metals combine to present a picture that would certainly be hellish to a rural, aristocratic and agrarian audience.

The demons usually inflict torments from the outside, but there are also vipers in many of the visions that infest the "bodies" of the souls and torture them by consuming their bones and flesh. Contemporary films, like *The Alien* and *Aliens,* attest to the perennial power of these hellish images found in works like *Tundale's Vision.*

As the visionary moves from hell toward heaven, he is often aware of a sweeter smell, more light, less noise or even sweet music. Heaven often is described in a mixed way including both ideal urban and natural elements.[7] The later are derived from descriptions of places like the Elysian Fields and are characterized by an abundance of trees, flowers and fruit. Often these scenes include the brightly colored pavilions that would usually be described in medieval romances.

The urban details are tied to both the developing urban sensibility in medieval Europe and an understanding of the Heavenly Jerusalem, which comes out of the *Book of*

Revelation. Yet the urban descriptions, though a highly developed medieval genre, are somewhat limited in these visions, as if their authors were not sure about what went into making an ideal city, and perhaps their audiences were really more likely to associate a real city with hell. These urban descriptions, however, always include beautiful walls, constructed of bright and precious materials. They might seem like gold and, like the Heavenly Jerusalem, are often full of gems and precious stones. There are buildings, often described as halls without walls, so that one can enter from all sides. The idea of entry seems important in these fanciful urban descriptions, because just as the halls or houses have no doors, which might be closed, the walls often have no gates, and the visionary finds himself miraculously on the other side of every wall he encounters.

As the visionary ascends through heaven he meets higher and higher levels of the blessed. It is a hierarchical society; but unlike earth where position is tied to birth, here one's place is determined by the spiritual achievements of the soul while it lived. The visionary moves among the married who maintained purity, the builders and defenders of churches, the virgins, and the martyrs. The next step is God. The visionary is often prevented from progressing just at this point and suddenly finds himself back inside his own body. Only the Monk of Evesham is shown Christ before he returns to his body, and this vision is the one that most closely resembles a mystical vision, with an ascent from purgation to illumination ending in union with the divine.[8] Most of the visions collected here, however, offer the visionary purgation and some degree of illumination, but definitely stop before divine union.

Purgation of the visionary occurs during his journey through hell. In many cases he is threatened with the torments that he will suffer if he does not amend his life when he is returned to his body. With *Furseus' Vision,* we encounter the first instance of a visionary, a soul, actually being punished. In hell he is hit by the soul of a sinner and burned on his face and shoulder. Tundale, who is a more serious sinner than Furseus, suffers incredible torments on his journey through hell. He is so handsomely described and so severely punished that we are obviously expected to sympathize with his plight and rejoice in his final salvation. Owen in *St. Patrick's Purgatory,* who has entered the Purgatory body and soul together for the sake of doing penance, is also tormented.

Illumination of the visionary is also an important feature of the vision. The soul goes on his "journey" for a specific purpose, and it is his enlightenment, so that either he himself will repent and reform or he will encourage others whom he knows or is about to meet on his return to repent and reform. He is generally counseled by his guide on what is expected of him after he returns to life. Sometimes the prophets or saints whom he meets in heaven tell him what he should concentrate on when he returns to his body. Occasionally he meets old acquaintances in hell or heaven who advise him. Only Thurkill seems to return from his vision with a weak idea of what is expected of him. Perhaps this is because his vision ends prematurely. His friends and relatives splash his body with cold water to see if they can revive him, and his guide, fearing that they will kill Thurkill by drowning him, quickly returns him back to his body. Thurkill, a generally reticent fellow, is then given another brief vision to let him know that he is expected to tell people what he has seen. The guide wants him to know that they did not go through all the trouble to provide him with a vision for him to waste their efforts by remaining silent about it. Wetti, on the other hand, is so traumatized by the injunctions made during his vision to tell everything exactly as it happened that he wants to disturb the whole monastery in the middle of the night so he can be sure to have his vision written down.

Again, these visions were written in the era before the concepts of heaven, hell, and purgatory were rigidified into tight intellectual and geographical compartments. Very often one of the most important messages brought back from the otherworld by the visionary is that those suffering in hell, who are slowly progressing toward heaven, could certainly benefit from the efforts of the living on their behalf. The visionary was often exhorted to encourage others to offer Masses, vigils, prayers, and alms for the souls of the dead.

THE NATURE OF THE VISION IN EXPERIENCE AND TEXT

The word "vision" is generally used to designate this type of work, but in fact "vision"[9] may not always be completely appropriate and may even be contrary to the spirit of some of these works. Although in all cases we are dealing primarily with a visual experience, in these works a great emphasis is often put on the visionary's experience of the otherworld through his other senses, such as smell, hearing and even taste. But most importantly, these visions are certainly presented as totally physical experiences, since the visionary often suffers pain and brings back the scars of torture from these "visions." Furseus and Tundale both suffer actual physical punishment. The knight Owen in *St. Patrick's Purgatory* also suffers a great deal, but unlike Tundale and Furseus, whose souls and bodies are separated for this experience, Owen enters the Purgatory with body and soul together.

In certain cases "voyage" is undeniably a more suitable word. It best describes what happens in *St. Brendan's Voyage,* where there is no separation of the soul from the body. The body and soul of the saint together actually get into a boat with seventeen companions and set sail in search of the Land of Promise of the Saints. They travel to hell and heaven and back, but these places are not found in a trance or dream or some superconscious state, but in the waters of the Atlantic.

Ultimately the best word might be "experience;" and this book, then, is a collection of experiences of heaven and hell, because what we are primarily dealing with is the religious experience of an individual.[10]

When the visionary returns from his voyage or vision he describes his experiences. The vision then takes on a life beyond the original visionary. When we are dealing with the text of a vision we are already removed by at least one person for the original visionary. The vision itself has already taken on a life of its own, as happens to all artistic works, even artistic works based on a profoundly personal and religious experience. In the end we are relying on the words of the writer and not the words of the visionary.

But for a moment let us consider further what this vision means to the original visionary. We can derive some basic information about the visionary's experience from what the writer tells us of the life of the visionary afterwards. His life often undergoes a profound change.

The worse the character of the visionary, the more obvious the change. The result of the vision is often a profound conversion, which is, after all, the primary characteristic of a religious experience. Visionaries sell everything, give all away to the poor, join monasteries, travel to Jerusalem and then spend the remainder of their days in penance, poverty, and prayer. They may take up preaching the Gospels or they may retire as hermits.

Although these visions have been discussed in other places as mystical visions, this term is not completely appropriate. The classic mystic ascent is a slow upward journey. With the help of God the mystic draws himself or herself through purgation to illumination and finally union. Our visionaries seldom seek this experience; they are seldom prepared for it in the way that a mystic would be prepared. Some of our visionaries are actually carried along screaming and kicking.[11] They are, however, purged and illuminated. They return repentant, converted and enlightened. The union is only hinted at and remains something that is promised for the reformed soul. The *Monk of Evesham's Vision* is the exception here, since the monk actually sees Christ and seems to undergo a mystical experience. Most of our other visionaries are brought into the ranks of the blessed and then returned to earth with a promise of glory if they accomplish what the purpose of their journey has been.

If we accept the premise that these are narratives about the actual religious experience of an individual, we are reading them as the authors hoped we would. The authors of these visions, who are at least once, and often twice, removed from the original visionaries themselves, went to great literary lengths to prove that these visions actually took place and were not strictly literary works. In attempting these proofs, the authors often resorted to a whole array of literary conventions or topoi. Often the presence of these topoi leads readers to assume that the work is strictly a literary invention rather than the literary documentation of a true religious experience. However, following the prescribed formulas is the best way to gain credibility.[12] We would certainly expect a lawyer to follow prescribed formulas attempting to prove a legal case, and for medieval society this reliance on formula as a means of ascertaining truth was certainly fundamental.

Our authors have their own formulas. They often will attempt to establish a connection between what was seen in the otherworld and something concrete in this world. In *St. Paul's Apocalypse* the author tells us that the box containing this narrative was found under the floor in Paul's old house in Tarsus. Paul's shoes were also in the box. The assumption is that certainly neither Paul nor his friends would have put his shoes in a box with a false document. In *Wetti's Vision* the author mentions things that were described years before to someone else but were unknown to Wetti. Wetti then rediscovers these things during his vision. There is apparently no way that Wetti could have discovered these things except through a true vision. Most authors hold the most convincing proof of the truth of the vision to be the changed life of the visionary. The conversion, which accompanies all true religious experience, is proof of Tundale's vision, Thurkill's vision and numerous others.

In addition to the literary conventions used by the authors, it is important to consider that in describing anything, imaginary or actual, one must rely on the whole body of language conventions to make a description understandable to an audience. How much more would this be the case when describing a vision of the other-world? Considering the magnitude of these visions and the physical and emotional shock of the experience, it is no wonder that in recounting these visions, the visionaries themselves had to rely on what would make sense in words. Often, because the descriptions would resemble one another so closely in the details, readers might be skeptical about the true and unique nature of the vision. However, in an attempt to express himself and to convince an audience that he had actually seen something – and had not just been sleeping for three days – the visionary would have to rely on the words that would come to mind, words that made sense to his audience. Between the vision itself and its narration by the visionary we have already passed to another level, one where we have to rely on words, an already established vocabulary, to describe a mystical or deeply religious experience that might not actually be describable in words.[13]

Now when the vision passes from the tongue of the teller to the person who will recount it to others, either in speech or writing, we pass on to the next stage of the development of the work. In no case here does the visionary act as the scribe of his own vision, so by the time it reaches written form there is another hand and mind involved. Considering the situation of literacy during the period from which most of these visions derive, the fact that the written word was primarily in the hands of churchpeople, and the likely presence of a priest or cleric at the recounting of the vision, when the vision goes beyond an oral account of a religious experience it is likely that it becomes a literary text and a religious document at the same time.

However, in the Middle Ages this distinction would not necessarily be considered in the same light as it would be today. We probably would make a distinction between the literary and the religious. And we would have to conclude that religion was the primary impetus for both initially recording these visions and later for translating, copying and disseminating them. The clergy and certainly particular orders within the church community viewed them as works that were likely to encourage the conversion of individual sinners and also to encourage the community to help obtain mercy for the dead who were already suffering for their sins in the otherworld.

As time went on and the written vision was transmitted through manuscript copying and translation the balance between the literary and religious importance of the work was likely to shift. In the example of *Tundale's Vision,* described above, the recounting of his religious experience did have a strong and long life primarily as a religious document, copied for the edification and conversion of the Christian population; but toward the end of this period its importance as a literary work is what keeps it alive. Because of their value as literary works these visions were preserved, translated and transmitted far beyond what would have resulted from the first wave of religious enthusiasm for them.

SURVIVAL AND INFLUENCE

The genre of medieval visions of heaven and hell culminates with Dante's *Divine Comedy*.[14] He was completely familiar with the tradition; and based on the centuries of speculation that preceded his work, Dante was able to prepare a cohesive, imaginative, literary and brilliant summation of the subject. After him the topic, in effect, dies. There are certainly other factors, intellectual and religious, responsible for the end of the genre, but with Dante it does not whimper away but enjoys a final, glorious apotheosis.

The influence of this genre does, however, survive. In painting, especially in the works of Bosch and Bruegel, and in medieval sculpture the hellish images of these visions is perpetuated. Imaginative literature continues to draw on this genre, right up to contemporary Science Fiction, and especially the branch designated "speculative fiction," which examines the possibilities of the unknown world. In speculative works by Ursula Le Guin and Doris Lessing we encounter descriptions of otherworlds, not vaguely reminiscent of, but strongly resembling these medieval visions of heaven and hell.

In addition to inspiring our imaginative literature, these medieval visions present for us a narrative by which we can understand the nature and mythology of the otherworld as it was constructed by Christians in the Middle Ages. There are other sources for this information, such as philosophical and theological texts, but the narratives presented here clearly provide an understanding of what the idea of the otherworld might be for a popular Christian audience. Thus these visions can be read as testimonies of personal religious experience, as bearers of archetypes and symbols, as documents in the history of the medieval church, and as powerful and enduring literary and spiritual works.

*

NOTES

1. See for example Colleen McDannell and Bernhard Lang, *Heaven: A History* (New Haven, CT and London: Yale University Press, 1988); Carol Zaleski, *Otherworld Journeys* (New York: Oxford University Press, 1987); Jeffrey Burton Russell, *The Prince of Darkness* (Ithaca, NY: Cornell University Press, 1988).

2. See Ernest J. Becker, *A Contribution to the Comparative Study of the Medieval Visions of Heaven and Hell* (Baltimore, MD: John Murphy Co., 1899), pp. 9-25; and Martha Himmelfarb, *Tours of Hell: An Apocalyptic Form in Jewish and Christian Literature* (Philadelphia: University of Pennsylvania Press, 1983).

3. For general information on the penitentials, see Ludwig Bieler, "The Irish Penitentials," *Scriptores Latini Hiberniae* 5 (Dublin: Dublin Institute for Advanced Studies, 1963); and Bieler, "Penitentials," *New Catholic Encyclopedia* (Washington, DC: Publishers Guild, and New York: McGraw Hill, 1967), 11:86-87; Gabriel Le Bras, "Pénitentiels," *Dictionnaire de théologie catholique,* ed. A. Vancant, E. Mangenot and E. Amann (Paris: Letouzey et Ané, 1903-72), 12(1933): 1160-79; John T. McNeill and Helen M. Gamer, *Medieval Handbooks of Penance* (New York: Columbia University Press, 1938); C.P. Oakley, "Cultural Affiliations of Early Ireland in the Penitentials," *Speculum* 8 (1933): 489-500; Cyrille Vogel, *Le pécheur et la pénitence au Moyen Age* (Paris: Editons Cerf, 1969); Oscar Daniel Watkins, *A History of Penance,* 2 vols. (London: Longmans, 1920); Allen J. Frantzen, *The Literature of Penance in Anglo-Saxon England* (New Brunswick, NJ: Rutgers University Press, 1983); and Frantzen, "The Penitentials Attributed to Bede," *Speculum,* 58, 3 (1983): 573-97.

4. Jacques Le Goff, *The Birth of Purgatory,* trans. Arthur Goldhammer (Chicago: Chicago University Press, 1984), pp. 1-17.

5. From the references to primary sources in the Notes many examples are evident of these visions appearing in the chronicles of Bede, Roger of Wendover, Vincent of Beauvais, Gregory of Tours, Helinand de Froidmont, William of Malmesbury, and Hariulf.

6. See "An Edition of the Middle English 'Vision of Tundale,'" ed. Eileen Gardiner (Ph.D. Diss.: Fordham University, 1980), pp. 21-29; and *Visio Tnugdali: The German and Dutch Translations and Their Circulation in the Later Middle Ages,* ed. Nigel F. Palmer (Munich and Zurich: Artemis, 1982), esp. pp. 363-76.

7. For a discussion of heaven in the Middle Ages see McDannell and Lang, pp. 69-110.

8. Evelyn Underhill, *Mysticism* (New York: Dutton, 1961), pp. 167-76.

9. OED defines vision as "an appearance of a prophetic or mystical character, or having the nature of a revelation supernaturally presented to the mind either in sleep or in an abnormal state."

10. For useful background on religious experience see Henry James, *Varieties of Religious Experience* (New York: Macmillan, 1961), esp. pp. 143-210; Wayne Proudfoot, *Religious Experience* (Berkeley, CA: University of California Press, 1985); and Aldous Huxley, *The Perennial Philosophy* (London: Chatto & Windus, 1946).

11. New works on mysticism, such as Matthew Fox, *The Cosmic Christ* (San Francisco: Harper & Row, 1988), are attempting a broader definition of mysticism, which might actually encompass the experiences described here; but certainly the classic definitions do not cover these visions.

12. Zaleski, pp. 81-85.

13. Zaleski, p. 190.

14. See for example M. Dods, *Forerunners of Dante* (Edinburgh, 1902); Alessandro D'Ancona, *I precursori di Dante* (Florence: Sansoni, 1874); and C.S. Boswell, *An Irish Precursor of Dante* (London: Nutt, 1908).

t. Peter's Apocalypse

This is the story of Christ's second coming and of the resurrection of the dead, revealed to St. Peter by Christ, who died for their sins because they did not keep the commandment of God their creator. Peter pondered this revelation so that he might understand the mystery of the Son of God, the merciful one and lover of mercy.

When the Lord was seated on the Mount of Olives, his disciples came to him. And we implored and entreated him individually and prayed to him, saying, "Declare to us what are the signs of your coming and of the end of the world, so that we may understand and mark the time of your coming and instruct those who come after us. To them we preach the word of your Gospel, and over them we sit in your church, so that when they hear it they may pay attention and mark the time of your coming."

The Lord answered us saying, "Take care that no man deceives you and that you are not doubters and serve other gods. Many shall come in my name saying, 'I am the Christ.' Do not believe them or draw near them. For the coming of the Son of God shall not be ordinary, but as lightning flashes from the east to the west, so will I come upon the clouds of heaven with a great host in my majesty. Shining seven times brighter than the sun I will come in my majesty with all my saints and angels. And my Father will set a crown on my head so that I may judge the living and the dead and repay every one according to his or her works. And you should learn a parable from the fig-tree. As soon as the shoot comes forth from it and the twigs are grown, the end of the world will come."

I, Peter, answered and said to him, "Interpret the fig-tree for me. How will we perceive it, for all through its days the fig-tree sends forth shoots, and every year it brings forth its fruit for its master. What then does the parable of the fig-tree mean? We do not know."

The Master answered and said to me, "Do you not understand that the fig-tree is the House of Israel? It is like a man who planted a fig-tree in his garden that brought forth no fruit. He sought fruit from it for many years, and when he did not find any, he said to his gardener, 'Root up this fig-tree so that it does not make our land unfruitful.' And the gardener said to God, 'Let us rid it of weeds and dig the ground around it and water it. If it then bears no fruit, we will remove its roots from the garden straight-away and plant another in its place.'

"Have you not understood that the fig-tree is the House of Israel? I say to you, when its twigs have sprouted forth in the last days, then shall false Christs come and awake expectation, saying, 'I am the Christ, who am now come into the world.' And when they perceive the wickedness of their deeds they will turn away with them and deny him whom our fathers praised, the first Christ whom they crucified and so sinned a great sin. But this deceiver is not the Christ. And when they reject him he will slay with the sword, and there will be many martyrs. Then will the twigs of the fig-tree, that is the House of Israel, shoot forth. Many will become martyrs at his hand. Enoch and Elias will be sent to teach them that this is the deceiver who must come into the world and do signs and wonders to deceive. Therefore those who die by his hand will be martyrs and will be counted among the good and righteous martyrs who have pleased God in their life."

And in his right hand he showed me the souls of all people. On the palm of his right hand was the image of what will happen on the last day; and how the righteous and the sinners shall be separated, and how they succeed who are moral in their hearts, and how the evil-doers will be rooted out for all eternity. We saw how the sinners wept in great affliction and sorrow, until all who saw it also wept, the righteous, the angels, and also he himself.

And I asked him and said to him, "Lord, let me speak your word concerning the sinners. It would be better for them if they had not been created." The Savior answered and said to me, "Peter, why do you speak in this way, as if not to have been created would be better for them? You resist God. You would not have more compassion than he does for his image; for he has created them and brought them forth out of nothing. Now because you have seen the lamentation that shall come upon the sinners in the last days your heart is troubled; but I will show you the works by which they have sinned against the Most High."

Now see what will happen to them in the last days when the day of God and the day of the judgment of God comes. From east to west all the children of humanity will be gathered together before my Father who lives forever. And he shall command hell to open its bars of adamant and give up all who are in there.

And he will command the wild beasts and fowl to restore all the flesh that they have devoured, because he wills that men and women should appear. For nothing perishes before God, and nothing is impossible with him, because all things are his.

3

For at the word of God all things come to pass on the day of decision, on the Day of Judgment. And as all things were accomplished when he created the world and commanded all that is in it, and it was done, even so will it be in the last days; for all things are possible with God. Therefore he says in the scripture, "Son of man, prophesy upon bones and say to the bones: bone to bone in joints, sinew, nerves, flesh and skin and hair thereon and soul and spirit." And great Uriel will give them soul and spirit at the commandment of God, for God has set him over the rising of the dead again at the Day of Judgment.

Behold and consider the grains of wheat that are sown in the earth. Men sow them in the earth like things that are dry and without soul; and they live again and bear fruit, and the earth restores them as a pledge entrusted to it. The human race is what dies and is sown as seed in the earth and then becomes alive and restored to life.

On the Day of Judgment will not God raise up even more those who believe in him and are chosen by him, and for whose sake he made the world? The earth will restore all things on the Day of Judgment, for it will also be judged with them, and heaven with it.

On the Day of Judgment this will come upon those who have fallen away from faith in God and have committed sin: floods of fire will be let loose, and darkness and obscurity will come up and clothe and veil the whole world, and the waters will be changed and turned into coals of fire, and all that is in them will burn, and the sea will become fire. Under heaven there will be a bitter fire that cannot be quenched and that flows to fulfill the judgment of wrath. The stars will fly into pieces like flames of fire, as if they had not been created, and the vaults of heaven will pass away for lack of water, and it will be as if they had never been. Heaven will turn to lightning, and the lightning will terrify the world. The

4

spirits of the dead will also be like the lightning and will become fire at the commandment of God.

As soon as all creation dissolves, the people in the east will flee to the west, and those in the west to the east; those in the south will flee to the north, and those in the north to the south. In all places the wrath of a fearful fire will overtake them; and an unquenchable flame will drive them and bring them to the judgment of wrath, to the stream of unquenchable fire that flows, flaming with fire. When its burning waves part from one another, there will be a great gnashing of teeth among the children of humanity.

Then they will all see me coming upon an eternal cloud of brightness. With the angels of God I will sit on the throne of my glory at the right hand of my heavenly Father, and he will set a crown upon my head. And when the nations see it, every nation will weep independently.

Then he will command them to enter the river of fire while the deeds of every one stand in front of them, each according to his or her deeds. As for the elect who have done good, they will come to me and not see death by the devouring fire. But the unrighteous, the sinners, and the hypocrites will stand in the depths of darkness that will not pass away; and their punishment is fire. Angels will bring forward their sins and prepare for them a place where they will be punished forever.

Uriel, the angel of God, will bring forth in order, according to their transgression, the souls of those sinners who perished in the flood, the spirits who dwelt in all idols, in every molten image, in every object of desire, and in images, and those who dwelt in all hills and in stones and by waysides, those whom people called "gods." They will burn them with their dwelling places in everlasting fire. And after all of them are destroyed with their dwelling-places, they will be punished eternally.

5

Then men and women will come to the place prepared for them. Those who have blasphemed the way of righteousness will be hung up by their tongues. Spread under them is unquenchable fire so that they cannot escape it.

In another place there is a pit, great and full of fire. In it are those who have denied righteousness, and angels of punishment chastise them there and kindle on them the fire of their torment.

And there are women. They hang them up by their necks and by their hair; they will cast them into the pit. These plaited their hair, not for the sake of beauty but to turn men to fornication, so that they might ensnare their souls to perdition. And the men who laid with them in fornication will be hung by their loins in that place of fire, and they shall say one to another, "We did not know that we would come to everlasting punishment."

They will cast the murderers and those who have made common cause with murderers into the fire, in a place full of venomous beasts, and they will be tormented without rest, feeling their pains; and their worms will be so many in number as to form a dark cloud. The angel Ezraël will bring forth the souls of those who have been slain, and they will see the torment of those who slew them and say to one another, "Righteous and just is the judgment of God. We heard but we did not believe that we would come to this place of eternal judgment."

Nearby this flame will be a pit, great and very deep, and from above into it flows all manner of torment, foulness, and discharge. Women are swallowed up to their necks in it and tormented with great pain. These are the ones who have caused their children to be born before their time and have corrupted the work of God who created them. Opposite them there will be another place where their children sit alive, and they will cry to God. And lightning bursts from those children and pierces the eyes of those who have caused their destruction for the sake of fornication.

Other men and women will stand above them, naked; and their children will stand opposite them in a place of delight and sigh and cry to God because of their parents, saying, "These are the ones who have despised and cursed and transgressed your commandments and delivered us to death. They have cursed the angel who formed us and have hung us up and withheld from us the light that you have given to all creatures." The milk of their mothers will congeal as it flows from their breasts; and from it flesh-devouring beasts will spring and turn and torment forever those women and their husbands, because they abandoned the commandments of God and slew their children. As for their children, they will be delivered to the angel Temlakos. And they who slew them will be tormented eternally, for so God wills it.

Ezraël, the angel of wrath, will bring men and women, with half of their bodies burning, and cast them into a place of darkness, the hell of humanity. A spirit of wrath will punish them with all kinds of torment, and a worm that does not sleep will devour their entrails. These are the persecutors and betrayers of my righteous people.

Beside those who are there, other men and women will be gnawing their tongues, and they will torment them with red-hot irons and burn their eyes. These are the ones who slander and doubt my righteousness.

Other men and women whose works were done in deceitfulness will have their lips cut off; and fire will enter their mouths and their entrails. These are the false witnesses.

Beside them, in a place nearby, upon a stone, will be a pillar of fire, and this pillar is sharper than swords. And there will be men and women clad in rags and filthy garments, and they will be cast on it to suffer the judgment of a torment that does not cease. These are the ones who trusted in their riches and before God despised the widows and the woman with fatherless children.

Into another place nearby full of filth they cast men and women up to their knees. These are the ones who lent money and took usury.

Other men and women cast themselves down from a high place and return again and run, and devils drive them. These are the worshippers of idols, and the devils drive them to the end of their wits and to the top of the height, where they cast themselves down. They do this continually and are tormented forever. These were the ones who defiled their bodies, behaving like women; and the women who were with them were those who laid with one another as a man with a woman.

Beside them there will be a brazier, and beneath them the angel Ezraël will prepare a place of great fire. All the idols of gold and silver, all idols, the work of men's hands, and the semblances of images of cats and lions, of creeping things and wild beasts, and the men and women who have prepared these images will be in chains of fire and will be punished because of their error before the idols; and this is their judgment forever.

Beside them other men and women will be burning in the fire of the judgment, and their torment is everlasting. These are the ones who have abandoned God's commandment and followed the persuasions of devils.

There will be another place, very high. There will be a furnace and a brazier in which fire will burn. The fire that burns will come from one end of the brazier. The men and women whose feet slip will go rolling down into a place where there is fear. And again while the fire that is prepared flows, they will rise up and fall down again and continue to roll down. Thus they will be tormented forever. These are the people who did not honor their fathers and mothers and of their own accord withdrew from them. Therefore they will be punished eternally.

Furthermore the angel Ezraël will bring children and maidens to show them those who are tormented. They will be chastised with pains, with hanging and with a multitude of wounds that flesh-devouring birds will inflict upon them. These are the ones who boast of their sins and do not obey their parents and do not follow the instruction of their fathers, and do not honor those who are older than they.

Beside them will be young women dressed in a garment of darkness, and they will be severely punished, and their flesh will be torn in pieces. These did not keep their virginity until they were given in marriage, and with these torments they will be punished and will feel them.

There will be other men and women gnawing their tongues without ceasing, tormented with everlasting fire. These are the slaves who were not obedient to their masters, and this is their judgment forever.

Near this place of torment there will be men and women dumb and blind, whose raiment is white. They will crowd one another and fall on coals of unquenchable fire. These are the ones who give alms and say, "We are righteous before God," whereas they have not sought righteousness.

Ezraël, the angel of God, will lead them out of this fire and make a decisive judgment: a river of fire will flow, and all who are judged will be drawn down into the middle of the river. And Uriel will set them there. There are wheels of fire, and men and women hung on them by the force of their whirling. And those who are in the pit will burn: now these are the sorcerers and sorceresses. A countless number of those wheels will be found in all punishments involving fire.

9

Afterward the angels will bring my elect and righteous, who are perfect in all uprightness, and bear them in their hands and clothe them with the garment of heavenly life. They will see justice carried out on those who hated them, when Ezraël punishes them, and the torment of every one will be forever, according to his or her deeds.

All who are tormented will say with one voice, "Have mercy on us, for now we know the judgment of God, which he declared to us before, but which we did not believe." And the angel Tatîrokos will come and punish them with still greater torment, and say to them, "Now you repent, when it is no longer the time for repentance, and nothing of life remains." And they will say, "Righteous is the judgment of God, for we have heard and seen that his judgment is good; for we are paid according to our deeds."

Then I will give my elect and righteous the baptism and the salvation that they sought from me in the field of Acherousia that is called Elysium. They will adorn the group of the righteous with flowers, and I will go and rejoice with them. I will cause these people to enter into my everlasting kingdom and show them that eternal life on which I have made them set their hope, I myself and my Father who is in heaven.

I have told this to you, Peter, and declared it to you. Go therefore to the land of the west and enter the vineyard that I will tell you of in order that the deeds of corruption may be sanctified by the sufferings of the Son who is without sin. As for you, who are chosen according to the promise that I have given you, spread my Gospel throughout the world in peace. Truly men will rejoice, my words will be the source of hope and life, and suddenly the world will be ravished.

And my Lord Jesus Christ our king said to me, "Let us go to the holy mountain." And his disciples went with him praying. There were two men there, and we could not look on their faces, for a light came from them shining greater than the sun, and their garments were also shining and cannot be described, and nothing in this world can be compared to them. No mouth can utter the sweetness or the beauty of their appearance, for it was astonishing and wonderful and shines greater than crystal. Like the flower of roses is their color. And upon their shoulders and on their foreheads were crowns of fragrant herbs woven of fair flowers. Like rainbows in water was their hair. And so was the beauty of their countenance adorned with all manner of ornament.

When we saw them, all of a sudden we marvelled. I drew near to the Lord Jesus Christ and said to him, "O my Lord, who are these?" And he said to me, "They are Moses and Elias." And I said to him, "Where then are Abraham and Isaac and Jacob and the rest of the righteous fathers?" And he showed us a great garden, open, full of fair trees and blessed fruits, and of the odor of perfumes. The fragrance of it was pleasant and came upon us. And I saw much fruit from this tree. And my Lord and God Jesus Christ said to me, "Have you seen the companies of the fathers? As is their rest, such also is the honor and the glory of those who are persecuted for the sake of my righteousness."

I rejoiced and believed, and believed and understood what is written in the book of my Lord Jesus Christ. And I said to him, "O my Lord, do you wish me to make three tabernacles here, one for you, one for Moses, and one for Elias?" And he said to me in anger, "Satan makes war against you and has veiled your understanding; and the good things of this world prevail against you. Your eyes therefore must be opened and your ears unstopped that you may see a tabernacle not made with men's hands, which my heavenly Father has made for me and for the elect." And we beheld it and were full of gladness.

Suddenly there came a voice from heaven, saying, "This is my beloved Son in whom I am well pleased; he has kept my commandments." And then over our heads there came a great and exceedingly white cloud that bore away our Lord and Moses and Elias. I trembled and was afraid; and we looked up, and the heavens opened and we saw there men in the flesh, and they came and greeted our Lord and Moses and Elias and went into another heaven. And the word of the scripture was fulfilled: "This is the generation that seeks him and seeks the face of the God of Jacob." And there was great fear and commotion in heaven, and the angels pressed upon one another so that the word of the scripture might be fulfilled that says, "Open the gates, you princes." Thereafter heaven, which had been open, was shut.

And we prayed and went down from the mountain, glorifying God, who has written the names of the righteous in heaven in the book of life.

aint Paul's Apocalypse

I: Introduction

During the consulate of Theodosius Augustus the Younger and Cynegius there was a certain honorable man then living at Tarsus, in the house that had been the house of St. Paul. An angel appeared to him at night and revealed to him that he should break up the foundation of the house and publish what he found. But he thought this was a lying vision.

But a third time the angel came and scourged him and forced him to break up the foundation. He dug and found a marble box inscribed on its sides. In it was the Revelation of Saint Paul and the shoes that he walked in when he taught the word of God. But the man was afraid to open that box and brought it to the judge.

Fearing that it might be something strange, the judge took it, sealed as it was with lead, and sent it to the emperor Theodosius. When the emperor received it, he opened it and found the Revelation of Saint Paul. He sent a copy of it to Jerusalem, and he kept the original with him. The following was written there.

*

II

Prologue

While I was alive I was caught up in my body to the third heaven. There the word of the Lord came to me, saying, "Tell this to the people. How long will you transgress and add sin upon sin and tempt the Lord who made you, saying that you are the children of God, doing the work of the devil, walking in the confidence of God, boasting in your name only but being poor because of your sins? Remember and know that all of creation is subject to God, but only humanity sins. It has dominion over all creation, and sins more than all nature."

Often has the sun, the great light, appealed to the Lord, saying, "O Lord God Almighty, I look upon the ungodliness and unrighteous of these people. Allow me, and I will deal with them according to my power, so that they may know that you alone are God." And there came a voice, saying, "I know all these things, for my eye sees and my ear hears, but my long-suffering bears with them until they convert and repent. But if they do not return to me, I will judge them all."

Sometimes the moon and the stars have appealed to the Lord, saying, "O Lord God Almighty, you have given us rule over the night. How long shall we look upon the ungodliness and fornications and murders that the children of humanity commit? Allow us to deal with them according to our powers, so that they may know that you alone are God." A voice came to them there, saying, "I know all these things, and my eye looks on them and my ear hears, but my long-suffering bears with them until they convert and repent. But if they do not return to me, I will judge them."

Often also the sea has cried out, saying, "O Lord God Almighty, these people have polluted your holy name in me. Allow me and I will rise up and cover every forest and tree and all the world until I blot out all the children of humanity from before your face, so that they may know that you alone are God." Again a voice came, saying, "I know all, for my eye sees all things, and my ear hears, but my long-suffering bears with them until they convert and repent. But if they do not return, I will judge them."

Sometimes the waters have also appealed against the children of humanity saying, "O Lord God Almighty, the children of humanity have all defiled your holy name." And there came a voice, saying, "I know all things before they happen, for my eye sees and my ear hears all things, but my long-suffering bears with them until they convert. And if not, I will judge them."

Often also the earth has cried out to the Lord against the children of humanity, saying, "O Lord God Almighty, I suffer more harm than all your creation, bearing these people's fornications, adulteries, murders, thefts, perjuries, sorceries and witchcrafts, and all the evils that they do, so that the father rises up against the son, and the son against the father, the stranger against the stranger, every one to defile his neighbor's wife. The father goes into his son's bed, and the son likewise goes up on the couch of his father; and with all these evils they who offer a sacrifice to your name have polluted your holy place. Therefore I suffer more harm than the whole of creation, and I do not wish to yield my excellence and my fruits to the children of humanity. Allow me and I will destroy the excellence of my fruits." A voice came there and said, "I know all things, and there is no one who can hide from his or her

15

own sin. And I know their ungodliness, but my holiness bears with them until they convert and repent. But if they do not return to me, I will judge them."

Behold then, you children of humanity. The creature is subject to God, but humanity alone sins.

III

The Guardian Angels

Children of humanity, you should bless the Lord God without ceasing at all hours and on all days, but especially when the sun sets. For in that hour all the angels go to the Lord to worship him and to present the deeds that men and women do from morning until evening, whether they are good or evil. And there is an angel who goes forth rejoicing from the person in whom he dwells.

When the sun has set, therefore, at the first hour of the night, in the same hour goes the angel of every person and of every man and woman, who protects and keeps them, because the person is the image of God. Likewise at the first hour of morning, which is the twelfth hour of the night, all the angels of men and women go to meet God and present all the work that every one has wrought, whether good or evil. Every day and night the angels present to God an account of all the deeds of humanity. To you, therefore, I say, O children of humanity, bless the Lord God without ceasing all the days of your life.

At the hour appointed all the angels, every one rejoicing therefore, come together before God to meet him and worship him. The angels came to worship in the presence of God, and the spirit came forth to meet them, and there was a voice saying, "Where do you come from, our angels, bringing burden of news?"

They answered and said, "We have come from those who have renounced the world for your holy name's sake, wandering as strangers and in the caves of the rocks, and weeping every hour that they dwell on the earth, and hungering and thirsting for the sake of your name, with their loins girt, holding in their hands the incense of their heart, and praying and blessing at every hour, suffering anguish and subduing themselves, weeping and lamenting more than all that dwell on the earth. We who are their angels mourn with them. Therefore, command us to go and minister wherever it pleases you, so that they will not do otherwise. But command us to minister to the poor more than to all others who dwell on the earth."

The voice of God came to them saying, "Know that from now on my grace will be established with you. My help, which is my dearly beloved Son, will be with them, ruling them at all times. He will minister to them and never forsake them, for their place is his habitation."

When these angels departed, then other angels came there to meet and worship there in the presence of the majesty; and they were weeping. The spirit of God went forth to meet them, and the voice of God came, saying, "Where do you come from, our angels, ministers of the news of the world, bearing burdens?" They answered and said in the presence of God, "We have come from those who have called on your name, and the snares of the world have made them wretched. They have devised many excuses at all times and not made so much as one pure prayer out of their whole heart all the time of their lives. Why then must we be with those who are sinners?" The voice of God came to them, "You must minister to them until they convert and repent. But if they do not return to me, I will judge them."

Know therefore, O children of humanity, that whatever you do, the angels tell it to God, whether it is good or evil.

IV

The Place of the Righteous

After I saw these things, I saw one of the spiritual ones coming toward me, and he caught me up in the spirit and carried me to the third heaven. And this angel said to me, "Follow me, and I will show you the place where the righteous are taken when they are dead. Thereafter I will take you to the bottomless pit and show you the souls of the sinners and the kind of place they are taken to when they are dead."

I went behind the angel, and he took me into heaven, and I looked upon the firmament and saw there the powers: there was forgetfulness, which deceives and draws human hearts to itself, and the spirit of slander, and the spirit of fornication, and the spirit of wrath, and the spirit of insolence; and there were the princes of wickedness. I saw these things beneath the firmament of heaven.

Again I looked and saw angels without mercy, having no pity, whose countenances were full of fury. Their teeth stuck forward out of their mouths, and their eyes shone like the morning star of the east, and sparks of fire went forth from the hair on their heads and out of their mouths. And I asked the angel, "Who are these, lord?" The angel answered and said to me, "These are the ones appointed to the souls of sinners in their hour of necessity,

even to those who have not believed that they had the
Lord for their helper and have not trusted in him."

I looked up and saw other angels whose faces shone
like the sun, and their loins were girt with golden girdles,
and they held palms in their hands and the sign of God.
They were clothed in garments on which was written the
name of the Son of God, full of all gentleness and mercy.
And I asked the angel, "Lord, who are these who are of
such great beauty and compassion?" The angel answered
and said to me, "These are the angels of righteousness
who are sent to bring the souls of the righteous in their
hour of necessity, even those who have believed that they
had the Lord for their helper." And I said to him, "Do the
righteous and the sinners necessarily meet when they are
dead?" The angel answered and said to me, "The way by
which all pass to God is one, but the righteous have a holy
helper with them and are not troubled when they go to
appear in the presence of God."

V

The Good Soul Departs from Its Body

I said to the angel, "I would like to see the souls of the
righteous and the sinners as they depart from the world."
The angel answered and said to me, "Look down on the
earth." I looked down from heaven upon the earth and
saw the whole world, and it was as if it were nothing to
my eyes. I saw the children of humanity as though they
were nothing and utterly failing. I marvelled and said to
the angel, "Is this the greatness of humanity?" The angel
answered and said to me, "This is it, and these are the ones

who do harm from morning till night." I looked and saw
a great cloud of fire spread over the whole world and said
to the angel, "What is this, lord?" And he said to me,
"This is the unrighteousness that is brewed by the princes
of sinners."

When I heard that I sighed and wept and said to the
angel, "I wish to wait for the souls of the righteous and the
sinners and see how they depart from the body." The
angel answered and said to me, "Look again upon the
earth." And I looked and saw the whole world. Men and
women were like nothing and utterly failing. I looked
and saw a certain man about to die, and the angel said to
me, "The one you see is righteous." Again I looked and
saw all the works that he had done in the name of God and
all his desires, those he remembered and those he did not
remember, all of them stood before his face in the hour of
necessity. And I saw that the righteous man had grown in
righteousness and found rest and confidence. Before he
departed from the world holy angels stood there by him
and also evil ones. I saw them all, but the evil ones found
no home in him, and the holy ones had power over his
soul and ruled it until it went from his body. They stirred
up the soul, saying, "O soul, take notice of your body,
which you have come out of, because you must return into
the same body at the Day of Resurrection to receive what
is promised to all the righteous."

They received the soul out of his body and straightway
kissed it as one who was acquainted with them every day,
saying to it, "Be of good courage, for you have done the
will of God while you lived on the earth." The angel that
watched this soul day by day came there to meet it, and he
said to it, "Be of good courage, soul. I rejoice in you
because you have done the will of God on earth, for I told
God all your works, how they stood." Likewise the spirit
came forth to meet it and said, "O soul, do not fear; do not

be troubled now that you have come to a place that you never knew; but I will be your helper, for I have found in you a place of refreshment while I dwelt in you when we were on the earth." And its spirit strengthened it, and its angel took it up and carried it into heaven. There also went out to meet it wicked powers, those that are under heaven. The spirit of error reached it there and said, "Where are you running, soul? Do you presume to enter heaven? Stay and let us see if there is anything of ours in you. Alas, we have found nothing in you. I see the help of God and also your angel; and the spirit rejoices with you because you did the will of God upon earth."

They brought it until it worshipped in the presence of God. When they ceased, Michael and all the host of angels fell and worshipped his footstool, and at his gates they said together to the soul, "This is the God of all, who made you in his image and likeness." The angel turned and declared, "Lord, remember his works, for this is the soul whose works I reported to you, Lord, according to your judgment." Likewise the spirit said, "I am the spirit of quickening that breathed upon it. I had refreshment while I dwelt in it, according to your judgment." And the voice of God came, saying, "Since this soul has not grieved me, neither will I grieve it, for since it has had mercy, I also will have mercy. Let it be delivered to Michael the angel of the covenant, and let him lead it into paradise, rejoicing that it becomes fellow-heir with all the saints."

Thereafter I heard the voices of thousands of thousands of angels and archangels and the cherubim and the four-and-twenty elders uttering hymns and glorifying the Lord and crying, "Righteous are you, O Lord, and just are your judgments, and there is no respect of persons with you, but you reward every person according to your judgment."

And the angel answered and said to me, "Do you believe and know that whatever every one of you has done, he sees it at the hour of your judgment?" And I said, "Yes, lord."

VI

Evil Souls Depart from Their Bodies

The angel said to me, "Look down again upon the earth and wait for the soul of a wicked man leaving his body, one who has provoked the Lord day and night saying, 'I know nothing else in this world. I will eat and drink and enjoy the things that are in the world. For who is he who has gone down into hell and come up again and told us that there is a judgment there?'"

I looked again and saw all the malice of the sinner and all he did, and they stood assembled before him in the hour of necessity. And it happened that in the hour when he was led out of his body to the judgment he said, "It would have been better for me if I had not been born." After that the holy angels and the evil ones and the soul of the sinner came together, and the holy angels found no place in it. But the evil angels threatened it, and when they brought it forth out of the body, the angels admonished it three times, saying, "O wretched soul, look on the flesh that you have come out of, because you must return into your flesh at the Day of Resurrection to receive the due reward for your sins and your wickedness."

When they had brought it forth, its accustomed angel went in front of it and said to it, "O miserable soul, I am the angel that stuck to you and day by day reported to the Lord your evil deeds, whatever you wrought by night or day. If it had been in my power I would not have ministered to you for even one day; but I could do nothing about this because God is merciful and a just judge, and he commanded us not to cease ministering to your soul until you should repent, but you have missed the time for repentance. Indeed I have become a stranger to you and you to me. Let us go then to the just judge. I will not leave you until I know that from this day on I am a stranger to you." And the spirit confounded it, and the angel troubled it.

Therefore when they came to the Principalities, and it would now attempt to enter heaven, one burden was laid upon it after another: error and forgetfulness and whispering met it, and the spirit of fornication and the rest of the powers, and said to it, "Wherever are you going, wretched soul, and how do you dare run forward into heaven? Stay here so that we can see whether we have property of ours in you, for we do not see a holy helper with you." After that I heard voices in the height of the heavens, saying, "Present this miserable soul to God, so that it may know that there is a God, whom it has despised."

When it entered heaven, therefore, all the angels, thousands upon thousands, saw it, and all cried out with one voice, saying, "Woe to you, miserable soul, for the works that you did on earth. What answer will you make to God when you draw near to worship him?" The angel who was with it answered and said, "Weep with me, my dearly beloved, for I have found no rest in this soul." The angels answered him and said, "Let this soul be taken away out of our midst, for since it came in its stench has passed up to us angels." Then it was presented to worship in the presence of God. The angel showed it the Lord

23

God who made it after his own image and likeness. And its angel ran before it, saying, "O Lord God Almighty, I am the angel of this soul, whose works, not done according to your judgment, I presented to you day and night." Likewise the spirit said, "I am the spirit that dwelt in it ever since it was made, and I know it in itself, and it did not follow my will. Judge it, Lord, according to your judgment."

The voice of God came to it and said, "Where is the fruit that you have yielded, which is worthy of those good things that you received? Did I put a distance of even a day between you and the righteous? Did I not make the sun rise on you even as on the righteous?" It was silent, having nothing to answer. Again the voice came, saying, "Just is the judgment of God, and there is no respect of persons with God, for whoever has had mercy, he will have mercy on them, and who has not had mercy, neither will God have mercy on them. Let him therefore be delivered to the angel Tartaruchus who is set over the torments, and let him cast him into the outer darkness, where there is weeping and gnashing of teeth, and let him be there until the great Day of Judgment." After that I heard the voice of the angels and archangels saying, "Righteous are you, O Lord, and just is your judgment."

Again I saw a soul who was brought by two angels, weeping and saying, "Have mercy on me, righteous God, O God the judge, for today it is seven days since I left my body, and I was delivered to these two angels, and they have brought me to those places that I had never seen." And God the righteous judge said, "What have you done? Since you have never been merciful, you were delivered to these angels, who have no mercy, and because you have not done right, neither have they dealt with you in pity in your hour of necessity. Therefore, confess the sin that you committed while you were in the world." The soul answered and said, "Lord, I have not sinned." The righteous Lord God was angered with indignation when the soul said, "I have not sinned," because it lied. And God said, "Do you think that you are still in the world? Although every one of you there hides and conceals your sin from your neighbor when you sin, here nothing is hidden, for when the souls come to worship before the throne, both the good works and the sins of everyone are made manifest." When the soul heard that, it held its peace, because it had no answer.

I heard the Lord God, the righteous judge, saying again, "Come, angel of this soul and stand in the middle." The angel of the sinful soul came holding a sheet of writing and said, "These, Lord, in my hands, are all the sins of this soul from its youth up to this day, from ten years after its birth. If you bid me, Lord, I can tell its acts since it was fifteen years old." And the Lord God the righteous judge said, "I say to you, O angel, I do not desire an account from you since this soul was fifteen years old, but declare its sins for the five years before it died and came here." Again God the righteous judge said, "For by myself and by my holy angels and by my power, I swear that if it had repented five years before it died, even for the length of one year, there would be forgetfulness of all the evil that it committed before, and it would have pardon and remission of sins, but now let it perish." The angel of the sinful soul answered and said, "Command, Lord, that angel to bring forth those souls."

In that same hour souls were brought forth into their midst, and the soul of the sinner knew them. And the Lord said to the soul of the sinner, "I say to you, soul, confess the deeds that you did to these souls whom you see, when they were in the world." It answered and said, "Lord, it is not yet a full year since I killed this one and shed its blood upon the earth, and with another I committed fornication, and not that only, but I did it much harm by taking away its substance." And the Lord God, the righteous judge, said, "Did you not know that if one does violence to another, and that if the one that suffered the violence dies first, that person is kept in this place until the one who did the harm dies, and then both of them appear before the judge? Then everyone receives according to what he or she did." Then I heard a voice saying, "Let that soul be delivered into the hands of Tartaruchus, and he must be taken down into hell. Let him take him into the lower prison, and let him be cast into torments and be left there until the great Day of Judgment." Again I heard thousands of thousands of angels singing a hymn to the Lord and saying, "Righteous are you, O Lord, and just are your judgments."

VII

The Third Heaven

The angel answered and said to me, "Have you understood all these things?" And I said, "Yes, lord." He said to me, "Follow me again, and I will take you and show you the places of the righteous." I followed the angel, and he took me up to the third heaven and set me before the door of a gate. I looked at it and saw, and the gate was gold, and there were two pillars of gold full of golden letters. The angel turned again to me and said, "Blessed are you if you enter by these gates, for it is not permitted to any to enter except those who have maintained the goodness and pureness of their bodies in all things." I asked the angel and said, "Lord, tell me why these letters are set upon these tables?" The angel answered and said to me, "These are the names of the righteous who minister to God with their whole hearts and who dwell on the earth." Again I said, "Lord, then are their names written while they are still on the earth?" And he said, "Not only are their names written in heaven, but also the countenance and the likeness of those who serve God is there, and they are known to the angels, because they know those who serve God with their whole hearts before they depart from the world."

When I had entered the gate of paradise an old man came there to meet me. His face shone like the sun, and he embraced me and said, "Hail, Paul, dearly beloved of God." He kissed me with a joyful face, but he wept, and I said to him, "Brother, why do you weep?" Sighing again and weeping he said, "Because we are vexed by humanity, and they grieve us sorely, because many are the good things that the Lord has prepared, and great are his promises, but many do not receive them." I asked the angel and said, "Who is this, lord?" And he said to me, "This is Enoch, the scribe of righteousness."

I entered that place, and straightway I saw Elias; and he came and saluted me with gladness and joy. When he had seen me he turned away and wept and said to me, "Paul, may you receive the reward for the labor that you have done among humanity. As for me, I have seen great and various good things that God has prepared for all the righteous, and great are the promises of God, but the greater part do not receive them; yet one and another hardly enters these places even with much toil."

The angel answered and said to me, "Whatever things I show you now here, and whatever you hear, do not reveal them to any on earth." He led me on and showed me, and I heard words there that it is not lawful for a human to say. Again he said, "Follow me again and I will show you what you must describe and tell openly."

VIII

The Second Heaven

He brought me down from the third heaven and led me into the second heaven, and he led me again to the firmament, and from the firmament he led me to the gates of heaven. The beginning of its foundation was on the river that waters all the earth. I asked the angel and said, "Lord, what river of water is this?" And he said to me, "This is the ocean." Suddenly I came out of heaven and saw that it is the light of heaven that shines on all the earth. There the earth was seven times brighter than silver. And I said, "Lord, what place is this?" He said to me, "This is the Land of Promise. Have you not yet heard what is written: 'Blessed are the meek, for they shall inherit the earth'? When they leave the body, the souls of the righteous are sent to this place for a time." I said to the angel, "Shall this land then be made manifest after a time?" The angel answered and said to me, "When Christ, whom you preach, comes to reign, then by the decree of God the first earth will be dissolved, and then this Land of Promise will be shown, and it will be like dew or a cloud. Then the Lord Jesus Christ, the eternal king, will be manifested and will come with all his saints to dwell here. He will reign over them a thousand years, and they will eat the good things that I will now show you."

I looked around that land and saw a river flowing with milk and honey. There were planted at the brink of the river trees full of fruit. Now every tree bore twelve harvests each year, and they had various and diverse fruits, and I saw the fashion of that place and all the work of God, and I saw there palm-trees of twenty cubits and others of ten cubits, and the land was seven times brighter than silver. The trees were full of fruit from the roots to the upper branches. And I said to the angel, "Why does every tree bring forth fruit in the thousands?" The angel answered and said to me, "Because the Lord God in his bounty gives his gifts in abundance to the worthy; because of their own will they also afflicted themselves when they were in the world, doing everything for the sake of his holy name."

Again I said to the angel, "Lord, are these the only promises that the most holy Lord God makes?" He answered and said to me, "No, because there are seven times greater than these. But I say to you that when the righteous are gone out of the body and see the promises and the good things that God has prepared for them, they will sigh and cry yet again, saying, 'Why did we utter a word from our mouths to provoke our neighbor even for a day?'" I asked again and said, "Are these the only promises of God?" The angel answered and said to me, "These that you now see are for those who are married and keep the purity of their marriage within restraints. But to the virgins, and to those who hunger and thirst after righteousness and afflict themselves for the name of the Lord, God will give things seven-times greater than these, which I will now show you."

IX

The City of Christ

After that he took me from that place, and there I saw a river; and its waters were exceedingly white, whiter than milk. I said to the angel, "What is this?" And he said to me, "This is Lake Acherusa where the City of Christ is, but not everyone is allowed to enter that city, for this is the way that leads to God, and if any are fornicators or ungodly, and convert and repent and bear fruits fitting for repentance, when they first come out of their bodies they are brought and worship God, and then by the commandment of the Lord they are delivered to Michael the angel, and he washes them in the Lake Acherusa and so brings them into the City of Christ with those who have not sinned." I marvelled and blessed the Lord God for all the things that I saw.

The angel answered and said to me, "Follow me, and I will bring you into the City of Christ." He stood by Lake Acherusa and set me in a golden ship. Angels, three thousand it seemed, sang a hymn before me until I came to the City of Christ. Those who dwelt in the City of Christ rejoiced greatly over me as I came to them, and I entered and saw the City of Christ. It was all gold, and twelve walls encircled it, and there were twelve towers inside, and every wall had a furlong between them round about. I said to the angel, "Lord, how much is one furlong?" The angel answered and said to me, "It is as much as there is between the Lord God and the men and women who are on earth, for the great City of Christ is separate."

There were twelve gates of great beauty in the circuit of the city, and four rivers encircled it. There was a river of honey and a river of milk and a river of wine and a river of oil. I said to the angel, "What are these rivers that encircle this city?" He said to me, "These are the four rivers that flow abundantly for those who are in this Land of Promise. These are their names: the river of honey is called Phison, and the river of milk Euphrates, and the river of oil Geon, and the river of wine Tigris. Since the righteous did not use their power over these things when they were in the world, but hungered and afflicted themselves for the Lord God's sake, therefore when they enter this city the Lord will give them these things without number and without any measure."

When I entered by the gate I saw before the doors of the city great and high trees with no fruit, but only leaves. I also saw a few people scattered in the midst of the trees, and they mourned sorely when they saw anyone enter the city. Those trees did penance for them, humbling themselves and bowing down, and raising themselves up again.

I saw this and wept with them, and I asked the angel and said, "Lord, who are these who are not permitted to enter the City of Christ?" He said to me, "These are the ones who earnestly renounced the world day and night with fasting but had a proud heart above others, glorifying and praising themselves, and doing nothing for their neighbors. For some they had a friendly greeting, but to others they did not even say 'Hail;' and they opened for those whom they wished to, and if they did any small thing for a neighbor they were puffed up." And I said, "What then, lord? Has their pride prevented them from entering the City of Christ?" The angel answered and said to me, "The root of all evil is pride. Are they better than the Son of God who came to the Jews in great humility?" I asked him and said, "Why is it then that the trees humble themselves and are again raised up?" The angel answered and said to me, "Despite all the time that they spent on

31

earth serving God, and despite the fact that they were ashamed for a time and humbled themselves because of the shame and reproaches of others, they were not grieved, nor did they repent or cease their pride. This is why the trees humble themselves and are raised up again." I asked and said, "Why are they allowed up to the gates of the city?" The angel answered and said to me: "Because of the great goodness of God, and because this is the entrance of all his saints who enter this city. Therefore they are left in this place so that when Christ the eternal king enters with his saints, when he comes in, all the righteous will entreat for them. Then they will enter the city with them. Yet none of them is able to have the confidence those have who humbled themselves, serving the Lord God all their life long."

But I went forward, and the angel led me and brought me to the river of honey, and I saw there Isaiah and Jeremiah and Ezekiel and Amos and Micah and Zachariah, even the lesser and greater prophets, and they greeted me in the city. I said to the angel, "What path is this?" And he said to me, "This is the path of the prophets. When anyone who has grieved his soul and not done his own will for God's sake has departed from the world and has been brought to the Lord God and has worshipped him, then by the commandment of God that soul is delivered to Michael, who brings it into the city to this place of the prophets. There they greet the soul as their friend and neighbor, because it performed the will of God."

Again he led me to the river of milk, and I saw there all the children that King Herod killed for the name of Christ. They greeted me, and the angel said to me, "All those who are chaste, when they leave the body, after they worship the Lord God, they are delivered to Michael and brought to the children; and they greet them, saying,

'They are our brothers and sisters and friends and members.' Among them they will inherit the promises of God."

Again he took me and brought me to the north side of the city and led me to the river of wine. There I saw Abraham, Isaac, and Jacob, Lot and Job and other saints, and they greeted me. I asked and said, "What is this place, lord?" The angel answered and said to me, "All those who are entertainers of strangers, when they leave the world, first worship the Lord God and then are delivered to Michael and brought by this path to the city. All the righteous greet this soul as a son or daughter and a brother or sister and say, 'Because you have maintained kindness and hospitality to strangers, come and have an inheritance in the city of our Lord God.' Every one of the righteous will receive the good things of God in the city according to his or her deeds."

Then he took me to the river of oil on the east side of the city. There I saw people rejoicing and singing psalms, and said, "Who are these, lord?" And the angel said to me, "These are the ones who have devoted themselves to God with their whole heart and had no pride in them." For all who rejoice in the Lord God and sing praises to the Lord with their whole heart are brought here into this city.

He took me to the middle of the city, near the twelve walls. Now there was a higher wall inside, and I asked and said, "Is there a wall in the City of Christ more excellent in honor than this one?" The angel answered and said to me, "The second is better than the first, and likewise the third than the second; for one excels the other right up to the twelfth wall." I said, "Why, lord, does one excel the other in glory? Explain it to me." The angel answered and said to me, "Through all who have even a little slander or envy or pride in them, something is taken away from this glory, even if he or she is in the City of Christ. Look behind you."

I turned and saw golden thrones set at the gates, and upon them were people with golden crowns and jewels; and I looked and saw among these twelve thrones set in another order, which appeared to be of so much glory that no one could declare their praise. I asked the angel and said, "Lord, who is on the throne?" The angel answered and said to me, "These are the thrones of those who had goodness and understanding of heart and yet made themselves foolish for the Lord God's sake, knowing neither the Scriptures nor many psalms. But keeping in mind one chapter of the precepts of God, they performed it with great diligence and had the right intention before the Lord God. For these great wonder will take hold of all the saints before the Lord God, who will speak together, saying, 'Look and see the unlearned who know nothing, and how they have earned such fair raiment and such great glory because of their innocence.'"

In the middle of the city I saw a very high altar. And there was one standing by the altar whose face shone like the sun, and he held in his hands a psalter and a harp and sang praises, saying, "Alleluia." And his voice filled the whole city. When all who were on the towers and the gates heard him, they answered, "Alleluia," so that the foundations of the city were shaken. I asked the angel and said, "Who is this, lord, that is so mighty?" And the angel said to me, "This is David. This is the city of Jerusalem. When Christ the king of eternity comes in the fullness of his kingdom, he will again go before him to sing his praises, and all the righteous will sing praises together, answering, 'Alleluia.'" I said, "Lord, how is it that only

David above all the rest of the saints began singing the Psalms?" The angel answered and said to me, "When Christ the Son of God sits on the right hand of his Father, David will sing praises before him in the seventh heaven; and as it is done in the heavens, so is it done below, for without David it is not lawful to offer a sacrifice to God; but it must be that David sings praises at the hour of the offering of the body and blood of Christ. As it is performed in heaven, so is it also on earth."

I said to the angel, "Lord, what is 'Alleluia'?" The angel answered and said to me, "You examine and inquire about all things." And he said to me, "'Alleluia' is spoken in Hebrew, which is the speech of God and the angels. Now the interpretation of 'Alleluia' is this: *tecel cat marith macha.*" And I said, "Lord, what is *tecel cat marith macha* ?" The angel answered and said to me, "*Tecel cat marith macha* means 'Let us bless him all together.'" I asked the angel and said, "Lord, do all those who say 'Alleluia' bless God?" The angel answered and said to me, "Yes, and if any sing 'Alleluia,' and those who are present do not sing together, they sin in not singing together." I said, "Lord, does one also sin if one is doting or very aged?" The angel answered and said to me, "No, but whoever is able and does not sing together is a despiser of the word, because it would be proud and unworthy if he or she did not bless the Lord God their creator."

When he had ceased speaking to me, he led me outside the city through the midst of the trees and back from the place of the land of good things and set me at the river of milk and honey, and after that he led me to the ocean that bears the foundations of the heaven.

X

The Regions of Hell

The angel turned and said to me, "Do you realize that you are leaving here?" And I said, "Yes, lord." He said to me, "Come, follow me, and I will show you the souls of the ungodly and the sinners, so that you may know what kind of place they have." I went with the angel, and he took me in the direction of the sunset, and I saw the beginning of heaven founded on a great river of water, and I asked, "What river of water is this?" He said to me, "This is the ocean that surrounds the whole earth." When I was beyond the ocean, I looked and there was no light in that place, only darkness and sorrow and sadness, and I sighed.

I saw there a river of fire burning with heat, and in it there was a multitude of men and women sunk up to their knees, and others up to their navels; others also up to their lips and others up to their hair; and I asked the angel and said, "Lord, who are these in the river of fire?" The angel answered and said to me, "These are neither hot nor cold, for they were not among either the righteous or the wicked; for they passed the time of their lives on earth with some days in prayer but other days in sins and fornication, until their death." I asked and said, "Who are these, lord, who are sunk up to their knees in fire?" He answered and said to me, "These are the ones who when they came out of church occupied themselves in disputes and idle talk. But these who are sunk up to their navels are the ones who, after they received the body and blood of Christ, went and committed fornication and did not cease from committing their sins until they died. And those who are sunk up to their lips slandered one another when they gathered in the church of God. Those who are sunk up to their eyebrows beckoned one another and secretly plotted evil against their neighbors."

On the north side I saw a place of various and diverse torments full of men and women, and a river of fire flowed down upon them. And I saw pits exceedingly deep, and in them were many souls, and the depth of that place was like three thousand cubits. I saw them groaning and weeping and saying, "Have mercy on us, Lord." No one had mercy on them. I asked the angel and said, "Who are these, lord?" And the angel answered and said to me, "These are the ones who did not trust in the Lord so that they could have him as their helper." I inquired and said, "Lord, if these souls continue like this, with thirty or forty generations cast one upon another, unless they are cast down still deeper, I believe the pits will not contain them." And he said to me, "The abyss has no boundary, for beneath it there follows also what is beneath; and so if someone strong took a stone and threw it into a very deep well, after many hours it would reach the bottom. This abyss is also like that. For when souls are thrown into it, they hardly come to the bottom after five hundred years."

When I heard this, I mourned and lamented for the human race. The angel answered and said to me, "Why do you mourn? Are you more merciful than God? For since God is good and knows that there are torments, he bears patiently with humanity, leaving every one to do his or her own will for the time that he or she dwells on earth."

Yet I looked again on the river of fire, and I saw there a man caught by the throat by angels, keepers of hell, who had in their hands an iron with three hooks with which they pierced that old man's entrails. I asked the angel and said, "Lord, who is this old man upon whom such torments are inflicted?" The angel answered and said to me, "He was a priest who did not fulfill his ministry well, because when he was eating and drinking and whoring he offered the sacrifice to the Lord at his holy altar."

I saw another old man not far off. Running quickly, four evil angels brought him, and they sank him up to his knees in the river of fire and struck him with stones and wounded his face like a tempest and did not allow him to say, "Have mercy on me." I asked the angel and he said to me, "He was a bishop, and he did not fulfill his episcopal office well, for indeed he received a great name, but he did not enter into the holiness of him who gave him that name all his life. He did not give righteous judgment and did not have compassion for widows and orphans. But now he is recompensed according to his iniquity and his actions."

I saw another man in the river of fire sunk up to the knees, and his hands were stretched out and bloody, and worms came out of his mouth and his nostrils, and he was groaning and lamenting and crying out and said, "Have mercy on me for I suffer more harm than the rest who are in this torment." I asked, "Who is this, lord?" And he said to me, "He was a deacon who devoured the offerings and committed fornication and did not do right in the sight of God; therefore he pays the penalty without ceasing."

I looked and saw beside him another man whom they hastily brought and cast into the river of fire, and he was there up to his knees. The angel who was over the torments came with a great razor, red-hot, and with it he cut that man's lips and also his tongue. I sighed and wept and asked, "Who is this man, lord?" And he said to me, "He was a lector and read to the people, but he did not keep the commandments of God. Now he also pays his own penalty."

I saw another great multitude of pits in the same place, and in the middle of them was a river filled with a multitude of men and women with worms devouring them. But I wept and sighed and asked the angel, "Lord who are these?" And he said to me, "These are the ones who extorted usury on usury and trusted in their riches, not having hope in God as their helper."

After that I looked and saw a very straight place, and there was some kind of wall and around it fire. Inside it I saw men and women gnawing their tongues and asked, "Who are these, lord?" He said to me, "These are the ones who mocked the word of God in church, not paying attention to it, but acting as if God and his angels were nothing. Now, therefore, they likewise pay their due penalty."

I looked in and saw another pool under the pit, and it appeared to be like blood. I asked and said, "Lord, what is this place?" He said to me, "Into this pit flow all the torments." I saw men and women sunk up to their lips and asked, "Who are these, lord?" And he said to me, "These are the sorcerers who gave men and women magical enchantments, and they found no rest until they died."

Again I saw men and women of a very black countenance in a pit of fire, and I sighed and wept and asked, "Who are these, lord?" And he said to me, "These are whoremongers and adulterers who had wives of their own and committed adultery. Likewise the women committed adultery in the same way, although they had their own husbands. Therefore they pay this penalty without ceasing."

I saw there girls clothed in black garments, and four fearful angels held in their hands red-hot chains and put them on their necks and led them away into darkness. And again I wept and asked the angel, "Who are these, lord?" And he said to me, "These are the ones who were virgins but defiled their virginity, and their parents did not know it. Therefore they pay their due penalty without ceasing."

Again I saw men and women there with their hands and feet cut off. They were naked in a place of ice and snow, and worms devoured them. When I saw this I wept and asked, "Who are these, lord?" He said to me, "These are the ones who injured the fatherless and the widows and the poor and did not trust in the Lord. Therefore they pay their due penalty without ceasing."

I looked and saw others hanging over a channel of water, and their tongues were very dry, and many fruits were set in their sight, and they were not allowed to take any of them. I asked, "Who are these, lord?" And he said to me, "These are the ones who broke the fast before the appointed time. Therefore without ceasing they pay this penalty."

I saw other men and women hanging by their eyebrows and their hair, and a river of fire provoked them, and I said, "Who are these, lord?" And he said to me, "These are the ones who did not give themselves to their own husbands and wives but to adulterers, and therefore they pay their due penalty without ceasing."

I saw other men and women covered with dust, and their appearance was like blood, and they were in a pit of pitch and brimstone and carried down in a river of fire. I asked, "Who are these, lord?" And he said to me, "These are the ones who committed the wickedness of Sodom and Gomorrah, men with men, therefore they pay their penalty without ceasing."

I looked and saw men and women dressed in white apparel, and their eyes were blind, and they were set in a pit, and I asked, "Who are these, lord?" He said to me, "These are those heathen who gave alms and did not know the Lord God. Therefore without ceasing they pay their due penalty."

I looked and saw other men and women on a spit of fire, and beasts were tearing them, and they were not allowed to say, "Lord, have mercy on us." And I saw the angel of the torments laying the most fierce torments on them and saying, "Acknowledge the Son of God. For you were told before, but when the scriptures of God were read to you, you paid no attention. Therefore the judgment of God is just, because your evil actions have taken hold of you and brought you into these torments." But I sighed and wept, and I inquired and said, "Who are these men and women who are strangled in this fire and pay the penalty?" He answered me, "These are the women who defiled the creation of God when they brought forth children from the womb, and these are the men who lay with them. But their children appealed to the Lord God and to the angels who are over the torments, saying, 'Take vengeance for us on our parents, for they have defiled the creation of God. They had the name of God, but did not observe his commandments. They gave us as food to dogs and to be trampled on by swine, and others they cast into the river.' But those children were delivered to the angels of Tartarus so that they could be brought into a spacious place of mercy. But their fathers and mothers were hauled into everlasting torment."

After that I saw men and women dressed in rags full of pitch and brimstone of fire, and there were dragons entwined around their necks and shoulders and feet, and angels with horns of fire constrained them and struck them and closed up their nostrils, saying to them, "Why did you not know the time when it was right for you to repent and serve God?" And I asked, "Who are these, lord?" He said to me, "These are the ones who seemed to renounce the world, wearing our habit; but the snares of the world made them miserable. They showed no charity and had no pity on the widows and the fatherless; they did not take in the stranger and pilgrim, nor offered one holy gift, nor had pity on their neighbor. Their prayers did not go up pure to the Lord God even one day; but the many snares of the world held them back, and they were not able to do right in the sight of God. And the angels surrounded them in the place of torments; and those who were in the torments saw them and said to them, 'Indeed when we lived in the world we neglected God, and you did so also. When we were in the world we knew that we were sinners, but it was said of you: 'These are righteous and servants of God.' Now we know that you were only called by the name of the Lord.' Therefore they also pay their due penalty."

I sighed and wept and said, "Woe to humanity! Woe to the sinners! To what end were they born?" And the angel answered and said to me, "Why do you weep? Are you more merciful than the Lord God who is blessed forever, who has established the judgment and left everyone to choose good or evil of their own will and to do as they please?" Still I wept again very pained; and he said to me, "Do you weep now, when you have still not seen the greater torments? Follow me, and you will see seven times worse than these."

XI

The Pit of Hell

He took me from the north side and put me over a well, and I found it sealed with seven seals. The angel who was with me said to the angel of that place, "Open the mouth of the well so that Paul, the dearly beloved of God, can see; for the power has been given to him to see all the torments of hell." And the angel said to me, "Stand far off so that you will be able to endure the stench of this place."

When the well was opened, therefore, a hard and very evil stench immediately arose there out of it. It surpassed all the other torments; and I looked into the well and saw masses of fire burning on every side, and anguish, and the mouth of the pit was so narrow that it took only one in at a time. The angel turned and said to me, "If any are thrown into the well of the abyss, and it is sealed over them, there will never be any recollection made of them in the presence of the Father and the Son and the Holy Ghost or of the holy angels." And I said, "Who are these, lord, who are cast into this well?" He said to me, "They are whoever does not confess that Christ has come in the flesh and that the Virgin Mary bore him and whoever says of the bread and the cup of blessing of the Eucharist that it is not the body and blood of Christ."

I looked from the north to the west and saw there the worm that does not sleep, and in that place there was a gnashing of teeth. The worms were the length of one cubit, and each had two heads. I saw there men and women who were gnashing their teeth in the cold. And I asked and said, "Lord, who are these in this place?" He said to me, "These are the ones who say that Christ did not rise from the dead, and that our flesh does not rise again." I inquired and said, "Lord, is there no fire or heat in this place?" And he said to me, "In this place there is nothing but cold and snow." Again he said to me, "Even if the sun rose upon them, they would not be warmed because of the extreme cold in this place and the snow." When I heard this I spread out my hands and wept and sighed, and again

I said, "It would be better for us if we were not born, since we all are sinners."

But when those who were there in that place saw me weeping, with the angel they also cried out and wept, saying, "Lord God, have mercy on us."

After that I saw heaven open and Michael the archangel come down out of heaven, and with him were all the host of the angels. They came to those who were set in torment. When they saw them they wept again and cried out and said, "Have mercy on us Michael, archangel, have mercy on us and on the human race, for it is by your prayers that the earth stands. We have now seen the judgment and have known the Son of God. It was not possible for us to pray for this before we came into this place, for we heard that there was a judgment before we departed from the world, but the snares and the life of the world did not allow us to repent." And Michael answered and said, "Listen when Michael speaks. I am he who always stands in the presence of God. As the Lord lives, before whose face I stand, I do not cease for one day or one night to pray continually for the human race. I indeed pray for those who are on earth, but they do not cease committing wickedness and fornication. They create nothing good while they are on earth. You have wasted in vanity the time when you ought to have repented. But I have always prayed, and now I entreat God to send dew and rain upon the earth, and still I pray until the earth yields her fruits. And I say that if anyone does just a little good I will strive for and protect that person until he or she escapes the judgment of torment.

"Where then are your prayers? Where are your repentances? You have wasted your time despicably. Yet weep now, and I and the angels who are with me together with the dearly beloved Paul will weep with you if possibly the merciful God will have pity and grant you refreshment." When they heard these words they cried out and wept sorely, and all said with one voice, "Have mercy on us, O Son of God." And I, Paul, sighed and said, "O Lord God, have mercy on your creatures, have mercy on the children of humanity, have mercy upon your image."

And I saw heaven shake like a tree that is moved by the wind; and suddenly they cast themselves down on their faces before the throne. I saw the four-and-twenty elders and the four beasts worshipping God. I saw the altar and the veil and the throne, and all of them were rejoicing, and the smoke of a sweet odor rose up beside the altar of the throne of God, and I heard a voice saying, "Why, our angels and ministers, do you entreat me?" They cried out saying, "We entreat you, witnessing your great goodness to humanity." Then I saw the Son of God coming down out of heaven, and on his head there was a crown. And when those who were in the torments saw him they all cried out with one voice, saying, "Have mercy on us, O exalted Son of God. You are he who has granted refreshment to all who are in heaven and on earth. Have mercy on us also, for since we saw you we have been refreshed."

And there went forth a voice from the Son of God throughout all the places of torment, saying, "What good works have you done that you should ask refreshment from me? My blood was shed for you, and you did not even repent. For your sake I wore a crown of thorns on my head. For you I received blows on my cheeks, and you did not even repent. I asked for water when I hung upon the cross, and they gave me vinegar mingled with gall. With a spear they opened my right side. For my name's sake they have killed my servants, the prophets and the righteous. And for all these things I gave you an opportunity for repentance, and you would not repent. Yet now because of Michael, the archangel of my

45

covenant, and the angels who are with him, and because of Paul, my dearly beloved whom I would not grieve, and because of your brethren who are in the world and do offer holy gifts, and because of your children – for my commandments are in them – and still more because of my own goodness on the day that I rose from the dead, I will always grant to all of you who are in torment refreshment forever for a day and a night." They all cried out and said, "We bless you, O Son of God, since you have granted us rest for a day and a night, for the refreshment of one day is better to us than the whole time of our lives when we were on earth. If we had known clearly that this place was appointed for those who sin, we would have done no other work whatever, neither traded nor done any wickedness. For what profit was our pride in the world? For this our pride that came out of our mouth against our neighbors is taken captive. This pain and our bitter anguish and tears and the worms that are under us, these are worse to us than the torments that we suffer."

As they thus spoke, the angels of torment and the evil angels were angry with them and said, "How long have you wept and sighed? You had no mercy. This is the judgment of God on those that did not have mercy. Yet you have received this great grace, refreshment for the night and day of the Lord's Day, because of Paul the dearly beloved of God who has come down to you."

Three Visions

from Gregory the Great

A certain Slav was a monk and lived with me here in this city in my monastery. He used to tell me that when he lived in the wilderness he knew a monk named Peter, who was born in Spain. He lived with him in the vast desert called Evasa. He said that Peter told him how, before he came to dwell in that place, he had died from an illness and was immediately restored to life again.

He declared that he had seen the torments and innumerable places of hell and many people, who were mighty in this world, hanging in those flames. As he himself was also carried to be thrown into the same fire, an angel in beautiful attire suddenly appeared. The angel would not allow him to be cast into those torments but spoke to him in this manner: "Go back again, and from now on look carefully after yourself and how you lead your life." After these words his body grew warm little by little. Waking out of this sleep of everlasting death, he reported all those things that happened around him. Then he devoted himself to such fasting and vigils that, although he said nothing, his very life and conversation still spoke of the torments that he had seen and still feared. Thus God's merciful providence arranged by his temporal death that he did not die forever.

But because the human heart is worse than obdurate and hard, it happens that though others have the same vision and see the same punishments, they do not always reap the same profit. The honorable man Stephen, whom you knew very well, told me himself that when he was on business, living in the city of Constantinople, he became sick and died. When they tried to find a surgeon to disembowel him and to embalm his body, they could not get anyone. All the following night he lay unburied. During this time his soul was carried to the dungeon of hell where he saw many things that he had little believed in when he heard of them before. But when he was brought before the judge who sat there he would not allow Stephen into his presence, saying, "I did not command this man, but Stephen the smith to be brought." With these words he was restored to life right away, and Stephen the smith, who lived nearby, departed from this life at that very hour. The smith's death showed that the words the first Stephen heard were true.

In this way the first Stephen escaped death at that time. Yet he ended his days three years later in that epidemic that lamentably wasted this city, in which, as you know, with their own eyes people saw arrows come from heaven and strike different men and women. At that time a certain soldier was also brought to the point of death. In a similar way his soul was carried out of his body, so that he lay void of any sense or feeling. But he quickly came to himself again. He told those who were present what strange things he had seen. He said – as many report that know it very well – that he saw a bridge. Under it a black and smokey river ran that had a filthy and intolerable smell. On its farther side there were pleasant green meadows full of sweet flowers. Here there were also different companies of men and women dressed in white.

There was such a delicate odor that the fragrant smell gave wonderful pleasure to all who dwelled and walked in that place. Different mansions were also there, all shining with brightness and light. One especially magnificent and sumptuous house was built of brick that seemed to be gold; but whose house it was he did not know.

On the bank of the river there were also a number of houses, but the stinking vapor that rose from the river reached some of them, and some others it did not reach at all. Now those who wanted to cross the bridge were subjected to the following trial. If anyone wicked attempted to cross, down he or she fell into the dark and stinking river. Those who were just and not hindered by sin, however, safely and easily crossed over to those pleasant and delicate places.

He said that there he also saw Peter who was the steward of the pope's family and who had died some four years before. He was thrust into a most filthy place where he was bound and kept down by a great weight of iron. Asking why he was treated in this way, the soldier was told what all of us who knew his life can confirm as true. He was told that Peter suffered that punishment because when he had to punish another he did it more to be cruel than to show his obedience. None who knew him can be ignorant of his merciless disposition. The soldier said that there he also saw a priest he knew who came to the bridge and passed over with great safety, since in this world he lived sincerely.

On the same bridge he said that he saw this Stephen, whom we spoke of before. He was about to go over when his foot slipped and his body hung in half over either side of the bridge. Terrible creatures rose out of the river and drew him down by the legs. Others, white and beautiful, pulled him up by the arms. While they competed like this, with the wicked spirits drawing him downward and the good ones lifting him upward, the soldier who saw this whole strange sight returned to life. He did not know what finally happened to Stephen.

By this miraculous vision we learn this about Stephen's life. In him the sins of the flesh competed with his works of charity. Just as he was drawn down by his legs and pulled up by his arms, it is apparent that he loved to give alms and yet did not perfectly resist the sins of the flesh that pulled him down. But which had victory in that secret examination of the supreme judge, neither we nor he who saw it know. Yet it is most certain that this Stephen, after he saw the places of hell, as we said before, returned to his body again but never did perfectly amend his former wicked life. Many years after he has departed from this world, he still leaves us in doubt whether he was saved or damned.

We can learn from this that when the torments of hell are shown to men and women, sometimes it is for their own benefit and sometimes as a witness for others. The first may see those miseries in order to avoid them; and the others may see them to be punished even more because they would not learn from the torments that they both knew and saw with their own eyes.

urseus' Vision

While Sigebert still governed the kingdom there came from Ireland a holy man named Furseus, renowned both for his words and actions and remarkable for exceptional virtues, for he wanted to live as a stranger for our Lord wherever an opportunity should offer itself. On coming into the province of East Anglia, he was honorably received by Sigebert. Performing his usual task of preaching the Gospel, by the example of his virtue and the efficacy of his discourse he converted many unbelievers to Christ and through his faith and love confirmed those who already believed.

While here he fell ill and was thought worthy to see an angelic vision. In it he was admonished to proceed diligently in the ministry of the Word, which he had undertaken, and indefatigably to continue his usual watching and prayers, since his end was certain, but its hour would be uncertain, according to our Lord who said, "Watch you therefore, because you know not the day nor the hour." Encouraged by this vision, he applied himself with all speed to build a monastery on the land that had been given to him by King Sigebert and to establish regular discipline in it.

This monastery was pleasantly situated in the woods with the sea not far off. It was built within the area of a castle, which in English is called Cnobheresburg, that is, Cnobher's town. Afterwards Anna, king of that province, and the nobility embellished it with more stately buildings and donations.

Furseus was of noble Scottish blood, but much more noble in mind than in birth. From his youth he applied himself particularly to reading sacred books and following monastic discipline; and, as is most appropriate to holy men, he carefully practised all that he learned was to be done.

In short, he built himself the monastery where he might have time for his heavenly studies. Falling sick there, as the book about his life informs us, he fell into a trance, and leaving his body from evening until the cock crowed, he was found worthy to see the choirs of angels and to hear the praises that are sung in heaven. He used to declare that among other things he distinctly heard this: "The saints shall advance from one virtue to another," and, "The God of gods shall be seen in Sion."

Restored to his body at that time and again taken from it three days later, he not only saw the greater joys of the blessed but also extraordinary combats of evil spirits, who with frequent accusations wickedly tried to obstruct his journey to heaven; but with the angels protecting him, all their efforts were in vain. If anyone desires to be more fully informed concerning the details of his jour-

ney, let that person read the little book of his life that I
have mentioned, and I believe he or she will reap much
spiritual profit from it. That book describes with what
subtle fraud the devils represented both his actions and
superfluous words and even his thoughts, as if they had
been written down in a book. It tells what pleasing or
disagreeable things he was informed of by the angels and
saints and what just men and women appeared to him
among the angels.

But there is one thing among all the rest that we have
thought may be beneficial to many if it is inserted in this
history. When Furseus had been lifted up on high, he was
ordered by the angels who conducted him to look back on
the world. Then casting his eyes down, he saw what
seemed to be a dark and obscure valley below him. He
also saw four fires in the air, not far from each other.
Then asking the angels what those fires were, he was told
they were the fires that would kindle and consume the
world. One of them was falsehood, when we do not fulfill
what we promised in baptism to renounce the devil and all
his works. The next is covetousness, when we prefer the
riches of the world to the love of heavenly things. The
third is discord, when we do not fear to offend those close
to us even in needless things. The fourth is iniquity, when
we look upon it as no crime to rob and to defraud the
weak.

These fires, increasing by degrees, extended to meet
one another, and being joined, became an immense flame.
When it drew near, fearing for himself, Furseus said to
the angel, "Lord, behold the fire draws near me." The
angel answered, "What you did not kindle shall not burn
you; for though this appears to be a terrible and great
fire, yet it tries everyone according to the merits of his or
her works; for everyone's concupiscence shall burn in the
fire; for as everyone burns in the body through unlawful

pleasure, so when discharged from the body, that person shall burn in the punishment that he or she has deserved."

Then he saw one of the three angels who had been his guides throughout both visions go first and divide the flame of fire, while the other two, flying on both sides, defended him from the danger of that fire. He also saw devils flying through the fire, raising conflagrations of wars against the just. Then followed accusations of the wicked spirits against him, the defense of the good angels in his favor, and a more extended view of the heavenly troops and also of the holy men of his own nation, who, as he had long ago been told, had been deservedly advanced to the level of priesthood. From them he heard many things that might be very salutary to himself or to all others who would listen to them.

When they had ended their discourse and returned to heaven with the angelic spirits, the three angels, of whom we have spoken before and who were to bring Blessed Furseus back to his body, remained with him. When they approached this immense fire, the angel divided the flame as he had done before; but when the man of God came to the passage opened amid the flames, the unclean spirits laid hold of one of those whom they tormented in the fire and threw him at Furseus and, touching his shoulder and jaw, burned them. Furseus knew the man and remembered that he had received this man's garment when he died; and the angel, immediately laying hold, threw the man back into the fire; and the malignant enemy said, "Do not reject him whom you received before; for since you accepted goods from him who was a sinner, so you must take part in his punishment." The angel replying said, "He did not receive them through avarice, but in order to save that man's soul." The fire ceased, and turning to Furseus the angel added, "What you kindled burned you; for had you not received the money from that man who died in sin, his punishment would not burn you." Proceeding in his discourse, he gave him wholesome advice for what ought to be done for the salvation of people like this who repented.

When he was restored to his body, and throughout his whole life, on his shoulder and jaw he bore the mark of the fire that he had felt in his soul, visible to all men. In an amazing way his flesh publicly showed what the soul had suffered in private. He was always careful, as he was before, to persuade all men to practice virtue both by his example and by preaching. But he would only tell his visions to those who wished to learn of them from holy zeal and desire for reformation.

An ancient brother of our monastery is still living who often declares that a very sincere and religious man told him that he had seen Furseus himself in the province of East Anglia and heard of those visions from his own mouth, adding that though it was in the most bitter winter weather and there was a hard frost, Furseus was sitting in a thin garment when he related his visions; and yet he sweated as if in the middle of the heat of summer, either through excessive fear or spiritual consolation.

rythelm's Vision

At this time a miracle, remarkable like those of former days, occurred in Britain. So that the living might be saved from the death of the soul, a certain person who had been dead for some time rose to life again and told many remarkable things that he had seen, some of which I have decided to mention here briefly.

There was a head of a household in the district of the Northumbrians that is called Cuningham, who led a religious life with his family. This man fell sick, and with his illness increasing daily he was brought to the final point, and he died at nightfall; but at dawn he suddenly came to life again and sat up. All those who sat weeping around his body fled away in great fright. Only his wife, who loved him best, remained with him though trembling and quaking. Comforting her he said, "Do not fear, for I am now truly risen from death, where I was held, and permitted again to live among people, but not as I used to; I am to live in a very different manner from before."

Rising, he immediately went to the oratory of their house and continuing in prayer until day, he then divided all his wealth into three parts; one he gave to his wife, another to his children and the third, belonging to himself, he instantly distributed to the poor. Not long after, free from the concerns of the world, he went to the monastery of Melrose, which is almost enclosed by the winding of the river Tweed, and he accepted the tonsure and went into a private dwelling that the abbot had provided. There he continued till the day of his death in such extraordinary contrition of mind and body that even though his tongue was silent, his life declared that he had seen many things either to be dreaded or desired, which others knew nothing of. He told what he had seen in the following way.

He who led me had a shining countenance and a bright garment, and we went on silently toward, I thought, the place where the sun rises on the solstice. Walking on, we came to a valley of great breadth and depth, but of infinite length. On the left it appeared full of dreadful flames, and the other side was no less horrid on account of the violent hail and cold snow flying in all directions. Both places were full of human souls, which seemed by turns to be tossed from one side to the other as if by a violent storm, because when the wretches could no longer endure the excess of heat, they leaped into the middle of the cutting cold; and finding no rest there, they leaped back again into the middle of the unquenchable flames. Now since an innumerable multitude of deformed spirits were alternately tormented here and there without any intermission as far as could be seen, I began to think that this perhaps might be hell, whose intolerable flames I had often heard discussed. My guide, who went before me, answered my thought saying, "Do not believe it, for this is not the hell you imagine."

When he had conducted me by degrees to the farther end, I was very frightened by that horrid spectacle; and all of a sudden I saw the place begin to grow dim and to be filled with darkness. When I entered the darkness, it gradually grew so thick that I could see nothing except the darkness and the shape and garment of my guide. As we went on through the shades of night, all of a sudden there appeared before us frequent globes of black flames, rising out of a great pit and falling back again into it. When I had been conducted there, my guide suddenly vanished and left me alone in the middle of darkness and this horrid vision, while those same globes of fire alternately flew up and fell back into the bottom of the abyss without intermission. As they ascended, I observed that all the flames were full of human souls, which were sometimes thrown up high like sparks flying up with smoke and again, when the vapor of the fire ceased, dropped down to the depth below. Moreover, an insufferable stench spread with the vapors and filled all those dark places.

After standing there a long time in fear, not knowing what to do, which way to turn, or what end I might expect, suddenly I heard behind me the noise of a most hideous and wretched lamentation, and at the same time a loud laughing, like that of a rude multitude insulting captured enemies. When that noise grew plainer and came close to me, I observed a gang of evil spirits dragging the howling and lamenting souls of people into the middle of the darkness, while the devils themselves laughed and rejoiced. Among those people, from what I could see, there was one shorn like a clergyman, a layman and a woman. The evil spirits who dragged them went down into the midst of the burning pit; and as they went down deeper, I could no longer distinguish between the lamentation of the people and the laughing of the devils, yet I still had a confused sound in my ears.

In the meantime, some of the dark spirits ascended from that flaming abyss, and running forward, attacked me on all sides and confounded me with their glaring eyes and the stinking fire that came from their mouths and noses. They threatened to lay hold of me with the burning tongs that they had in their hands; yet they dared not touch me, although they frightened me. While I was thus surrounded on all sides with enemies and darkness, and looked about on every side for help, behind me from the way that I came there appeared the brightness of a star shining amid the darkness, which increased by degrees and came rapidly toward me. When it drew near, all those evil spirits who sought to carry me away with their tongs dispersed and fled.

He whose approach put them to flight was the same one who led me before. Turning toward the right, he then began to lead me toward what seemed the place where the sun rises in winter, and bringing me out of the darkness, conducted me into an atmosphere of clear light. While he was leading me in open light in this way, I saw a vast wall before us, the length and height of which seemed to be altogether boundless in every direction. I began to wonder why we went up to the wall, since I saw no door, window or path through it. When we came to the wall, all of a sudden – I don't know how – we were on the top of it. Within it there was a vast and delightful field, so full of fragrant flowers that the odor of its delightful sweetness immediately dispelled the stink of the dark furnace that had pierced me through and through. So great was the light in this place that it seemed to exceed the brightness of day or the sun in its meridian height. In this field were innumerable assemblies of men and women in white and many groups seated together rejoicing. As he led me through the middle of those happy inhabitants, I began to think that this might, perhaps, be the kingdom of heaven, of which I had often heard so much. He answered my thought, saying, "This is not the kingdom of heaven, as you imagine."

When we had passed those mansions of blessed souls and gone further on, I discovered before me a much more beautiful light and there heard the sweet voices of people singing, and so wonderful a fragrance proceeded from the place that the other place, which I had thought before most delicious, then seemed to me only very indifferent; even as that extraordinary brightness of the flowery field, compared with this, appeared mean and inconsiderable. When I began to hope that we would enter that delightful place, my guide suddenly stood still and then, turning around, led me back the way we came.

When we returned to those joyful mansions of the souls in white, he said to me, "Do you know what all these things are that you have seen?" I answered that I did not; and then he replied, "That valley you saw so dreadful because of the consuming flames and cutting cold is the place to try and punish the souls of those who delay to confess and amend their sins, but eventually have recourse to repentance at the point of death, and so depart from this life. Nevertheless, because they finally confessed and repented at death, they will all be received into the kingdom of heaven at the Day of Judgment. Many, however, are aided before the Day of Judgment by the prayers, alms and fasting of the living, and more especially by Masses.

"That fiery and stinking pit that you saw is the mouth of hell, and whoever falls into it shall never be delivered for all eternity. This flowery place, in which you see these most beautiful young people, so bright and merry, is the reception place for the souls of those who depart from the body after doing good works, but who are not so perfect as to deserve to be admitted immediately into the kingdom of heaven. Yet at the Day of Judgment they shall all see Christ and partake of the joys of his kingdom; for they who are perfect in thought, word and deed immediately enter the kingdom of heaven as soon as they depart from their bodies. That is in the place with the fragrant odor and bright light where you heard the sound of sweet singing.

"As for you, who are now to return to your body and live among men and women again, if you will try carefully to examine your actions and direct your speech and behavior in righteousness and simplicity, after death you will have a place of residence among these joyful troops of blessed souls; for when I left you for a while, it was to know how you were to be disposed of."

When he said this to me, I hated very much to return to my body, since I was delighted with the sweetness and beauty of the place I saw and with the company of those I saw in it. However, I dared not ask him any questions, but in the meantime I suddenly found myself alive among men and women.

Now these and other things that this man of God saw he would not relate to lazy people or those who lived negligently; but only to those who are terrified with the dread of torments or delighted with the hopes of heavenly joys and would make use of his words to advance in piety.

In the neighborhood of his cell lived one Hemgils, a monk, eminent in priesthood, which he honored by his good works. He is still living and leading a solitary life in Ireland, supporting his declining age with coarse bread and cold water. He often went to that man and, asking several questions, heard from him all the particulars of what he had seen when he was separated from his body. Through his retelling we also came to know those few particulars that we have briefly set down.

He also related his visions to King Aldfrith, a man most learned in all respects, and was so willingly and attentively heard by him that at his request he was admitted into the monastery mentioned above and received the monastic tonsure. When this king happened to be in those regions, he very often went to hear him. At that time the religious and humble abbot and priest,

Ethelwald, presided over the monastery and now with worthy conduct possesses the episcopal see of the church of Lindisfarne.

He had a more private place of residence assigned to him in that monastery, where he might apply himself to the service of his creator in continual prayer. Since that place lay on the bank of the river, he often used to go into it to do penance to his body, and many times to dip completely under the water and to continue saying psalms or prayers in the water as long as he could endure it, standing still sometimes up to his middle and sometimes to his neck in water. When he came ashore, he never took off his cold and frozen garments until they grew warm and dry on his body. In the winter when the half-broken pieces of ice were swimming around him, which he had broken himself to make room to stand or dip himself in the river, those who saw it would say, "It is wonderful, Brother Drythelm (for that was his name) that you are able to endure such harsh cold." He simply answered (for he was a man of simple character and moderate nature) "I have seen greater cold." And when they said, "It is strange that you will endure such austerity." He replied, "I have seen more austerity."

Thus through an indefatigable desire of heavenly bliss, he continued to subdue his aged body with daily fasting until the day he was called away. And so he helped the salvation of many by his words and example.

etti's Vision

On Saturday Brother Wetti, along with certain of our other brothers, took a potion to promote bodily health. Although the others took it in good health, Wetti had great difficulty and began to throw up what he had taken and immediately to hate the sight of food, which he had to consume to nourish his body. At dawn on the next day, which was Sunday, he felt better and went with the others to take bodily sustenance, and he ate; but in disgust he suffered the same aversion. Although he was already anxious, he did not think that he was in danger of dying because the nourishment that he took on the second and third day of the week encouraged his hope for his present life.

At dusk on the third day of the week, when the brothers were sitting at dinner, he said to them that he was not able to wait with them until the end of the meal. In the meantime he had his bed litter carried from the assembly room into another cell next to the one in which they were eating. This was separated by only one wall, so that he could wait for the end of their dinner while he rested there, and he made his way to bed.

He was resting his limbs on the bed with his eyes only just closed, but not yet sleeping, as he himself later revealed. An evil spirit appeared, assuming the figure of a cleric. He was so deformed by a shadowy and dark face that no trace of his eyes was apparent. In his hand he carried different kinds of instruments of torture. Standing near Wetti's head he congratulated him very much, as if he would torture him tomorrow. While he was being threatened by this great terror, a great crowd of evil spirits immediately filled the whole space of this cell from all sides and surrounded him with shields and lances, making a structure like an Italian fort to enclose him. They surrounded Wetti in such great horror and intolerable terror and made him so anxious that he already had no hope of escaping the signs of his death.

But see how divine compassion came to him there. All of a sudden magnificent men in monastic habit with honorable faces appeared in this same cell, sitting on benches. One in the middle of them said these words in Latin – and so they are written just as he revealed them – "It is not just that these useless spirits do this. This man needs rest. I order them to withdraw." After the gathering of evil spirits heard his voice they withdrew and disappeared.

Once this enormous terror abated, a shining angel of incredible beauty enrobed in purple garments came and stood at his feet. He addressed him in a friendly voice and said, "I have come to you, most beloved spirit." The brother answered him in Latin, saying, "If my Lord wishes to forgive my sins, let him do this mercy, otherwise, we are in his hands. Let him do what seems best. For the patriarchs, prophets, apostles and all the other dignitaries work for humanity either in heaven or on earth, and you ought to work most strenuously in this way since we are in most fragile times." This first vision ended with this conversation between our brother and the angel. These were the words exchanged, which we have had written down as he recalled them. Adding nothing of our own and taking nothing away, we committed this to writing.

When this brother woke up he sat up looking around. As soon as he came to himself, he discovered that two brothers, the prior of his monastery and another monk, were left to take care of him. The others were already dismissed after dinner to go to bed. Wetti called these two to him, and he told them everything in the order that they were shown to him in this short span of time. This written account has been kept close to what he said.

He trembled all over with the horror of the preceding vision, to the point that he completely forgot the graveness of his physical illness, so that his whole body was totally oppressed by an insupportably violent fear. Anxious in the immensity of this fear, he fell down in the presence of these brothers, his body in the shape of a cross, so that they prayed for his sins with all the strength that they had. While he was prostrated these brothers began to sing the seven penitential Psalms for him, and they even added others that occurred to them to sing for him in his great anxiety.

When they finished he rose and sat on his bed, asking for someone to read to him from the *Dialogs* of Gregory. While he listened, the beginning of the last book of the *Dialogs* were read to him up to the end of the ninth or tenth page. At the end of the reading he advised the brothers that they should relieve the tiredness brought on by this vigil by sleeping during the small part of the night that remained and also allow him time to rest.

They moved away from him and gathered in quiet in a part of this cell. After such exhaustion of the soul as well as the body Wetti fell asleep; and the same angel who appeared to him in the first vision stood at his feet clothed in white garments shining with incredible splendor. The angel praised him, speaking with caressing words, because he turned to God when he was placed in distress and concentrated on psalms and readings. He warned Wetti to continue to act in the same way without fail. He advised him to repeat often among others, Psalm 118, since moral virtue is described in it. He was very pleased when he saw that at the same instant he was able to please God with the reading and the intention of the psalm, if it was done truly and not feigned.

When he said this the angel raised him up and led him along a very pleasant and beautiful path. While they went along it, the angel showed Wetti immeasurably high and incredibly beautiful mountains that seemed to be made of marble. A great river of fire surrounded them. An innumerable multitude of the damned was held enclosed in it for punishment. Wetti acknowledged that he knew many of them. In other places he saw souls crucified with numerous different kinds of torments. He saw among these as many priests of major orders as of minor orders who were standing in clinging fire, tied in back with straps. The women defiled by them were tied in a similar way in front of them. They were immersed in the same fire up to their genitals. The angel said that every third day without fail they were beaten on their genitals with rods. Wetti said that he knew many of them.

The angel said that a great many priests who desired worldly advantages were devoted to the business of the court. They think they are pious by elevating themselves in the cult of clothes and the pomp of banquets. They do not concern themselves about gaining their souls. Abounding in luxuries, they rush into whoredom; and so it happens that they cannot intercede for themselves or for others. In a world afflicted by plague and famine they might be able to help if they wished to turn their wealth to God with all their strength. So in the end they would be given the same payment since they deserved it by their earlier merits.

Wetti revealed that he himself saw there a certain building like a castle, built very irregularly with wood and stone and discolored by soot, with smoke rising out of it. When he asked what it was, the angel said that this was the dwelling place of monks from different places and regions gathered together for their purgation. One of them was mentioned especially. It was said that he ought to wait for the Last Judgment enclosed in a lead box because of his particular deed, which, like Anania and Saffira, corrupted the integrity of the life of the community.

Ten years earlier this same thing was revealed about this cursed brother to a certain pilgrim swept up in ecstasy at the end of his life. His fate was then made known, but it was already forgotten in oblivion. This similar vision was recalled on account of the one heard from Wetti. It was apparent from this that when one thing that turned out badly repeats itself twice, it ought to be recorded more frequently so that more monks do not turn their own special work into the heaviness of lead.

The height of a mountain was also shown to him. He was told by the angel about a certain abbot who had died ten years before. He was sent to the top of this summit not for eternal damnation, but to purge his sins. There he endured all the discomfits of weather, the unpleasantness of wind and rain. The angel added that a certain bishop who had recently died should have come to the aid of this abbot by obtaining pardon through the compensation of his prayers. He was ordered to do this through a cleric who learned this in a vision. But this bishop dealt with this in a negligent way and did not feel the fire of charity strongly enough, so that he did not help him in the struggle to which he had been invited.

The angel said, "Because of this he is not even able to help himself." The soul asked, "Where is he?" The angel said, "See there. On the other side of the mountain he pays the penalty of his damnation." We heard this vision, of which we have offered a little sample, from him who saw it three years ago. He said, "I entered a small hut that appeared abandoned. The same abbot sat in it with his legs bleeding and called me. 'Hail,' he said, 'tell the bishop that this dwelling given to me and another comrade here has become filthy because of two knights, who wash themselves in a bath. They create an intolerable stench that splashes down from there on top of us and makes this place uninhabitable. Let him try to shut the openings on all sides by collecting and gathering donations. But if he does not have enough to close it by what he gathers he should send delegates to specified monasteries. These would supply all that is necessary for closing this since they usually give help joyfully.' When he heard this the bishop said, 'The deliriums of dreams are not to be listened to.'" But the angel in this vision warned the soul again that the bishop did not help by providing the comfort of his prayers, not even to the dead from his community. This brother reported from below to the world above all these things that he did not know before.

He also said that he saw a certain prince standing there who formerly ruled the kingdoms of the people of Rome and Italy. His genitals were mangled by animal bites, while the rest of his body remained immune from laceration. Wetti was stunned by a strong stupor and wondered how such a man, who seemed to be very special among others in defending the Catholic faith and the rule of the Holy Church in the modern world, could be afflicted by a punishment so degrading. Immediately he was answered by the angel, his guide, that although he did many things admired and praised and accepted by God – and he would not be deprived of the recompense for them – he was dissipated by the charms of sexual defilement. He wished to finish his life by offering his other good deeds to God so that the little obscenity and the freedom allowed to the frailty of humanity might be buried and destroyed by the greatness of so many good deeds. He said, "Nevertheless, he is destined to the fate of the elect in eternal life."

He saw there among cloths, pompously set out for exhibition by evil spirits, innumerable and magnificent gifts, silver vases and horses made to shine white with the finest linens. He asked whose they were and what they signified. The angel said, "They belonged to the counts who have the rule of different provinces, so that when they come here they will find them and know them, because they are accumulated by extortion, avarice and rapine." Naming some of them expressly, he said the gifts would never be ended or destroyed until these came here and received them in their laps.

Who can relate the terrible pronouncement on the regular behavior of the counts that he introduced? He said that they were not punishers of crimes, but like the devil, persecutors of men, damning the righteous and justifying the defendant, in union with thieves and robbers. He said, "Blinded by the expectation of gifts, they do nothing for the rewards of the future. While they are supposed to administer earthly laws to restrain the boldness of evil men and women, they damage the law by inflicting it instead on debtors. Thus, procuring bribes again and again, without mercy they put themselves on the side justly befitting their greed. They never exercise justice in the hope of the future life, but when they ought to offer it free to all for the reward of eternity, they instead always offer it for sale, just like their souls." The angel named some already judged, just as the Gospel says of nonbelievers, "Those who do not believe are already judged."

Wetti recalled that he also saw a countless number of lay people and others from the monastic orders, from different regions and convents, some of them in glory and others sunk in punishment.

After he had seen these and innumerable other things – which we will exclude in our haste on account of the quick style of this composition – the angel led him to a most beautiful place, a structure built by nature, with arches of gold and silver, decorated with sculpted works that were so high and great, and made so bright with incredible beauty, that no one could conceive with thoughts nor express with the human tongue the greatness of this work. The King of Kings and the Lord of Lords came forward with the multitude of saints shining with so much glory and majesty that with physical eyes a person could not judge the splendor of such light and the dignity of the glory of the saints that appeared there.

The angel, who was his leader and guide, said to him, "Tomorrow you must leave, but meanwhile we will struggle for mercy." With the angel leading they then went on together to where the assembly of the blessed priests was in inestimable glory and dignity. Then the angel said to him, "These are crowned by God for the merits of their good works. You arrange service in the church for them. We will ask them to obtain mercy for you with God." When he had said this, making supplications they prayed to them for intercession. Rising immediately the holy priests approached the throne; and they prostrated themselves before the throne, requesting mercy for this brother. While these were interceding the angel stood apart from them with Wetti. While they prayed before the throne to obtain mercy, a voice from the throne was heard in response saying to them, "He should have given edifying examples to your brothers, but he did not do it." Nothing more was added in answer. In this esteemed group Wetti said that he recognized such illustrious holy priests as Dionysius, Martin, and Hilary of Aniane.

Then with the angel encouraging him, they turned back to their path, where an innumerable multitude of blessed martyrs was revealed in inestimable glory. The angel said, "Glorious triumph in the struggle advanced these here to this glory. You honor them in church to the honor and praise of God. You ought to seek them as intercessors for the forgiveness of your sins."

With a similar prayer these two prostrated themselves on the ground. Immediately, without any delay, the martyrs prostrated themselves at the throne of divine majesty and earnestly asked grace for the indulgence of his sins. From the throne a voice came to them as before saying, "These sins are forgiven if he who enticed them, teaching evil with the example of his depravity, and who led them away from the way of truth to the way of error, corrects them and leads them back to the way of truth." When they asked how it was possible for him to correct them to attain the remission that they requested, a voice from the throne said to them, "Let him call all those whom he has entrapped to do wrong by his example or teaching, and let him cast himself down before them and confess that he did or taught evil. Let him ask pardon and request from the all-powerful God and all the saints that those whom he taught neither teach nor do evil." While this was taking place Wetti and the angel stood a long way off, just as they did before during the prayers of the priests. Among those that Wetti said he recognized were St. Sebastian and St. Valentine.

From there, with the angel always going in front, they headed to the place in which an innumerable multitude of holy virgins lingered, shining with the incomparable dignity and splendor of twinkling light. He said, "These are holy women for whom you prepare ecclesiastical services in honor of the name of Christ. We ought to send them before God to ask for your eternal life." When he said this these two prostrated themselves before them in the same way as they did before. The virgins immediately rushed toward the throne and requested eternal life for him. Meanwhile, as before, these two stood apart. But before they could prostrate themselves on the ground to pray, the majesty of the Lord appeared in the way. Raising them up he said, "If he teaches good and leads them with good example and corrects them to whom he previously provided bad example, your request will be granted."

After this they went away from there, and the angel began to explain in how much evil filth humanity was groveling. He said, "In a great number of crimes humanity draws itself away from its creator and sells itself to the devil. But God is offended by nothing more than when a person sins contrary to nature. Therefore the struggle ought to be carried on with great vigilance everywhere so that sodomy does not turn a temple of God into a shrine of devils. For not only," he said, "does the violent contagion of this creeping disease infect the polluted soul of males who lie together, but it is even found in the ruin of many couples. Stirred up in madness by the instigation of devils and changed by the vexation of lust, they lose the natural goodness given by God to their own wives, so that both of the married ones change an immaculate marriage bed into a stain of disgrace as they prostitute themselves with devils. So you are ordered by divine authority to proclaim this publicly. Do not hide how much danger there is in the luxury of concubines. In the end, those polluted in this obscenity will never deserve entry to the kingdom of heaven." Wetti said to him, "Lord, I do not dare to pronounce this in public, since I do not consider nor feel myself suited to this on account of my limitations." The angel responded with great indignation, "What God wishes and commands you to do, through me, do not dare put off."

After this he began to warn him in a different way for his conversion. The angel said, "I am sent to watch over you. I was also assigned by God to Samson, described in the Book of Judges, from his birth. With the help of God I helped him in all his marvelous works up to the time that, softened by the charms of the flesh and incurring the offense of God with Delilah and selling his religious dedication to a harlot, he was abandoned by God. Then I left him. While you were a child, I was pleased with you, but after, as an adult, you began to live under your own control and you were very displeasing. But now, since you have turned your path to God with sorrow and penance, I am again happy with you.

"Warning should be given in the monasteries that when the roots of vice are dried up, the seeds of virtue can sprout, since the number of those who are held by the necessities of this world is greater than those who devote themselves to spiritual concerns in the spirit of God. The man of the world does not see what pertains to the spirit of God. Struggling with every strength is necessary so that the spiritual life does not become lukewarm through the great number of carnal people, and so that the abundance of evil does not silence the charity of many. Avoid avarice, because if it dominates, the spirit does not reach down to poverty, through which the entrance of heaven is opened. Gluttony of food and drink should be changed into a desire for only the food that is necessary.

75

Since it is natural," he said, "water should be praised as a drink. Dressing for elegance should be changed into dressing as necessary to prevent nudity and to moderate the cold. The swelling of pride should be changed into true humility. Some bend their heads, but pride is still in their hearts. In this way the life of apostolic order is thrown into confusion, since the virtues are colored by the vices. The fault that enters under the guise of piety becomes habitual, already defended as if it is the law of just living. Therefore in the western regions of Germany and Gaul especially, men of the just order should be warned to follow true humility and voluntary poverty of Christ, so that they are not repelled from the entrance of eternal life. This should be done by God through me to you, proclaiming this with horror.

"Do not be silent about how much this fault grows in the congregations of women and how the confusion of the order is advanced and injury made to God to the advantage of the devil. For when," the angel said, "dead women are placed above the living – since a widow living in pleasure is dead – her subjects change from living to dead through joining in the works of the dead. These riches, which were accumulated by the faithful for preserving the chastity of the heavenly life, are given to those with an unsatisfied thirst for earthly riches, turning them regularly in confusion to earthy and perishable riches."

"Where," Wetti asked, "is the rule of the apostolic life preserved uncorrupted?" "In regions across the sea," the angel said, "the constancy of apostolic rigor still flourishes, since they choose the reign of heaven with the poverty of spirit and without the obstacle of any earthly impediments."

When this was said, again and again the angel introduced a discussion of the sin of sodomy. He mentioned only once the other vices to avoid; while this deadly sin of the soul against nature, suggested by the cleverness of the devil, he mentioned five times and more that it should be avoided.

Then Wetti asked him why such a great number of people die in the assault of the plague. He said, "It is the punishment of sinners for the great number of sins committed in the world. And it is a sign announced by God with which he predicts the rapid approach of the end of the world."

Among other things the angel warned that the celebration of the service of God be conducted in church regularly with all unembarrassed strength and diligence and without any boredom or negligence seeping in.

The angel also spoke of a certain knight named Geroldus, who was sharing in heaven in the glory of the martyrs. He said, "With zeal for God, in defense of the holy church he met the hoard of the infidel and suffered with the loss of his temporal life, so that he is made a participator in eternal life."

When the angel had shown him and told him of all these innumerable sufferings, which we are excluding from this work for the sake of brevity, this same brother was awakened while the approaching day was already making itself known. When he called together his brothers who had spent the night watching him, he was moved by the greatness of the vision and shaken by the anxiety of intolerable fear. He explained the secrets of his vision one by one. He wanted the head of the monastery to come immediately so that his words might be copied down. They told him that they did not dare disturb the silence of the cloister since the brothers were busy with their nocturnal meditations. He said, "In the meantime, imprint this in liquid wax, so when dawn comes it will already be prepared. I fear that my tongue will become numb and will not be able to reveal what I have heard and seen, since I was commanded with so much obligation to declare this in public that I am afraid I will be condemned without pardon if I am struck silent and cannot reveal what I saw and heard; for the last intercession of the holy virgins, which was made to God for my long life, left me in doubt whether it was to extend the length of eternal life or this temporal life. So, therefore, if because of that intercession, of which I spoke before, an extension of this temporal life is not granted to me, tomorrow I will be carried away, disregarding every scruple, according to the solemn promise of my angel-guide." Therefore, exhorted by these words, they impressed everything learned from him in order on wax.

In the meantime, when the morning hymns were finished, the father of the monastery came with certain other brothers to visit him. While he stood by him, the sick one sought privacy. When the others had left, the abbot remained, keeping four other brothers with him.

Drawing out the tablets that were impressed in the silence of the night with frantic speed, Wetti again told everything with words and writing. Then, rising from the bed and prostrating himself on the ground, he asked pardon for the sins he committed and asked them to pray to God for him.

Since they did not see his color change, nor that he was wasted away in his thinness, nor that he complained excessively about the pains in the parts of his body, and when they touched him they did not find any lack of pulse or any lethal signs, with consoling words they encouraged him with all confidence in the hope of the present life. To them he gave the same response as he did before; that he did not doubt that he would die the next day.

Therefore that whole day and the following night and for all of the following day up to vespers he spent in this way: explaining the fear of his approaching call, laboring with sighs and groans, now commending himself to each of his brothers and sending letters to different friends in various destinations asking for prayers for the absolution of his sins.

At the very end of the evening of the following day, now already night, he called his brothers and announced that he was at the end of his present life; and he requested them to arrange themselves around to sing the Psalms. Beginning them as if he were the leader of the choir he made them sing all the antiphons and the beginning of the Psalms.

When the singing ended he still breathed for a little while; and when his brothers went to their beds again, he was agitated, walking here and there. With great speed he fell on his bed and, taking the Viaticum, he completed the last hour of this unsure life.

aint Brendan's Voyage

I: Introduction

St. Brendan, the son of Finnlug Ua Alta, of the race of Eoghan, was born in the marshy district of Munster. He was famous for his great abstinence and his many virtues, and he was the patriarch of nearly three thousand monks. While he was waging his spiritual warfare at a place called Ardfert-Brendan, a certain father named Barinthus, of the race of King Nial, came to him one evening. When St. Brendan questioned him during their frequent conversations, he could only weep and prostrate himself and continue longer in prayer. But Brendan raised him up, embraced him, and said, "Father, why should we be grieved on the occasion of your visit? Have you not come to give us comfort? You ought, indeed, make better cheer for the brethren. In God's name, tell us the divine secrets and refresh our souls by recounting to us the various wonders you have seen upon the great ocean."

Then Barinthus, in reply, proceeded to tell of a certain island. He said, "My dear child, Mernoc, the guardian of the poor of Christ, fled from me to become a hermit and found, near the Stone Mountain, an island full of delights. After some time I learned that he had many monks there under his charge, and that through him God had worked many marvels. I therefore went to visit him, and when I was within three days' journey, he came out to meet me with some of his brethren, for God had revealed my approach to him.

"As we sailed to the island the brethren came from their cells towards us like a swarm of bees, for they dwelt apart from each other, though their relationship was harmonious, well grounded in faith, hope, and charity. They had one refectory and one church where all of them performed the divine offices. No food was served but fruit and nuts, roots and vegetables of other kinds. After compline the brethren passed the night in their respective cells until the cock crowed or the bell tolled for prayer.

"When my dear son and I had crossed the island, he led me to the western shore, where there was a small boat, and he then said, 'Father, enter this boat, and we will sail on to the west toward the island called the Land of Promise of the Saints, which God will grant to those who succeed us in the latter days.'

"When we entered the boat and set sail, clouds overshadowed us on every side. They were so dense that we could scarcely see the prow or the stern of the boat. After an hour or so, a great light shone around us, and land appeared, spacious and grassy, and bearing all kinds of fruits. And when the boat touched the shore, we landed and walked around the island for fifteen days, yet we could not reach its boundaries. We saw no plant there without its flower, no tree without its fruit, and all the stones there were precious gems. But on the fifteenth day we discovered a river flowing from the west toward the east, and being at a loss what to do, although we wished to cross the river, we waited for the direction of the Lord.

"While we thus considered the situation, a certain man suddenly appeared there before us, shining with a great

light. He called us by name and addressed us thus:
'Welcome, worthy brothers, for the Lord has revealed to
you the land he will grant to his saints. There is one-half
of this island up to this river, which you are not permitted
to cross. Return, therefore, to where you came from.'

"When he stopped speaking, we asked him his name
and where he had come from. But he said, 'Why do you
ask these questions? Should you not ask instead about this
island? As you now see it, it has continued since the
beginning of the world. Do you need food or drink now?
Have you been weighed down by sleep or shrouded in the
darkness of the night? Know then for sure that here it is
forever daytime, without a shadow of darkness, for the
Lord Jesus Christ is its light; and if men had not transgressed the commandment of God, they would have
always dwelt in this land of delights.'

"When we heard this we were moved to tears, and
after we rested awhile, we set out on our return journey.
This man accompanied us to the shore, where our boat
was moored, and when we had entered the boat, he was
taken from our sight, and we went on into the thick
darkness that we had passed through before, and thus to
the Island of Delights. But when the brethren there saw
us, they rejoiced with great joy at our return, since they
had long regretted our absence. They said, 'Why, O
fathers, did you leave us, your little flock, to stray without a shepherd in the wilderness? We knew, indeed, that
our abbot frequently departed somewhere from us and
remained away sometimes a month, sometimes a
fortnight, or a week more or less.'

"When I heard this I tried to console them and said,
'Brethren, think no thought of evil, for your lives here
are certainly passed at the very portals of paradise. Not
far away from you lies the island called the Land of
Promise of the Saints, where night never falls and day

never ends. There your abbot, Mernoc, goes, as the angels of God watch over it. Do you not know by the fragrance of our garments that we have been in the paradise of God?' They replied, 'Yes, father, we knew well that you had been in the paradise of God, for on the garments of our abbot we often found this fragrance, which lingered about us for nearly forty days.' I then told them that I had stayed there with my dear son for a fortnight, without food or drink. Yet, so complete was our bodily refreshment that to others we would seem to have been quite full. When forty days had passed, after we received the blessings of the abbot and the brethren, I came away with my companions, so that I could return to my little cell to which I will go tomorrow."

Having heard all this, St. Brendan and his brethren threw themselves on the ground, giving glory to God in these words: "Righteous are you, O Lord, in all your ways, and holy in all your works. You have revealed to your children so many and such great wonders. May you be blessed for your gifts. Today you have refreshed us all with this spiritual meal." When these discussions ended, St. Brendan said, "Let us now proceed to have a meal and perform the New Commandment. When night had passed, St. Barinthus received the blessing of the brethren and returned to his own cell.

II

St. Brendan Sets Sail

Soon after, St. Brendan selected fourteen monks from his whole community. The venerable father took these apart and went with them into an oratory where he addressed them thus: "Dearly beloved fellow-soldiers, I ask your advice and assistance, because my heart and my mind are firmly set on one desire. If it is God's holy will, I have resolved in my heart to look for the Land of Promise of the Saints, which Father Barinthus told us about. What do you think? What is your advice?"

But they knew well the purpose of their holy father and replied with one voice, "Father-abbot, your will is also our will. Have we not left our parents? Have we not turned our back on our family prospects? Have we not committed our very bodies into your hands? We are, therefore, ready to go with you, whether to life or to death, provided only we discover that to be God's will."

St. Brendan and these brethren then decided to fast for forty days, taking food only every third day, and afterward to depart. After those forty days elapsed, St. Brendan affectionately took leave of his monks and commended them to the special care of the prior of his monastery, who afterwards was his successor there. Brendan sailed toward the west with fourteen brethren to the island where St. Enda lived, and he remained there for three days and nights. He received the blessing of this holy father and all his monks, and then he proceeded to the most remote part of his own country, where his parents lived. However, he did not wish to visit them, but he went up to the summit of the mountain there, which extends far into the ocean, where St. Brendan's Seat is.

There he set up a tent near a narrow creek, where a boat could enter. Then, using iron implements, St. Brendan and his companions built a light vessel with wicker sides and ribs, like those usually made in that country, and covered it with cow-hide tanned in oak-bark, tarring its joints; and they put on board enough provisions for forty days, with butter enough to dress hides for covering the boat and all the utensils needed by the crew. He then ordered the monks to embark in the name of the Father, and of the Son, and of the Holy Ghost.

But while he stood on the shore and blessed the little creek, three more monks from his monastery came up and cast themselves at his feet saying, "O dearest father, allow us, for the love of Christ, to accompany you on your voyage, otherwise we will die here of hunger and thirst, for we are resolved to travel with you all the days of our lives." When the man of God saw their great urgency, he ordered them to embark, saying, "Have your wish, my children," but adding, "I know well why you have come here. One of you has acted well, for God has provided you with an excellent place; but for the other two he has appointed harm and judgment."

St. Brendan then embarked, and they set sail toward where the sun rises at the summer solstice. They had a fair wind, and therefore no work, only to keep the sails properly set. But after twelve days the wind fell to a dead calm, and they had to row until their strength was nearly exhausted. Then St. Brendan would encourage and exhort them saying, "Fear not, brothers, for God will be our helper, a mariner, and a pilot. Take in the oars and helm, keep the sails set, and may God do to us, his servants and his little vessel, as he wishes." They always took refreshment in the evening, and sometimes a wind sprung up; but they did not know from what point it blew, or in what direction they were sailing.

III

First Landing

At the end of forty days, when all their provisions were
gone, a very rocky and steep island appeared there toward
the north. When they drew near it, they saw that its cliffs
were perpendicular like a wall, and many streams of
water rushed down into the sea from the summit of the
island. But they could not discover a landing-place for
the boat. The brethren were very distressed with hunger
and thirst and got some vessels to catch the water in as it
fell. But St. Brendan cautioned them, saying, "Brothers,
do not do such a foolish thing. As long as God does not
wish to show us a landing-place, you are taking this
without his permission, but after three days the Lord
Jesus Christ will show his servants a safe harbor and
resting-place where you can refresh your weary bodies."

After they had sailed around the island for three days,
about the hour of nones on the third day they saw a small
cove where the boat could enter. St. Brendan rose immediately and blessed this landing-place, where on every
side rocks stood wonderfully steep like a wall. When all
the brethren had disembarked and stood on the beach, St.
Brendan ordered them to remove nothing from the boat.

Then a dog appeared there, approaching from a small
path. He came to fawn upon the saint, as dogs will often
fawn upon their masters. "Has not the Lord," said St.
Brendan, "sent us a good messenger. Let us follow him."
And the brethren followed the dog until they came to a
large mansion, in which they found a spacious hall laid
out with couches and seats and water for washing their
feet.

When they had rested, St. Brendan warned them saying, "Beware that Satan does not lead you into temptation, for I can see him urging one of the three monks who followed us from the monastery to a wicked theft. Pray for his soul, for his flesh is in Satan's power." The mansion where they stayed had walls hung with vessels made of various metals, with bridle-bits and horns inlaid with silver.

St. Brendan ordered the serving brother to bring the meal that God had sent to them. Without delay the table was laid with napkins and with white loaves and fish for each brother. When everything was laid out, St. Brendan blessed the meal and the brethren: "Let us praise God in heaven who provides food for all his creatures." Then, giving thanks to the Lord, his brethren ate and drank as much as they pleased. When the meal was finished and the divine office performed, St. Brendan said, "Go and rest now. Here you see couches well prepared for each of you, and you need to rest those limbs over-tired by your labors during our voyage."

When his brethren had gone to sleep, St. Brendan saw the demon, in the guise of a little black boy, at his work. He had a bridle-bit in his hands and was beckoning to the monk mentioned before. Then Brendan rose from his couch and remained all night in prayer.

When morning came the brethren hurried to perform the divine offices, because they wanted to sail off again; but they found the table laid for their meal, as on the previous day, and so for three days and nights God provided meals for his servants. Afterward St. Brendan set out again on his journey with his brethren, first cautioning them not to take any property away from the island.

"God forbid," they said, "that any of us would dishonor our journey by theft." St. Brendan responded,

"The brother I spoke to you about the other day has concealed in his clothes a silver bridle-bit, which the devil gave him that night." When the brother in question heard this he threw away the bridle-bit and fell at the feet of the saint, crying aloud, "O father, I am guilty. Forgive me, and pray that my soul may not be lost." And all the brethren cast themselves on the ground earnestly praying to the Lord for his soul's sake. When they rose from the ground, and St. Brendan had raised up the guilty brother, they all saw a little black boy leap out of his chest, howling loudly, "Why, O man of God, do you expel me from my home, where I have lived for seven years, and drive me away as a stranger from my secure possession?"

Then St. Brendan said, "I command you, in the name of the Lord Jesus Christ, that you injure no one until the Day of Judgment." Then turning to the penitent brother, he told him to prepare to receive the body and blood of the Lord without delay, because his soul would soon depart from his body, and here would be his burial-place, but that the other brother who accompanied him from the monastery would be buried in hell. Soon after he received the Holy Viaticum, the soul of the brother departed from this life and was taken up to heaven by angels of light in the sight of his brethren, who gave him a Christian burial in that place.

St. Brendan and his brethren came to the shore where the boat lay and embarked at once. Then a young man presented himself to them, bearing a basketful of loaves of bread and a large bottle of water, and said, "Accept this blessing from your servant, for a long way lies ahead of you before you will have the comfort that you seek, but this bread and water will not fail you from today until Pentecost." With this blessing they sailed forth on the ocean, taking food only every second day, while the boat was borne along in different directions, until one day they came within view of an island, not far off, towards which they sailed with a favorable wind.

IV

Sheep Island & Jasconius

When the boat reached a landing-place, the man of God ordered all to disembark, and he was the last to leave the boat. In making a circuit of the island, they saw great streams of water flowing from many fountains full of all kinds of fish. St. Brendan said to his brethren, "Let us perform the divine office here and sacrifice to God the Lamb without spot, for this is the feast of the Last Supper." And they remained there until Easter Saturday.

On the island they found many flocks of sheep, all pure white, and so numerous that they could hide the face of the land. Then the saint directed his brethren to take from the flocks what they needed for the feast, and they caught one sheep, which they tied by the horns, and it followed at their heels as if it were tame. He also told them to take one spotless lamb. When they had obeyed those orders, they prepared to celebrate the office of the next day, and a man came to them there with a basket of hearth-cakes and other provisions, which he laid at the feet of the man of God, prostrating himself three times and saying with tears, "O, precious pearl of God, how have I deserved that you should take food at this holy season from the labor of my hands?" Then, raising him up from the ground, St. Brendan said, "My son, our Lord Jesus Christ has provided a suitable place for us to celebrate his holy resurrection."

Afterwards he proceeded to perform the washing of the feet and to prepare what was necessary for tomorrow's feast. When the supply of provisions was taken into the vessel, the man who brought them said to St. Brendan, "Your boat can carry no more now, but after eight days I will send you enough food and drink to last until Pentecost." Then the man of God said to him, "How can you know for certain where we will be after eight days?" He replied, "Tonight you will spend on that island you see near you, and also tomorrow until noon. Then you will sail on to the island not far from it toward the west, called the Paradise of Birds, and there you will stay until the octave of Pentecost."

St. Brendan also asked him why the sheep were so very large on that island, larger even than oxen, and he told him that they were so much larger than in the lands known to St. Brendan because they were never milked and did not feel the stress of winter, since at all seasons they had abundant pasture.

They then went on board their vessel, and after giving and receiving parting blessings, they proceeded on their voyage. When they drew near the closest island, the boat stopped before they reached a landing-place, and the saint ordered his brethren to get out into the sea and fasten the vessel stem and stern until they came to some harbor. There was no grass on the island, very little wood, and no sand on the shore. While the brethren spent the night in prayer off the vessel, the saint remained on it, for he knew well what kind of island this was. He did not wish to tell his brethren, however, since they might be too afraid.

When morning dawned, he told the priests to celebrate Mass, and after they had done so, and he himself had said Mass in the boat, the brethren took out some uncooked meat and fish they had brought from the other island and put a caldron on a fire to cook them. After they had put more fuel on the fire, and the caldron began to boil, the island moved about like a wave. They all rushed toward the boat and begged the protection of their father, who took each one by the hand and drew them all into the vessel. Then leaving behind what they had brought onto to the island, they cast their boat loose to sail away, when all at once the island sunk into the ocean.

Afterwards they could see the fire they had kindled still burning more than two miles off. Then St. Brendan explained the occurrence, saying, "Brethren, you wonder at what has happened to this island." "Yes, father," they said, "we wondered and were seized by a great fear." "Do not fear, my children," said the saint, "for last night God revealed to me the mystery of all this. It was not an island you were on, but a fish, the largest of all that swim in the ocean. It is always trying to make its head and tail meet, but cannot succeed because of its great length. Its name is Jasconius."

When they had sailed beside the island where they had already been for three days and reached the end of it, they saw another island toward the west, not far off across a narrow sound. It was very grassy, well-wooded, and full of flowers. They sailed off toward its landing place.

V

The Paradise of Birds

When they had sailed to the southern side of this island they found a brook flowing into the sea, and there they brought the boat to land. The saint ordered them to leave the boat and tow it up the stream, which was only wide enough for it. So they towed it for a mile up to the source of the brook, the saint sitting on board all the while.

After some consideration, St. Brendan said to them, "My brothers, God has provided a suitable place for us to stay during Easter time. If we had no other provisions, this fountain would, I believe, serve as food as well as drink." The fountain was truly a very wonderful one. A large tree of marvelous width but no great height hung over it. It was covered with snow-white birds, so that they hid its boughs and leaves entirely. When the man of God saw this, he was wondering why this immense number of birds was brought together in one group, and the question grew to bother him so much that with tears he asked the Lord on his bended knees, "O God, who knows what is unknown and reveals what is hidden, you see the anxious distress of my heart. Therefore I ask you to grant me, in your great mercy, to reveal your secret in what I see here before me. Not because I deserve it, but because you are merciful, I presume to ask this favor."

In answer one of the birds flew off the tree over to the boat where the man of God was seated, and in flight his wings had a tinkling sound like little bells. Perching on the prow, it spread out its wings in token of gladness and looked complacently toward St. Brendan. Then the man of God, realizing from this that his prayer was granted, addressed the bird, "If you are a messenger from God, tell me from where have those birds come, and why there is this gathering of them here?" The bird at once answered, "We share in the great ruin of the ancient enemy, because soon after our creation we fell, not by sin of our will or consent, but our ruin resulted from the fall of Lucifer and his followers. The almighty God, however, who is righteous and true, has condemned us to this place, where we suffer no pain and where we can partially see divine presence. But we must remain apart from the spirits who were faithful. We wander about the world, in the air and earth and sky, like the other spirits on their missions. But on feast days we take the shapes you see, remain here, and sing the praises of our Creator. You and your brethren have been on your voyage for one year now, and six more years of journeying await you. Where you celebrated Easter this year, you will celebrate it every year, until you find what you have set your hearts on, the Land of Promise of the Saints." When the bird had said this, it rose from the prow of the vessel and flew back to the other birds.

At the approach of the hour of vespers, clapping their wings in unison, all the birds began to sing: "A hymn, O Lord, becomes you in Sion, and a vow will be paid to you in Jerusalem;" and they alternately chanted the same psalm for an hour. The melody of their warbling and the accompanying clapping of their wings sounded like a delightful harmony of great sweetness.

Then St. Brendan said to his brethren, "Take some refreshment now, for the Lord has filled your souls with the joys of his divine resurrection." When supper was over and the divine office performed, the man of God and his companions retired to rest until the third watch of the night, when he woke them all from their sleep, chanting the verse: "O Lord, you will open my lips." Then all the birds with voice and wing warbled in response, "Praise the Lord, all his angels, praise him all his virtues." Thus they sang for an hour every night, and when morning dawned they chanted, "May the splendor of the Lord God be upon us" in the same melody and measure as their matin praises of God. Again, at terce, they sang the verse: "Sing to our God, sing; sing to our King, sing wisely;" at sext: "The Lord has caused the light of his countenance to shine on us, and may he have mercy on us." At nones they sang: "Behold how good and how pleasant it is for brethren to dwell in unity." Day and night those birds praised God. St. Brendan, seeing all this, gave thanks to the Lord for all his wonderful works. And the brethren were thus feasted with spiritual food until the octave of the Easter festival.

At the end of the feast days St. Brendan said, "Let us now share the water from this fountain. Up to now we needed it only to wash our hands or feet." Soon after this the man who had been with them three days before Easter, and who had supplied them with provisions for the Easter season, came to them with his boat full of food and drink. He laid it all before the holy father and said, "My brothers, you have here enough to last until Pentecost, but do not drink from that fountain because its waters have a peculiar virtue. Anyone drinking from it, though it seems to have the taste and quality of ordinary water, is seized with sleep and cannot awaken for twenty-four hours." After this, once he received the blessing of St. Brendan, he returned to his own place.

St. Brendan remained where he was with his brethren until Pentecost, the singing of the birds being a delight always new to them. On the feast of Pentecost, when St. Brendan and the priests had celebrated Mass, their venerable provider brought enough food for the feast, and when they sat down together at their meal, he said to them, "My brothers, you still have a long journey before you. Therefore, take from this fountain vessels full of its water and dry bread that will keep for another year, and I will supply as much as your boat can carry." He then departed with a blessing from all, and eight days later St. Brendan had the boat laden with the provisions brought by this man and all the vessels filled with water from the fountain.

When they had brought everything down to the shore, the bird mentioned before flew towards them and landed on the prow of the boat. The saint, who understood that it wanted to let him know something, stood still where he was. Then the bird, in human voice, addressed him: "This year you have celebrated Easter time with us. You will celebrate it with us again next year. And where you have been this past year on the feast of the Last Supper, there you will also be on that same feast next year. You will also celebrate the feast of Easter as you did before on the back of the great fish Jasconius, and after eight months you will find the Island of St. Ailbe, where you will celebrate Christmas." After the bird said these things, it returned to its place on the tree.

VI

The Island of St. Ailbe

The brethren got the boat ready and set sail into the ocean, while all the birds sung in concert, "Hear us, O God our Savior, the hope of all the ends of the earth, and in the sea afar off." After this St. Brendan and his brethren were tossed back and forth on the waves of the ocean for three months. During this time they could see nothing but the sea and sky, and they ate and drank only every second day.

One day, however, an island came into view not far off, but when they drew near the shore the wind drove them aside, and so for forty days they sailed around the island without finding a landing-place. The brethren meanwhile prayed to the Lord with tears that he would help them, since their strength was almost exhausted because of their great fatigue. When they had persevered in frequent prayer and also in fasting for three days, they finally found a narrow creek fit to receive one boat. Beside it were two fountains, one foul and the other clear. When the brethren rushed to take some of the water, the man of God said to them, "My children, do nothing that may be unlawful. Take nothing here without the permission of the venerable fathers who are on this island, and they will freely give what you would take by stealth."

When they had all landed and were considering in what direction they should go, an old man worn away by great age came to them. His hair was white as snow and his face transparent like glass. He prostrated himself three times, before he went to embrace the man of God, who, raising him up from the ground, embraced him, as did all the brethren. Then this aged man, taking the holy father by the hand, led him to the monastery, which was about a furlong away. St. Brendan stood at the entrance and asked his guide whose monastery this was and who its superior was. He asked him various questions in this way but could get no reply, only gestures very gently indicating silence. As soon as the holy father realized that silence was the rule of this place, he warned his brethren: "Hold your tongues from too much talking, so that these monks here will not be scandalized by your foolish speeches."

After this eleven monks in their habits and crosses came forth to meet them. They were chanting the verse, "Arise, you holy ones from your dwellings, and come forth to meet us, sanctify this place, bless this people, and vouchsafe to guard us, your servants, in peace." When the verse ended, the abbot embraced St. Brendan and his companions in their due order, and in a similar way his monks embraced the brethren of the holy man. When the kiss of peace was thus mutually given and received, they conducted the guests into the monastery, according to the custom in western countries, and the abbot and his monks proceeded to wash the feet of their guests, and to chant the New Commandment.

Then the abbot led them all into the refectory, in strict silence, and when they had washed their hands he gave them a signal to take their seats. On a given signal one of the monks rose and provided the table with marvelously white loaves of bread and roots of delicious flavor. The monks had taken places at the table between their guests, according to rank, and to each pair a whole loaf was served. The ministering brother also set before them some drink.

The father abbot cheerfully told his guests: "Brothers, from the fountain, out of which you wished to drink secretly today, now make a loving cup in gladness and in the fear of the Lord. In the other fountain of foul water, which you saw, the feet of the brethren are washed, because it is always tepid. We do not know where those loaves of bread, which you now see in front of you, are prepared, or who brings them to our cellar. But we do know well that they are supplied to us by the free gift of God, as a charity by some obedient creature of his. In our respect the words of divine truth are thus fulfilled: 'Those who fear God want for nothing.' Here we are twenty-four brothers. Each day we have twelve loaves for our support, one loaf for two brothers. But on Sundays and great feasts the Lord allows us a full loaf for each brother, so that we can have a supper from what is left. And now, with your arrival, we have a double supply. From the days of St. Patrick and St. Ailbe, our patriarchs, for eighty years until now, Christ has provided for us with sustenance in this way. Moreover neither old age nor bodily illnesses increase upon us here, nor do we need cooked food, nor are we oppressed with heat or distressed with cold, but we live here as if it were in the paradise of

God. When the hours for the divine office and for Mass arrive, the lamps in our church, which we brought with us from our own country under God's guidance, are lit and always burn without diminishing."

When the meal was over, and they had taken some drink three times, the abbot gave the usual signal, and all the brethren rose from the table in great silence, giving thanks to God, and preceded the fathers to the church. At the door of the church they met twelve other monks who readily genuflected as they passed. St. Brendan said, "Father abbot, why have those monks not eaten with us?" "For your sakes," said the abbot, "because our table could not seat us all together. They will now have their meal, because by God's holy will they will lack nothing. We will now enter the church and sing vespers, so that the brethren who are now dining may sing the office afterwards in proper time."

When vespers had ended, St. Brendan noticed the structure of the church. It was a perfect square of equal length and width. In it were seven lamps arranged so that three of them hung before the central altar, and two before each of the side altars. All the altars were of crystal, and the chalices, patens, cruets, and the other vessels required for the Mass were also of crystal. Around the church were arranged twenty-four benches, with the abbot's seat between the two choirs of monks in rows on either side. No monk from either choir was allowed to intone the chant of the office, only the abbot; and throughout the monastery no voice was heard, nor any sound whatever. But if a brother needed anything, he went to the abbot and on his knees he made signs that he wanted something; and then the father wrote on a tablet what God had intimated to him that the brother needed.

While St. Brendan was considering all these things, the abbot said to him, "Father, it is now time to return to the refectory, so that all may be done during daylight, since it is written, 'He who walks in the light, does not stumble.'" So it was done, and when all things were completed in the usual order of the daily routine, all hurried swiftly to compline. Then the abbot intoned the verse: "Incline to my aid, O Lord," invoking at the same time the most Holy Trinity; and they added the antiphon: "We have sinned; we have acted unrighteously; we have worked iniquity; you, O Lord Jesus Christ, who are all mercy, have pity on us. In peace to the same, I will sleep and take my rest." And they proceeded to chant the office of compline.

When the office had concluded, the brethren went to their cells, taking their guests with them. But the abbot remained with St. Brendan in the church to wait for the lighting of the lamps. The saint asked the father abbot about the rule of silence they observed: how such a method of communication was possible in a community of flesh and blood. The abbot replied with much reverence and humility, "Holy father, before the Lord I declare that during the eighty years that have passed since we came to this island, not one of us has heard from another the sound of human voice, except when we sing the praises of God. Among us twenty-four brothers no voice is raised, but signs are made with the fingers or the eyes, and this is only permitted for the elder monks. Since we came here none of us has suffered any illness of the body or mind that may be fatal to the human race."

When he heard this St. Brendan said with many tears, "Grant, I pray you, father abbot, to tell us whether we are permitted to remain here or not." The abbot answered, "You are not permitted to stay, for this is not the will of God. But why do you ask me? God revealed to you what you must do before you came to us. You must return to your country, where God has prepared a burial place for you and for fourteen of your companions. Concerning the other two monks, one will have his pilgrimage on the Island of Anchorites, but the other will suffer in hell the worst of all deaths." These events later came to pass.

While they were talking, as they looked on, a fiery arrow passing in through a window lit all the lamps that hung in front of the altars, and passing out through the same window left the lamps burning. Then St. Brendan asked who would put out those lamps in the morning, and the abbot replied, "Come and see the secret of all this. You see those tapers burning in the vases, yet none of them is consumed, nor do they diminish, nor do any ashes remain in the morning, for the light is entirely spiritual." "How," said St. Brendan, "can a spiritual flame burn in a material substance?" "Have you not read," said the abbot, "of the burning bush, near Mount Sinai, which remained unconsumed by the burning?" "Yes," said the saint, "I have read of this, but what analogy has it to this case?"

After they had remained on watch until morning, St. Brendan asked permission to leave the island, but the abbot replied, "No, O man of God, you must celebrate the feast of Christmas with us and give us the joy of your company until the octave of Epiphany." So the holy father with his brethren remained on the Island of St. Ailbe until that time.

VII

Island of the Soporific Spring, Return to Sheep Island, Jasconius & The Paradise of Birds

When those feast days had passed, St. Brendan, with the blessing of the abbot and all his monks, and with a supply of the necessary provisions, sailed into the ocean; and there the vessel, without oar or sail, drifted about in various directions until the beginning of Lent.

One day they saw an island not far off and quickly sailed toward it; for they were hungry and thirsty, since their supply of food and water had been exhausted three days before. When St. Brendan had blessed the landing-place, and all had landed, they found a spring of clear water, and different kinds of herbs and vegetables around it, and many sorts of fish in the stream that flowed from it to the sea.

Then St. Brendan said, "Brothers, surely God has given us comfort after our wearisome labors. Take enough fish for your meal and prepare them on the fire, and also gather those herbs and roots that God has provided for his servants." When this was done, they poured out some of the water to drink, but the man of God warned them: "Take care, my brethren, to use this water in moderation." But the brethren did not pay equal attention to this warning. While some drank only one cup of the water, others drank two cups, and others drank three, so that a sudden stupor, which lasted for three days and nights, fell on some of them. On others it fell for only one day and night. But St. Brendan prayed without ceasing to God for them, as they incurred this great danger through their ignorance.

When three days had passed, the father said to his companions, "My children, let us hurry away from this fatal place, so that greater evil does not befall you. The Lord has given you refreshment, but you have turned it to your detriment. Go from this island, therefore, taking with you as much fish as you might want for a meal on every third day until the feast of the Last Supper, and also one cup of this water for each man, with a similar supply of the vegetables." When the boat was filled with these provisions, as the man of God directed, they sailed into the ocean on a northerly course.

After three days and nights the wind ceased, and the calm was so great that the sea became like a thick curdled mass. Then the holy father said, "Take in your oars and cast loose the sails, for the Lord will guide our boat wherever he wishes." In this way the boat was kept in motion for about twenty days until at length God sent a favorable wind. Then they put up the sail and rowed in an easterly direction, taking refreshment every third day.

One day an island came into view like a cloud in the distance. St. Brendan asked the brethren whether they recognized it. When they replied that they did not recognize it, the holy father said to them, "I know it well, my children, for we were on it last year, on the feast of the Last Supper, and our good provider lives on it." When the brethren heard this they rowed vigorously with great joy, putting out all their strength. But the man of God said to them, "You are senseless to tire out your limbs in this way. Is not almighty God the pilot of our vessel? Leave her, therefore, in his hands, for he will guide her course as he wishes."

When they drew near to the island, their provider came out to meet them, and giving glory to God he led them to the same landing-place where they had landed the year before, where he embraced the feet of St. Brendan and all the brethren, saying, "Wonderful is God in his saints." When they finished the verse, and everything was removed from the boat, he set up a tent and prepared a bath for them, because it was the feast of the Last Supper. He also provided new garments for all the brethren, as well as for St. Brendan, and performed all other services for them as he was accustomed to do.

The brethren then celebrated the feast of the passion of our Lord with great diligence until Holy Saturday. When all the offices and ceremonies of the day ended, and the feast of the Last Supper was fully completed, the provider said to them, "Go now to your boat, so that you can celebrate the vigil of Easter where you celebrated it last year, and also Easter itself, until the hour of sext. Then sail on to the Paradise of Birds, where you were last year from Easter until the octave of Pentecost. Take with you all the food and drink you need, and I will visit you a week from next Sunday." And the brethren did as he said.

Giving his blessing to this good brother, St. Brendan embarked with all his brethren and sailed to another island. When they drew near the landing-place they found the cauldron that in their flight the year before they had left on the back of Jasconius. Then going on land, St. Brendan sang the "Hymn of the Three Children" to the end, and then he warned his brethren, "Watch and pray, my children, that you do not enter into temptation. Consider carefully how the almighty God has placed under us, without difficulty, this greatest monster of the deep." The brethren made their vigils here and there over the island, until the morning watch, when all the priests said their Masses until the hour of terce; but St. Brendan, getting into the boat with the brethren, there offered to God the holy sacrifice of the Immaculate Lamb, saying, "Last year we celebrated our Lord's resurrection here; and I desire, if it be God's holy will, to celebrate it here also this year."

Proceeding from there they came to the island called the Paradise of Birds. When they reached the landing-place, all the birds sang together, "Salvation to our God, who sits on the throne, and to the Lamb;" and again: "The Lord is God, and he has shone upon us. Appoint a solemn day, with shady boughs, even to the horn of the altar." And so with voice and wing they warbled until St.

Brendan and his companions were settled in their tent, where they passed the Easter season until the octave of Pentecost.

The provider mentioned above came to them, as he had promised, on the Sunday after Easter, bringing what they needed for their nourishment, and in mutual joy all gave thanks to God. When they were seated at their meal the bird mentioned before perched on the prow of the boat, spreading out and clapping its wings with a loud sound, like a great organ; and St. Brendan knew that it wished to give him this message, which it spoke as follows, "The almighty and merciful God has appointed for you four certain places, at four different seasons of the year, until the seven years of your pilgrimage are ended. On the feast of the Last Supper each year you will be with your provider, who is present here; the vigil and feast of Easter you will celebrate on the back of the great whale. With us here you will spend the Easter season until the octave of Pentecost. And on the Island of St. Ailbe you will remain from Christmas until the feast of the Purification of the Blessed Virgin Mary. After those seven years, through many and different dangers, you will find the Land of Promise of the Saints, which you are seeking, and there you will remain for forty days. Then God will guide your return to the land of your birth."

When St. Brendan had heard this he prostrated himself with many tears, as did the brethren, giving thanks and praise to the great Creator of all things. The bird then flew back to its place on the tree, and when the meal was ended, the provider said, "With God's help I will come to you again on Pentecost Sunday with provisions." And with a blessing from all he left.

VIII

The Sea Monster

The venerable father remained here for the appointed time and then ordered his brethren to prepare the boat and to fill all the water vessels from the fountain. When the boat was launched, the provider met them in his boat, loaded down with provisions, which he quickly transferred into the boat of the man of God. With a parting embrace he returned to where he had come from, but the saint sailed forward into the ocean, and the boat was carried along for forty days.

One day a fish of enormous size appeared swimming after the boat, spouting foam from its nostrils and ploughing through the waves in rapid pursuit to devour them. Then the brethren cried out to the Lord, "O Lord, who has made us, deliver us, your servants!" And to St. Brendan they cried aloud, "Help, O father, help us!" The saint begged the Lord to deliver his servants so that this monster would not devour them, while he also sought to give courage to his brethren in these words: "Do not fear, you of little faith, for God, who is always our protector, will deliver us from the jaws of this monster and from every other danger."

When the monster was drawing near, immense waves rushed before it up to the gunwale of the boat, which caused the brethren to fear more and more; but St. Brendan, with his hands raised up to heaven, earnestly prayed, "Deliver, your servants, O Lord, as you delivered David from the hands of the giant Goliah, and Jonah from the power of the great whale."

Once these prayers were uttered, a great monster came into view from the west rushing against the other, spouting flames from its mouth, and immediately attacked it. Then St. Brendan said, "See, my children, the wonderful work of our Saviour. See here the obedience of the creature to its Creator. Wait now for the end in safety, for this conflict will bring no evil to us but only greater glory to God." The rueful monster that pursued the servants of God was immediately slain and cut up into three parts in front of them, and its slayer returned to where it came from.

The next day they saw at a distance a wide and grassy island. When they drew near it and were about to land, they found the back portion of the monster that was slain. "See," said St. Brendan, "what sought to devour you. Now make your food from it, and fill yourselves abundantly with its flesh, for you will have a long delay on this island. Draw the boat higher up on the land, and seek a suitable place where we can set up our tent."

When the father had selected a site for their tent, and his brethren had placed the requisite fittings in it, in compliance with his directions, he said to them, "Now take enough of this monster's flesh for three months, since tonight its carcass will be devoured by the great fish of the sea." The brethren acted accordingly and took as much of its flesh as was needed. But they said to St. Brendan, "Holy father, how can we live here without water to drink?" "Is it more difficult," said the saint, "for the Almighty to give us water than to give us food? Go to the southern side of the island, and there you will find a spring of clear water and an abundance of herbs and roots, of which you will take enough to satisfy your needs." And they found everything as the man of God had told them.

107

St. Brendan remained on this island for three months, since violent storms prevailed at sea, and hail and rain caused very difficult weather. The brethren went to see what had become of the remains of the great monster that the saint had spoken of; and where its carcass had lain they found only its bones, as the father had told them. When they mentioned this to him, he said, "If you need to test the truth of my words, I will give you another sign. Tonight a large part of a fish will break loose from a fishing net, be cast ashore here, and tomorrow you will have your meal from it." Next day they went to the place he indicated, and they found there what the man of God had predicted. They brought away as much fish as they could carry. The venerable father then said to them, "Keep this carefully, and salt it, for we will surely need it, since the Lord will grant calm weather today and tomorrow; and on the third day, when the turbulence of the sea and the waves has subsided, we will leave this island."

IX

The Island of the Three Choirs of Saints Or the Island of Anchorites

When these days had passed, St. Brendan ordered them to load their boat with the skins of water-vessels filled from the fountain and with as much of a supply of herbs and roots as might be needed. (From the time the saint was ordained a priest, he ate nothing in which there had been the breath of life.) After they loaded the boat, they sailed in a northerly direction. One day they saw an island far off, and St. Brendan said to his brethren, "On that island, now in view, there are three classes of people: boys, young men, and elders. One of our brothers will have his pilgrimage there." The brethren asked him which one it was, but he was reluctant to say. When, however, they pressed the question and seemed grieved at not being told, he said, "This is the brother who is to remain on this island." He was one of the monks who had come after the saint from his own monastery. St. Brendan had made a prediction about him when they embarked in their own country. Then they drew near the island until the boat touched the shore.

The island was remarkably flat, almost level with the sea, without a tree or anything that waved in the wind, but it was wide and covered with white and purple flowers. Here, as the man of God had said, there were three groups of monks, standing apart, about a stone's throw from each other, and keeping this distance apart when they moved in any direction. One choir, in its place, chanted, "The saints will advance from virtue to virtue; God will be manifest in Sion." Then another choir took up the same chant, and thus they chanted unceasingly. The first choir was boys robed in snow-white garments, the second was young men dressed in violet, and the third was older men in purple dalmatics.

When the boat reached the landing-place it was the fourth hour. And at the hour of sext all the choirs of monks sang together the psalm: "May God have mercy on us and bless us," to the end; and "Incline to my aid, O Lord;" and also the psalm, "I have believed, therefore have I spoken," with the proper prayer. In the same way, at the hour of nones they chanted three other psalms: "Out of the depths I have cried to you, O Lord;" "Behold how good and how pleasant it is for brethren to dwell together in unity;" and "Praise the Lord, O Jerusalem, praise your God, O Sion." Again at vespers they sang the psalms: "A hymn, O Lord, becomes you in Sion;" "Bless the Lord, O my soul;" and "Praise the Lord, you children, praise you the name of the Lord;" then, when seated, they chanted the fifteen gradual psalms.

After they had finished this chanting, a cloud of marvellous brightness overshadowed the island, so that they could not see what was visible before, but they heard the voices, without ceasing, in the same chant until the morning-watch, when they sang the psalms: "Praise the Lord from the heavens;" "Sing to the Lord;" and "Praise the Lord in his saints;" and then twelve psalms in the order of the psaltery, as far as the psalm: "The fool says in his heart."

At dawn this cloud passed away from the island, and then the choirs chanted three psalms: "Have mercy on me, O Lord;" "The Lord is my refuge;" and, "O God, my God." Again, at the hour of terce, they sang three other psalms: "Oh, clap your hands, all you nations;" "Save me, O God, by your name;" and, "I have loved, because the Lord will hear the voice of my prayer," with the Alleluia. Then they offered the Holy Sacrifice of the Immaculate Lamb, and all received the Holy Communion with the words: "This sacred body of the Lord and the blood of our Savior receive unto life everlasting."

When the Holy Sacrifice was ended, two members of the choir of young men brought a basketful of purple grapes and placed it in the boat of the man of God, saying: "Eat the fruit of the Isle of the Strong Men, and deliver our chosen brother to us, then depart in peace." St. Brendan then called this brother to him and said, "Give the kiss of peace to your brethren, and go with those who are inviting you. I say to you that in a happy hour did your mother conceive you, since you have deserved to live with so holy a community." Then St. Brendan, with many tears, gave him the kiss of peace – as did the brethren – and said to him, "Remember, my dear son, the special favors to which God has preferred you in this life. Go your way, and pray for us." Saying farewell to them all, the brother quickly followed the two young men to the companies of the saints, who, when they saw him, sang the verse: "Behold how good and pleasant it is for brethren to dwell together in unity," and in a higher key they intoned the *Te Deum laudamus,* and then, when they had all embraced him, he was admitted to their society.

St. Brendan sailed from this island, and when mealtime came, he told the brethren to refresh themselves with the grapes they got on the island. Taking up one of them, and seeing its great size and how full of juice it was, he said in wonder, "Never have I seen or read of grapes so large." They were all the same size, like a large ball, and when the juice of one was pressed into a vessel, it yielded a pound weight. The father divided this juice into twelve parts, giving a part to each of the brethren every day; and so for twelve days, one grape was enough for the refreshment of each brother, in whose mouth it always tasted like honey.

When those days had passed, St. Brendan ordered a fast for three days, after which a brilliantly shining bird flew toward the boat, bearing in its beak the branch of an unknown tree, on which there was a cluster of very red grapes. The bird dropped it near the man of God, then flew away. Brendan then said to the brethren, "Enjoy this feast the Lord has sent us." The grapes were as large as apples, and he gave some to each of them, and so they had enough food for four days, and after that they resumed their previous fasting.

Three days later, they saw nearby an island covered all over with trees, closely set, and laden with grapes like those in surprising abundance, so that all the branches were weighed down to the ground with fruit of the same quality and color. There was no fruitless tree or tree of a different kind on the whole island. The brethren then drew up to the landing-place, and leaving the boat, St. Brendan walked around the island, where the fragrance was like that of a house stored with pomegranates. The brethren stayed all this time in the boat waiting for his return, and the wind blew towards them full of those odors and feasted them with its fragrance, so that they paid no attention to their long fast. The venerable father found six fountains on the island watering the greenest grass and vegetables of different kinds. He then returned to the brethren, bringing with him some samples, as first-fruits of the island. He said to them, "Leave the boat now, and set up your tent here. Be cheerful and enjoy the excellent fruits of this land, that God has shown us." And so for forty days they feasted on the grapes and herbs and vegetables watered by those fountains.

After that time, they embarked again, taking with them some of the fruits of the island, and sailed along as the winds shaped their course, when suddenly there appeared flying towards them the bird called a griffin. When the brethren saw it, they cried out to the holy father, "Help us, O father. This monster comes to devour us." But the man of God told them not to fear it, for God was their helper. And then another great bird came into view, and in rapid flight flew against the griffin, engaging it in a combat that seemed for some time of doubtful outcome, but finally, tearing out its eyes, it vanquished and slew the griffin, and the carcass fell into the sea in front of all the brethren, who therefore gave thanks and praise to God, while the bird that gained the victory flew back to where it came from.

They went to the Island of St. Ailbe to celebrate Christmas; and afterward, taking leave of the abbot with mutual blessings, they sailed the ocean for a long time,

resting only at Easter and Christmas on the islands
mentioned before.

X

The Canopy & Column

On one occasion, when St. Brendan was celebrating the
feast of St. Peter in the boat, they found the sea so clear
that they could plainly see what was at the bottom. They
saw below them various monsters of the deep, and so
clear was the water that it seemed as if they could touch its
greatest depths with their hands; and the fish were visible
in great shoals, like flocks of sheep in the pastures,
swimming around, heads to tails.

The brethren entreated the man of God to say Mass in
a low voice, so that those monsters of the deep, hearing
the strange voice, would not be stirred up to attack them.
But the saint said, "I really wonder at your foolishness.
Why do you fear those monsters? Is not the largest of
them all already devoured? While seated – and often
chanting – on its back, have you not chopped wood and
kindled a fire and even cooked some of its flesh? Why,
therefore, should you fear those? Our God is the Lord
Jesus Christ, who can bring all living things to nothing."

After he said this, he proceeded to sing the Mass in a
louder voice, as the brethren were still gazing at the large
fish. When they had heard the voice of the man of God,
these rose up from the depths and swam around the boat
in such numbers that the brethren could see nothing but
swimming fish, which, however, did not come close to the
boat but swam around at some distance until the Mass was

ended. Then they swam away in different directions, out of view of the brethren. For eight days, even with a favorable wind and all sails set, they were scarcely able to pass out of this transparent sea.

One day, on which three Masses had been said, they saw a column in the sea, which seemed not far away, and yet they could not reach it for three days. When they drew near it, St. Brendan looked toward its summit, but could not see it because of its great height, which seemed to pierce the skies. It was covered with a rare canopy of material which they did not know, but its color was silver, and it was as hard as marble, while the column itself was of the clearest crystal. St. Brendan ordered the brethren to take in their oars, and lower their sails and mast, and directed some of them to hold on by the fringes of the canopy, which extended about a mile from the column, and about the same depth into the sea. When this had been done, St. Brendan said, "Now run the boat in through an opening, so that we can get a closer view of the wonderful works of God." And when they had passed through the opening and looked around, the sea seemed as transparent as glass, so that they could plainly see everything below them, even the base of the column, and the skirts or fringes of the canopy, lying on the ground, for the sun shone as brightly inside as outside.

St. Brendan then measured an opening between four pavilions, which he found was four cubits on every side. While they sailed along for a day on one side of the column, they could always feel the shade as well as the heat of the sun beyond the ninth hour. And after sailing around the column like this for four days, they found the measurement to be four hundred cubits. On the fourth day, they discovered on the south side a chalice of the same material as the canopy and a paten like that of the column, which St. Brendan at once took up, saying, "The

Lord Jesus Christ has displayed this great marvel to us and has given us two gifts from it in testimony of this fact for others."

The holy father then directed his brethren to perform the divine office and afterward to take refreshment, for they had taken none since they came in sight of this column. Next day they rowed toward the north, and passing out through an opening, they set up the mast and unfurled the sails again, while some of them held on by the fringes or skirts of the canopy until all was right in the boat. When they had set sail, a favorable wind came up behind them, so that they did not need to use the oars but only had to hold the ropes and the tiller. And so for eight days they were carried along toward the north.

XI

The Volcanic Island

When those days had passed, they came within view of a very rugged and rocky island covered with slag, without trees or grass, but full of smiths' forges. St. Brendan said to his brethren, "I am very distressed about this island. I do not wish to enter or even approach it, yet the wind is driving us directly toward it, as if it were the aim of our course."

When they had passed on further, about a stone's throw, they heard the noise of bellows blowing like thunder, and the beating of sledge hammers on the anvils and iron. Then St. Brendan armed himself all over his body with the sign of the Cross, saying, "O Lord Jesus Christ, deliver us from this sinister island." Soon one of the inhabitants appeared to do some work. He was hairy and hideous, blackened with fire and smoke. When he saw the servants of Christ near the island, he withdrew into his forge, crying aloud: "Woe! Woe! Woe!"

St. Brendan again armed himself with the sign of the Cross and said to his brethren, "Put on more sail, and ply your oars more briskly, so that way we can get away from this island." Hearing this, the savage man mentioned before rushed down to the shore, carrying in his hand a tongs with a great burning mass of the slag intensely hot, which he flung at once after the servants of Christ; but it did them no harm, since they were protected by the sign of the Cross. It passed them by about a furlong, where it fell into the sea. It fumed up like a heap of burning coals, and great smoke rose as if from a fiery furnace.

When they had passed about a mile beyond the spot where this burning mass had fallen, all those who lived on this island crowded down to the shore, each of them bearing a large mass of burning slag, which they flung, each one in turn, after the servants of God. Then they returned to their forges, which they blew up into mighty flames, so that the whole island seemed one globe of fire, and the sea on every side boiled up and foamed, like a cauldron set on a fire well supplied with fuel. All day the brethren, even when they were no longer within sight of the island, heard a loud wailing from its inhabitants, and a noxious stench was perceptible at a great distance. Then St. Brendan sought to stimulate the courage of the brethren, saying, "Soldiers of Christ, be strong in sincere faith and in the armor of the spirit, for we are now on the confines of hell. Watch, therefore, and act bravely."

XII

Judas Iscariot

On another day there came into view a large and high mountain in the ocean, not far off, toward the north, with misty clouds around it and great smoke issuing from its summit. Suddenly the wind drove the boat rapidly toward the island until it almost touched the shore. The cliffs were so high that they could scarcely see the top and were black as coal and upright like a wall. Here the last of the three monks who followed St. Brendan from his monastery leaped from the boat and made his way on foot to the cliff, wailing and crying aloud, "Woe is me! father, for I am forcibly torn away from you and cannot return."

But the brethren, seized with a great fear, quickly drew off from the shore and, lamenting loudly, cried to the Lord, "Have mercy on us, O Lord, have mercy on us!" St. Brendan plainly saw how the wretched man was carried off by a multitude of demons and was already burning among them, and he exclaimed, "Woe is yours, unhappy man, who has made so evil an end of your life."

Afterward a favorable breeze caught the boat and drove them southward. As they looked back, they saw the peak of the mountain unclouded and shooting flames up into the sky, which it drew back again to itself so that the mountain seemed like a burning pyre.

After this dreadful sight, they sailed for seven days toward the south, and then St. Brendan observed a very dense cloud. When they approached it there came into view the shape of a man, sitting on a rock with a veil in front of him as large as a sack, hanging between two iron prongs. He was tossed about like a small boat in a storm.

117

When the brethren saw this, some thought it was a bird, others that it was a boat; but the man of God told them to stop discussing it and steer directly toward the place, where on his arrival he found the waves motionless all around, as if frozen. They found a man sitting on a rugged and shapeless rock with waves on every side. As they flowed they beat on him, up to the top of his head, and as they ebbed they exposed the bare rock on which the wretched man was sitting. The wind tossed about the cloth that hung before him, so that it struck him on the eyes and forehead.

When the saint asked him who he was, for what crime he was sent there, and how he had deserved to suffer so great a punishment, he answered, "I am that most unhappy Judas, the most wicked of all traffickers. Not through any desert of mine, but through the unspeakable mercy of Jesus Christ, am I placed here. I expect no place for repentance, but through the forbearance and mercy of the Redeemer of the world and in honor of his resurrection I have this cooling relief, since now it is the Lord's Day. While I sit here I seem to be in a paradise of delights, considering the agony of the torments that are in store for me afterward, for when I am in my torments, I burn like a mass of molten lead, day and night, in the heart of that mountain you have seen. There Leviathan and his followers dwell, and I was there when it swallowed down your lost brother, for which all hell exulted and belched forth great flames, as it always does when it devours the souls of the reprobate.

But so that you may know the boundless mercy of God, I will tell you of the refreshing coolness I have here every Sunday from the first vespers to the second, from Christmas Day to the Epiphany, from Easter to Pentecost, on the Purification of the Blessed Virgin Mary, and on the feast of her Assumption. On all other days I am in torments with Herod and Pilate, with Annas and Caiphas. Therefore I beg you through the Redeemer of the world to intercede for me with the Lord Jesus, so that I may stay here until sunrise tomorrow, and that, because of your coming here, the demons may not torment me nor drag me off sooner to my heritage of pain, which I purchased at an evil price."

The saint then said, "The will of the Lord be done. You will not be taken away by the demons until tomorrow." He then asked him what that cloth in front of him meant. Judas replied, "This cloth I once gave to a leper when I was the purse-bearer of the Lord, but since it was not my own, I find no relief from it, but pain instead. These iron prongs that it hangs on I once gave to the priests for supporting their cauldrons, and the stone that I am sitting on I placed in a trench on a public road before I became a disciple of the Lord."

When evening came, a great number of demons gathered around in a circle, shouting: "Leave us, O man of God, for we cannot come near our comrade unless you move away from him, and we do not dare look on the face of our prince until we bring his pet victim back to him. Give us our prey, therefore, and do not keep it from us tonight." The saint then said, "I do not protect him, but the Lord Jesus Christ has permitted him to stay here tonight." The demons cried out, "How could you invoke the name of the Lord on behalf of the man who had betrayed him?" The man of God then commanded them in the name of Jesus Christ not to hurt him until morning.

When the night had passed, at early dawn, when St. Brendan was proceeding on his way, a countless number of demons covered the face of the deep, uttering dreadful cries: "O man of God, cursed be your coming and your going, for last night our chief scourged us with cruel lashes because we did not bring back his wretched cap-

119

tive." "Not on us," said the saint, "but on yourselves will those curses be, for blessed is he whom you curse, and cursed is he whom you bless." The demons shouted, "He will suffer double punishment for the next six days, because you saved him from his punishment last night." But the man of God warned them, "You have no power, neither has your chief, only whatever power God may give you, and I command you in the name of the Lord that you do not increase his torments beyond those you used to inflict before." "Are you," they said, "the Lord of all, that we should obey your commandment?" "No," answered the saint, "but I am the servant of the Lord of all, and whatever I command in his name is done, and I am his minister in only what he grants to me." In this manner they pursued him with their blasphemies until he was far away from Judas, and they bore off this wretched soul with great rushing and howling.

XIII

The Island of the Holy Hermit

Afterward St. Brendan sailed for some time toward the south, giving glory to God in all things. On the third day a small island appeared in the distance, toward which the brethren rowed briskly. The saint said to them, "Do not exhaust your strength, brothers. Seven years will have passed next Easter since we left our country, and now on this island you will see a holy hermit called Paul the Spiritual, who has dwelt here for sixty years without bodily food and who for twenty years previously received his food from a certain animal."

When they drew near the shore, the coast was so steep that they could not find a place to land. The island was small and circular, about a furlong in circumference, and on its summit there was no soil, the rock being quite bare. When they sailed around it, they found a small creek that was scarcely wide enough for the prow of their boat. The ascent from here was very difficult. St. Brendan told his brethren to wait there until he returned, for they should not enter the island without the leave of the man of God who dwells there. When the saint ascended to the highest part of the island, he saw two caves opening opposite each other on its eastern side and a small cup-like spring of water gurgling up from the rock at the mouth of the cave where the soldier of Christ dwelt.

As St. Brendan approached the opening of one of the caves, the venerable hermit came out of the other to meet him, greeting him with the words: "Behold how good and how pleasant for brethren to dwell together in unity." He then directed St. Brendan to summon all the brethren from the boat. When they came he gave each of them the kiss of peace, calling him by his proper name, at which they all marvelled because of this demonstration of the prophetic spirit. They also marvelled at the way he was dressed, for he was covered all over from head to foot with the hair of his body, which from old age was as white as snow, and he had no other garment except this.

Noticing this, St. Brendan was moved to grief, and heaving many sighs, said to himself, "Woe is me, a poor sinner who wears a monk's habit and rules over many monks, when I see here a man of angelic condition, dwelling still in the flesh, yet untroubled by the vices of the flesh." The man of God said in response, "Venerable father, what great and wonderful things has God shown to you that he has not revealed to our saintly predecessors, and yet you say in your heart that you are not worthy to wear the habit of a monk. I say that you are greater than any monk, for the monk is fed and clothed by the labor of his own hands, while God has fed and clothed you and all your brethren for seven years in his own mysterious ways. And I, wretch that I am, sit here upon this rock without any covering, save the hair of my body."

Then St. Brendan asked him how he came to this island, where he came from, and how long he had led this type of life. The man of God replied, "For forty years I lived in the monastery of St. Patrick and had the care of the cemetery. One day when the prior pointed out to me the place for the burial of a deceased brother, an old man appeared there before me. I did not know him, and he said, 'Brother, do not make the grave there, for this is the burial-place of another one.' I said 'Who are you, father?' 'Do you not know me?' he said. 'Am I not your abbot?' 'St. Patrick is my abbot,' I said. 'I am he,' he said, 'and yesterday I departed from this life, and this is my burial-place.' Then he pointed out another place to me, saying, 'Here you will bury our deceased brother, but do not tell anyone what I have said to you. Go down tomorrow to the shore, and there you will find a boat that will carry you to the place where you shall wait for the day of your death.'

"Next morning, in obedience to the directions of the abbot, I went to the appointed place and found what he promised. I got into the boat and rowed for three days and nights, and then I allowed the boat to drift wherever the wind drove it. On the seventh day this rock appeared, and I landed on it at once, and I pushed the boat off with my foot, so that it could return to where it had come from. It cut through the waves in a rapid course to the land that it had left.

"On the day of my arrival here, about the hour of none, a certain animal, walking on its hind legs, brought to me in its front paws a fish for my dinner and a bundle of dry brushwood to make a fire with. After it set these before me, it went away as it came. I struck fire with a flint and steel and cooked the fish for my meal. For thirty years, every third day, the same provider brought the same quantity of food, one fish at a time, so that I never felt a want of food or drink either, since, thanks to God, every Sunday there flowed from the rock enough water for me to satisfy my thirst and to wash myself.

"After thirty years I discovered these two caves and this spring-well. I have lived on its waters for sixty years without any other nourishment whatsoever. For ninety years, therefore, I have lived on this island, surviving for thirty years on fish and for sixty years on the water from this spring. I already had lived fifty years in my own country, so that all the years of my life amount now to one hundred and forty. And for what may remain, I have to wait here in the flesh until the day of my judgment.

"Proceed now on your voyage, and carry with you water-skins full from this fountain, for you will want it during the forty days' journey remaining before Easter Sunday. That feast of Easter, and all the Easter holidays, you will celebrate where you have celebrated them for the past six years, and afterward, with a blessing from your provider, you will proceed to the land that you seek, the most holy of all lands. There you will remain for forty days, after which the Lord your God will guide you safely back to the land of your birth."

XIV

The Land of Promise of the Saints

St. Brendan and his brethren received the blessing of the man of God and mutually gave the kiss of peace in Christ. They then sailed away toward the south during Lent, and the boat drifted about to and fro. Their sustenance all this time was the water brought from the island. They refreshed themselves with it every third day and were glad since they did not feel hunger or thirst. On Holy Saturday they reached the island of their former provider, who came to meet them at the landing-place and lifted every one of them out of the boat in his arms. As soon as the divine offices of the day were performed, he set a meal before them.

In the evening they again got into their boat with this man, and they soon discovered the great whale in its usual place. On his back they proceeded to sing the praises of the Lord all night and to say their Masses in the morning. When the Masses had concluded, Jasconius moved away, all of them still on its back, and the brethren cried aloud to the Lord, "Hear us, O Lord, the God of our salvation." But St. Brendan encouraged them, saying, "Why are you alarmed? Do not fear, for no evil will befall us, since here we have only a helper on our journey."

The great whale swam in a direct course toward the shore of the Paradise of the Birds, where it landed them unharmed, and on this island they stayed until the octave of Pentecost. When that solemn season was passed, their provider, who was still with them, said to St. Brendan, "Embark now on your boat, and fill all the water skins from the fountain. I will be your companion and the conductor of this journey from now on, for without my guidance you could not find the land you seek, the Land of Promise of the Saints." Then, while they were embarking, all the birds of the island, as soon as they saw St. Brendan, sang together in concert, "May a happy voyage under his guidance bring you safely to the island of your provider." They took with them provisions for forty days, since their course lay to the west for that amount of time. During this time their provider went before them, guiding their way.

At the end of the forty days, toward evening, a dense cloud overshadowed them, so dark that they could scarcely see one another. Then the provider said to St. Brendan, "Do you know, father, what darkness this is?" The saint replied that he did not know. "This darkness," he said, "surrounds the island you have sought for seven years. You will soon see that this is the entrance to it." After an hour had passed a great light shone around them, and the boat stood by the shore.

When they disembarked, they saw an extensive land thickly set with trees, laden with fruit, as in the autumn. All the time they were crossing that land, during their stay in it, there was no night. A light always shone, like the light of the sun in the meridian, and for the forty days they viewed the land in various directions, but they could not find its borders. One day, however, they came to a large river flowing towards the middle of the land, which they could not cross in any way. St. Brendan then said to the brethren, "We cannot cross this river, and we must therefore remain ignorant of the size of this country." While they were considering this matter, a young man of brightly shining features and very handsome appearance came to them and joyfully embracing and addressing each of them by his own name said, "Peace be with you, brothers, and with all who practise the peace of Christ.

Blessed are they, O Lord, who live in your house. They will praise you forever and ever."

He then said to St. Brendan, "This is the land you have sought after for so long, but you could not find it before now because Christ our Lord wished first to show you his various mysteries in this immense ocean. Return now to the land of your birth, bearing with you as much of those fruits and precious stones as your boat can carry, for the days of your earthly pilgrimage must draw to a close, when you can rest in peace among your saintly brethren. After many years this land will be shown to those who come after you, when days of tribulation come upon the people of Christ. The great river you see here divides this land into two parts, and just as it appears now, teeming with ripe fruits, so it always remains, without any blight or shadow whatever, for unfailing light shines on it."

When St. Brendan inquired whether this land would be revealed to all, the young man replied, "When the most high Creator has brought all nations under subjection, then this land will be made known to all his elect." Soon after, St. Brendan received the blessing of this man and prepared for his return to his own country. He gathered some of the fruits of the land and various kinds of precious stones, and taking a last farewell of the good provider who had each year supplied food for him and his brethren, he embarked once more and sailed back through the darkness again.

When they had passed through this, they reached the Island of Delights, where they stayed for three days as guests of the monastery. Then St. Brendan, with the abbot's parting blessing, sailed in a direct course, under God's guidance, and arrived at his own monastery, where all the monks gave glory to God for the safe return of their holy patron; and they learned from him the wonderful works of God that he had seen or heard during his voyage.

Afterward he ended the days of his life in peace, on the nones of July, our Lord Jesus Christ reigning, whose kingdom and empire endure for ever and ever. Amen!

Charles the Fat's Vision

Charles, king of Swabia, the son of Louis, king of the Norici, assumed the joint empire of the Franks and Romans in the year of the Incarnate Word 885, the third Indiction. His vision, which I think worth preserving, I here include.

*

In the name of God, most high, the king of kings. When I, Charles, by the free gift of God the emperor of the Franks, on the sacred night of our Lord's day, after properly performing the holy service of the evening, went to my bed to rest and sought the sleep of quietude, there came a tremendous voice to me, saying, "Charles, in a little while your spirit shall leave you for some time."

Immediately I was carried away in spirit, and he who carried me away was most glorious to see. In his hand he held a ball of thread emitting a beam of the purest light, such as comets shed when they appear. He began to unwind it and said to me, "Take the thread of this brilliant ball and wind and tie it firmly on the thumb of your right hand, for by it you will be led through the inextricable punishments of the

129

infernal regions." Saying this, he went before me, quickly unrolling the thread of the brilliant ball, and led me into very deep and fiery valleys that were full of pits boiling with pitch and brimstone and lead and wax and grease.

I found there the bishops of my father and of my uncles, and when in terror I asked them why they were suffering such dreadful torments, they replied, "We were the bishops of your father and of your uncles and instead of preaching and admonishing them and their people to peace and concord, as was our duty, we were the sowers of discord and the fomenters of evil. On account of this we are now burning in these infernal torments together with other lovers of slaughter and plunder. And here also will come your bishops and ministers who now delight to act as we did."

While I was fearfully listening to this, the blackest demons came flying around me with fiery claws trying to snatch away the thread of life, which I held in my hand, and to draw it to them; but repelled by the rays of the ball they were unable to touch it.

Next, running behind me, they tried to grip me in their claws and cast me head-first into those sulphurous pits; but my guide, who carried the ball, threw a thread of light over my shoulders, and doubling it drew me strongly after him. In this way we ascended lofty fiery mountains from which arose lakes and burning rivers and all kinds of burning metals where I found immersed innumerable souls of the vassals and princes of my father and brothers, some up to the hair, others to the chin, and others to the middle, who mournfully cried out to me, "While we were living together with you and your father and brothers and uncles, we were fond of battle and slaughter and plunder because we craved earthly things. Therefore we now suffer punishment in these boiling rivers and in various kinds of liquid metal."

While I was listening to these souls with the greatest alarm, I heard some others behind me crying out, "The great will suffer still greater torment." I looked back and on the banks of the boiling river saw furnaces of pitch and brimstone, filled with great dragons and scorpions and different kinds of serpents, where I also saw some of my father's nobles, some of my own, and some of those of my brothers and my uncles, who said, "Alas, Charles, you see what dreadful torments we suffer on account of our malice and pride and the evil counsel that we gave our kings and you for lust's sake."

When I could not help groaning mournfully at this, the dragons ran at me with open jaws filled with fire and brimstone and pitch and tried to swallow me up. My guide then tripled the thread of the ball around me, which overcame their fiery throats by the splendor of its rays. He then pulled me with greater force, and we descended into a valley, which was on one side dark and burning like a fiery furnace, but on the other so extremely enchanting and glorious that I cannot describe it.

I turned toward the dark part that emitted flames, and there I saw some kings of my race in extreme torture. Frightened beyond measure by this and reduced to great distress, I expected to be immediately thrown into these torments by some very black giants who made the valley blaze with every kind of flame.

I trembled a great deal, and with the thread of the clue of light assisting my eyes, I saw the light brightening somewhat on the side of the valley and two fountains flowing from there. One was extremely hot, the other clear and lukewarm. Two large casks were there besides. When I proceeded there, guided by the thread of light, I looked into the vessel containing boiling water and saw my father Louis, standing there up to his thighs. He was dreadfully oppressed with pain and agony and said to me, "Fear not, my lord Charles. I know that your spirit will again return to your body, and that God has permitted you to come here so that you might see for what crimes I, and all you have seen, suffer these torments. One day I am bathed in the boiling cask; the next I pass into that other delightful water. This reprieve is brought about by the prayers of St. Peter and St. Remigius, under whose patronage our royal race has reigned up to now. But if you and my faithful bishops and abbots and the whole ecclesiastical order will quickly assist me with Masses, prayers and psalms, and alms and vigils, I will shortly be released from the punishment of the boiling water. My brother Lothaire and his son Louis have had these punishments remitted by the prayers of St. Peter and St. Remigius, and they have now entered into the joy of God's paradise."

He then said to me, "Look on your left hand," and when I had done so I saw two very deep casks boiling furiously. "These," he said, "are prepared for you if you do not amend and repent for your atrocious crimes." I then began to be dreadfully afraid, and when my guide saw my soul thus terrified, he said to me, "Follow me to the right of that most resplendent valley of paradise." As we proceeded, I saw my uncle Lothaire sitting in great brightness, among glorious kings, on a topaz stone of unusual size, crowned with a precious diadem. Near him sat his son Louis crowned in the same manner.

Seeing me nearby, he called me to him in a kind voice, saying, "Come to me, Charles, now my third successor in the empire of the Romans. I know that you have passed through the place of punishment where your father, my brother, is placed in the baths appointed for him; but by the mercy of God he will soon be liberated from those punishments as we have been by the merits of St. Peter and the prayers of St. Remigius, to whom God has given a special charge over the kings and people of the Franks. But unless he continues to favor and assist the dregs of our family, our race must shortly cease from both the kingdom and the empire. Know, moreover, that shortly the rule of the empire will be taken out of your hand, nor will you survive long." Then Louis, turning to me, said, "The empire that you have held up to now by hereditary right, Louis the son of my daughter is to assume." And when he said this there seemed to appear immediately before me a little child, and looking on him Lothaire his grandfather said to me, "This infant seems like the one whom our Lord set in the midst of the disciples and said, 'Of such is the kingdom of God. I say to you that angels there always behold the face of my father who is in heaven.' But bestow on him the empire with the thread of the ball that you hold in your hand."

I then untied the thread from the thumb of my right hand and gave him the whole rule of the empire by that thread, and immediately the entire ball became rolled up in his hand like a brilliant sunbeam. After this wonderful exchange, my spirit returned to my body, extremely wearied and frightened.

Therefore let all people know, willingly or unwillingly, that according to the will of God the whole empire of the Romans will revert into his hands. And I cannot prevail against him, compelled by the conditions of my calling. Know also that God, who is the ruler of the living and the dead, will both complete and establish this, whose eternal kingdom remains forever and ever. Amen!

t. Patrick's Purgatory

A knight named Owen, who had served for many years under King Stephen, obtained the king's permission and went to visit his parents in Ireland, his native country. After spending some time there, he began to meditate on his wicked life, which from his cradle had been spent in plunder and violence. He particularly repented the violation of churches and invasion of ecclesiastical property, besides other enormous sins of which he had been guilty.

In this state of penitence he went to a bishop of that country, who, after hearing his confession, rebuked him severely, asserting that he had committed a great offense against God's mercy. The knight began to consider how he should show proper sorrow for his evil deeds. The bishop wished to impose on him a just penance, to which the knight replied, "If, as you say, I have so seriously offended my maker, I will submit to a penance more severe than usual, and for the remission of my sins I will enter the Purgatory of St. Patrick." The following is the account that the ancient Irish histories give us of this purgatory and its origin.

While the great Patrick was preaching the work of God in Ireland and gaining a great reputation for the miracles that he performed there, he sought to reclaim the bestial people of that country from the works of the devil through fear of the torments of hell and a desire for the happiness of heaven. But they told him plainly that they would not be converted to Christ unless they first saw with their own eyes the things that he told them. While St. Patrick entreated God for the salvation of those people, with fasting, watching and prayer, the Son of God, appearing to him, led him to a deserted place where he showed him a round cave, dark within, and said to him, "Whoever in true repentance and constancy of faith enters this cave for one day and night will be purified there from all the sins they have committed against God during all their lives and will also not only see there the torments of the wicked, but, if they persevere steadfastly in the love of God, they will also witness the joys of the blessed."

The Lord then disappeared, and St. Patrick, joyful both at having seen Christ and at the discovery of the cave, believed at last that he would be able to convert the wretched people of Ireland to the true faith of Christ. He immediately, therefore, constructed an oratory on the spot, and enclosing the cave that is in the cemetery in front of the church, placed a door there so that no one could enter without his permission. He next appointed a society of regular canons there and gave the key to the prior, with orders that whoever came to the prior with a license from the bishop of the district would be allowed to enter the purgatory. Many people took advantage of this privilege while St. Patrick was still alive, and when they came out they testified that they had seen the torments of the wicked, as well as the great and unspeakable happiness of the good.

The knight Owen, therefore, persevered in asking for the required license, and the bishop, seeing that he was inflexible, gave him a letter to the prior, requesting him to act in the usual way. After he read the letter the prior conducted the knight into the church where he remained fifteen days in prayer. At the end of this time the prior celebrated Mass and gave him Holy Communion. He then led him to the door of the cave, which was then opened; he sprinkled him with holy water and said, "You will enter here in the name of Jesus Christ and will walk through the cave until you come out on an open plain, where you will find a hall skillfully constructed. Enter it and God will send you guides who will tell you what you are to do." The man boldly entered this conflict with the demons, and commending himself to the prayers of all and signing his forehead with the sign of the holy cross, he bravely passed the gate. The prior, shutting the door after him, returned with the procession into the church.

The knight passed courageously through the cave until he was in total darkness. At last the light again broke upon him, and he found himself in the plain where the hall that he had been told of was. The light was no more than the twilight of evening, and the hall was not enclosed by walls, but by pillars, like a monastic cloister. He entered and sat down looking around him on all sides, admiring the beauty of the building.

When he had sat there a short time, fifteen men in white garments, looking like ecclesiastics, and lately shaven, entered the hall and sat down, saluting him in the name of the Lord. All kept silence, except one, who said, "Blessed be almighty God, who has inspired you with this good resolution to enter this purgatory for the remission of your sins. Unless you carry yourself manfully, however, you will perish, body and soul together. For when we leave this building, it will be filled with a great multitude of unclean spirits, who will torment you greatly and will threaten to torment you even more. They will promise to conduct you back to the gate by which you entered, if by chance they can deceive you, so that you would leave; but if you allow yourself to be overcome by their torments or terrified by their threats, or deceived by their promises, and yield to them, you will perish both in soul and body. If, however, you are firm in faith, rest all your hope in the Lord, and do not yield to their torments, their threats or their promises, but despise them with all your heart, you will be purified from all your sins and will see the torments of the wicked and the repose of the good. As long as these demons torment you, call on the name of the Lord Jesus Christ, and, by invoking his name, you will immediately be released from all their torments. Now we can stay here with you no longer, but we commend you to almighty God."

The knight, therefore, was left alone and prepared his mind for this new kind of conflict. He no sooner wrought up his soul to courage than a noise was heard around the building, as if all the people in the world, with the animals and beasts, were making it, and after this noise came a terrible apparition of ugly demons, of which an immense multitude rushed into the hall, and in derision addressed the knight. "Other men," they said, "who serve us are content to wait till they are dead before they come. But you honor this company of masters so much that you come to us, soul and body, while you are still alive. Have you come to receive punishment for your sins? You will have nothing but affliction and sorrow among us; but since you are so zealous a servant to us, if you wish to return through the door by which you came in, we will conduct you there unharmed so that you may again enjoy yourself in the world and all its pleasures."

Thus spoke the demons, wishing to deceive him either by threats or allurements, but Christ's soldier was neither terrified by their threats nor seduced by their allurements. He turned a deaf ear to them and contemptuously answered them without a word. Indignant at being treated with contempt, the demons kindled a large fire in the hall, and seizing the knight by the arms and legs, threw him into the middle of it, dragging him with iron hooks backwards and forwards through the fire. When he first felt the torture, he called on the name of Jesus Christ saying, "Jesus Christ, have mercy on me." At Christ's name the fire was put out, so that not a spark remained. Seeing this, the knight no longer feared them, because he saw that they were overcome by Christ's name.

The demons now left the hall and dragged the knight after them through a black and dark wilderness toward the place where the sun rises in summer, and now he began to hear lamentations, as if from all the people in the world. Finally he was dragged by the demons into a long and wide plain filled with woe and calamities. It was so long that it was impossible to see across it. It was full of people of both sexes and of every age, naked, and lying with their bellies on the ground, for their bodies and limbs were fastened horribly to the ground with hot iron nails driven into the earth. Sometimes in the anguish of their sufferings they gnawed the dust, crying and lamenting, "Spare us, oh, spare us; have mercy, have mercy on us!" though there was no one there to have mercy or to spare them.

The demons ran over these wretched beings, striking them with heavy blows as they passed, and said to the knight, "These torments, which you see, you will also suffer yourself unless you consent to be led back to the door by which you entered. If you like, you will be conducted there in safety." But the knight, remembering how God had released him before, turned a deaf ear to all they said.

They then threw him on the ground and tried to nail him down like the others; but, when he invoked the name of Jesus Christ, they were unable to do him further injury in that place and dragged him away into another open plain. Here he saw a difference between these and the first. In the first place they had their bellies to the ground, here all were lying on their backs. Fiery dragons were sitting on some of them and were gnawing them with iron teeth, to their inexpressible anguish. Others were the victims of fiery serpents, which, coiling round their necks, arms, and bodies, fixed iron fangs into their hearts. Toads, immense and terrible, also sat on the breasts of some of them and tried to tear out their hearts with their ugly beaks. Demons also ran along over them, lashing them as they passed, and they never let them rest a moment from their sufferings.

From there the demons dragged the knight into another plain of punishment, where there was so large a multitude that it seemed to surpass the population of the whole world. Some were suspended over fires of brimstone by iron chains fastened to their feet and legs, with their heads downward; others hung by their hands and arms, and some by the hair of their heads. Some were hung over the flames by hot iron hooks passed through their eyes and noses, others by their ears and mouths, others by their breasts and genitals, and in the middle of all their groans and lamentations the lash of the demons never ceased for a moment. Here also, as in the other place of punishment, the enemy sought to torment the knight, but he invoked the name of Jesus and was safe.

From this place of punishment the demons dragged the knight to a hot iron wheel, whose spokes and rims were fixed with red-hot nails. Men and women were suspended from it and they were grievously burned by the flame of brimstone-fire that rose from the ground. The demons turned this wheel with iron bars so rapidly that it was impossible to distinguish one from another. Because of the rapid motion they all looked like one mass of fire.

Others fixed to spits endured equal torments and were basted by the demons with liquid metal, while others were baked in ovens and fried in frying pans.

As his conductors dragged him away, the knight also saw a house containing numerous large cauldrons, which were full of liquid pitch, sulphur, and melted metals, where there were human beings of both sexes, and all ranks and ages. Some were completely immersed, some up to their eyes, others to their lips and necks, others to their breasts, and others again only to their knees and legs. Some had only one hand or foot immersed, others had both. All were howling and crying piteously because of the enormity of their sufferings. When the demons tried to plunge the knight into the cauldrons with the rest, he invoked the name of Christ, and that saved him.

The demons now hurried the knight to the top of a lofty mountain and showed him a large number of people of both sexes and of different ages. All were sitting naked, bent down on their toes, turned toward the north and apparently waiting in terror for the approach of death. Suddenly a violent whirlwind from the north swept them away, and the knight with them, and carried them weeping and lamenting to another part of the mountain into a cold and stinking river. When they tried to rise out of its chilling waters, the demons ran over the surface and again sank them into its depths. The knight, however, invoked the name of Christ and immediately found himself on the other bank.

The demons dragged him towards the south and showed him a noxious flame that arose with a stinking smell out of a well, over which there were naked men and women, apparently red-hot, who were shot into the air like sparks and again, fell into the pit beneath when the flame subsided. The demons said to the knight, "That fiery well is the entrance to hell where we live, and since you have served us so diligently up to now, you will remain here with us forever. If you enter this pit, you will perish body and soul together. But if you listen to us even now and return to the door by which you entered, you will pass unharmed." But the knight, trusting in the help of God, who had so often delivered him, turned a deaf ear to all their exhortations.

In indignation the demons then rushed into the fiery pit and dragged the knight with them. The deeper he went the wider it became, and the more terrible were the punishments that he saw. In that pit the knight also saw such woe and misery that for some time he forgot him who had helped him; but at last, by God's grace he invoked the name of Jesus and was immediately driven by the flames into the open air above, where he stood for some time dazed and thunderstruck. But sallying from the pit's mouth some new demons said to him, "Hey, you, who stand there. Our comrades told you that this was the mouth of hell, but it is not so. We are in the habit of telling lies, so that if we cannot deceive by the truth, we can do it by what is false. This is not hell, but we will now lead you there."

These new enemies dragged the knight with a terrible noise to a broad and stinking river, covered with flame and fire of brimstone and full of demons, who told him that under that river was hell. A bridge stretched across it that seemed to have three impossibilities connected with it. In the first place it was so slippery that even if it were broad hardly anyone could have had a firm footing on it. In the second place it was so narrow that no one could walk or even stand up on it. Third, it was so high above the river that it was dizzying to look down.

"You must cross that bridge," said the demons, "and the wind that blew you into the other river will blow you into this. You will then be caught by our comrades who are in the river and be sunk into the pit of hell." But the knight, invoking the name of Jesus Christ, bravely set foot on the bridge. The farther he went, the wider he found it, until it was as wide as a high road. The demons, seeing the knight walk so freely across the bridge, shook the air with their horrid cries, which alarmed the knight more than all the torments he had endured before from them. His other enemies under the bridge threw red-hot hooks of iron at him, but they could not touch him. In this way he crossed the bridge in safety, for he met nothing that could stop him.

Now released from the persecutions of these unclean spirits, the brave knight saw before him a high wall of wonderful workmanship. It had one gate, which was shut. This gate was adorned with precious stones and shone brilliantly. When the knight approached it, the gate opened, and so sweet a smell came from inside that he regained his courage and was revived from all the torments that he had suffered.

A procession, such as has never been seen in this world, came forth to meet him with crosses, tapers, banners, and branches of golden palm. It was followed by a multitude of men and women of every rank: archbishops, bishops, abbots, monks, priests, and ministers of every ecclesiastical degree, all clad in sacred garments, suited to their ranks. They welcomed the knight with pleasant greetings and led him inside the gate in triumph with concerts of unequalled harmony.

When the concert was ended, two archbishops conversing with him blessed the Lord for having provided his soul with the courage to resist the torments that he had passed through and suffered. As they conducted him through that region, they pointed out to him the most delightful meadows, adorned with different flowers and fruits of many kinds of herbs and trees. He thought he could live forever on their sweet odors. Darkness is never felt in that region, because it is illuminated by a celestial brilliancy that never fails. He saw there such a large multitude of men and women that he supposed all the rest of the world could hardly have held them. Choir followed choir, and all in sweet harmonious concert praised the Creator of all things. Some approached crowned like kings, others were clothed in golden garments, some with robes of different colors according to what they were when they were in this world. Some of them rejoiced in their own happiness, others at the freedom and happiness of the rest. When they looked at the knight, all thanked God for his arrival and congratulated him on his escape from the regions of death. No one felt heat or cold, nor did he see there anything that could create offense or injury.

Then the holy pontiffs who had shown the knight this delightful country said to him, "Since you have come uninjured among us, by the mercy of God, you must hear from us an account of all that you have seen. This region is the terrestrial paradise from which humanity was first expelled for its sins and plunged into that miserable condition in which humans die in the world. All of us who are here were born in the flesh and in original sin, and by the faith in the Lord Jesus Christ, which we received in baptism, we returned to this paradise. But since we all committed actual sins without number after we were baptized, it was only by being purged of our sins and being punished for them that we were able to reach this place. The penance that we undertook before our death or at the hour of death, but did not complete on earth, must still be discharged by suffering in the places of punishment that you have seen, according to the nature and magnitude of the sin.

"All of us who are here have been in those places of punishment for our sins, and all whom you saw there suffering punishment, except those who are within the mouth of the infernal pit, will come to this place of rest and at last be saved. For some of them come here every day, purified from their sins, and we go to meet them and bring them in, as we did with you. No one of us knows how long he or she will remain here. But by the Masses and psalms, by the alms and prayers of the universal church, as well as the special aid of their own friends, the torments of those in purgatory may be greatly lessened; or they may even receive a lighter kind of punishment in exchange for those to which they were first doomed, until they are released entirely in the end. Thus, as you see, we enjoy much tranquility here, although we are not yet worthy to enter the full happiness of heaven. When the time that God has set arrives, each of us will hereafter pass into the heavenly kingdom, as God will provide."

The reverend prelates now led the knight to the sloping side of a mountain and told him to look up. When he had done this, they asked him what color heaven was in comparison with the place where he stood. He replied that it was like the color of red-hot gold in a furnace. They said, "What you now see is the entrance to heaven and the celestial paradise. When anyone leaves us that person ascends this way to heaven. As long as we remain here God feeds us daily on heavenly food. Its nature we will now describe by letting you taste it." The words were hardly spoken when a ray of light descending from heaven covered the whole country, and the flame, settling in rays on the head of each, entered into the bodies of all.

The knight felt such a delicious sweetness pervade his heart and whole body that he hardly knew whether he was alive or dead, but this feeling was over in a moment. He would gladly have remained here forever if he could have enjoyed these delights, but in the next place he was told of other things not so pleasant.

"Since you have now set eyes," said the holy prelates, "on the happiness of the blessed, as you wished, and have also seen the torments of the wicked in part, you must now return by the same path that you came. If – God forbid! – when you return to the world you lead a wicked life, you have seen here what torments await you. If, however, you lead a good and religious life, you may rely on coming to us again when your spirit is released from the body. You need not fear the torments of the demons on your way back, for they will not be able to come near you, nor can their torments that you have seen hurt you."

The knight replied with tears, "I cannot return from this place, for I fear that the frailty of human nature will lead me to err, and I may be prevented from returning again." "No," they said, "these things are not as you wish, but according to the will of him who made both us and you." With sorrow and mourning the knight was then brought back to the gate, which was shut behind him, after he had reluctantly passed through it.

The knight Owen returned by the same path as he had gone to the hall mentioned before, but the demons whom he saw during his return fled from him in alarm; and the torments through which he had passed were unable to hurt him. As soon as he had entered the hall, the fifteen men described before glorified God for having given him such fortitude under the torments: "You must now go up with speed, for day is already dawning in your country, and if the prior does not find you when he opens the door, he will think you are lost, and shutting the door he will return to the church."

The knight then received their blessing, and hurrying away he met the prior at the moment that he opened the door. With praises and thanksgiving to Christ, he was led by him to the church, where he remained fifteen days in prayer.

After this he took the sign of the cross and set out to the Holy Land, seeking the Sepulcher of Our Lord and the other sacred places in holy mediation. From there, once he had discharged his vow, he returned home and prayed to his lord, King Stephen, that he might be allowed to pass the remainder of his life in the service of religion and become a soldier in the armies of the King of Kings.

It happened at this time, that Gervais, abbot of Louth, had obtained from King Stephen a grant of land on which to build an abbey in Ireland, and he sent one of his monks named Gilbert to the king to take possession of the land and to build the abbey on it. But Gilbert complained, when he came before the king, that he did not know the language of that country. The king replied that with God's help he would soon find him an able interpreter, and calling Owen before him, he bade him go with Gilbert and stay in Ireland.

This was agreeable to Owen, who gladly went with Gilbert and served him faithfully, but he would not assume the habit of a monk because he chose rather to be a servant than a master. They crossed over into Ireland and built an abbey, where Owen acted as the monk's interpreter and faithful servant in all he did. Whenever they were alone together, the monk asked him particularly about purgatory and the marvelous punishments that he had seen and felt there; but the knight, who never could hear about purgatory without weeping bitterly, told his friend for his edification and under the seal of secrecy all that he had seen and experienced and affirmed that he had seen it all with his own eyes. By the care and diligence of this monk all that the knight had seen was put in writing, together with the narratives of the bishops and other ecclesiastics of that country who for the sake of truth gave their testimony to the facts.

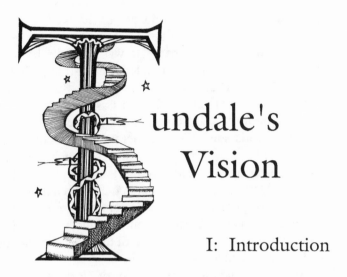

undale's Vision

I: Introduction

Hibernia is an island situated in the farthest western sea. It extends from south to north and is distinguished by rivers and lakes, planted with woods, very fertile with fruit, full of milk and honey and all kinds of fish and game. It lacks vineyards but is rich in wine. Serpents, frogs, toads, and all such wild poisonous animals, and all poisons known to destroy wood or rope or horn are unknown. It is famous enough for its holy men and women and is, moreover, well-known for its harsh warriors, for it has England close at hand in the south; in the east not only the Scots, but also the Britons, who are called the Gauls; in the north the Scandinavians and those from the Orkneys; and on the opposite side to the south the Spaniards. This island also has thirty-four extraordinary cities, which are under two main bishops. Armagh is the most famous city of northern Ireland, and Cashel is the most famous city in the south.

From Cashel there was a certain nobleman by the name of Tundale. He gave us the material for this work because, on account of his cruelty and power, he went against God's piety. He was a youth of a noble race with a cheerful face and elegant manner. He was carefully brought up, well-dressed, and high-minded, not ill-trained in the military arts, skillful, friendly and joyful. But I am not able to say without sorrow that, just as he trusted in the strength and form of his body, he disregarded the eternal salvation of his soul. So in general he often confessed with tears, because it oppressed him so much when he wanted to say anything, although brief, about the state of his soul. He neglected God's church and did not wish to even see the poor of Christ. For empty glory he gave whatever he had to buffoons, mimes and jesters. But when divine mercy wished, it saw fit to put an end for him to all his evils and to call him forth.

As many inhabitants of the city of Cork, who were present then, may testify, he lay dead for three days and three nights; and later he spoke bitterly of all that he suffered during this period because of his previous easy carelessness, as his present life bore witness. For he suffered the most incredible and intolerable kinds of tortures, the order of which is without name. So from this man, who saw and suffered, we now can tell you this, because it does not oppress us to write it so that you can increase your devotions.

Tundale had many faithful friends. Among them was one who was in debt to Tundale for three horses that they had traded. When the end of the term was approaching, Tundale visited his friend in time for the transaction. He remained there for three days, and he was well received; then he began to speak of this other business. When his friend told him that he did not have on hand what Tundale was seeking, Tundale decided to make his way back to where he had come from, since he was very angry. The debtor, however, wished to mollify his friend and asked him to consider eating with him before he went back. Since he was not able to say no to his entreaties, Tundale sat down again and, assured by the deposit that he held in his hand, he began to eat with his friend.

But divine piety prevented his appetite. Struck by a sudden stroke, he was not able to raise the hand that he extended to his mouth. Then he began in a frightened way to cry out for his ax, which he had previously put away. He then committed it to the care of his friend's wife, saying, "Take care of my ax, for I am dying." Then, as far as the word has any meaning, his body immediately sank to the ground, separated from his soul; and his spirit was no longer of any account there.

The signs of death were present: his hair fell out, his forehead became hard, his eyes wandered, his nose became pointed, his lips grew pale, his mind failed, and his whole body grew rigid. The household ran, the food was removed, arms-bearers cried out, the guests cried, the body was laid out, the standards trembled, the clerk ran, the people marveled, and all the excited citizenry were disturbed by the death of this good soldier.

Why do we die? From almost the tenth hour of the fourth day to the same hour on Saturday he lay dead with no signs of life remaining in him, except that those who tried diligently to coax his body back to life felt a little heat on his left side. Because of this warmth that they felt in this small part of him, they did not wish to bury his body.

Moreover, after this, when the clerk and the people present gathered around to bury him, he regained his soul and with a feeble breath, in almost a single hour, he began to revive. Everyone marveled, even the wise, saying, "Is this not the spirit going and returning?" Then Tundale, looking around with a weak gaze, was asked if he wished to receive Communion. He gave a sign to indicate that they should bring the body of the Lord; and when he had consumed and drank wine he began to praise God with thanks saying, "O God, your mercy is greater than my difficulty, although my difficulty may be great beyond measure. You showed me so many great tribulations and evils, and you led me back from the abyss to the way of earth, and you restored me back to life." When he had said this with everyone looking on he dispersed what he had and gave it to the poor, and he began to sign himself by the true healing sign of the cross, and he vowed for himself a pure life, abandoning his former ways. Moreover, all that he saw or experienced he told us afterward, as follows.

II

The Departure of Tundale's Soul

He said that when his soul left his body, and he knew he was dead, knowing he was guilty he grew terrified, and he did not know what he might do. He feared something, but he did not know what he feared. He wished to return to his body, but he was unable to enter it. He even wished to proceed on, but he was frightened on every side. And so, this most miserable soul, knowing he was guilty, had no confidence except in the mercy of God. So finally he went on weeping and crying and trembling, since he did not know what he ought to do.

Finally he saw a great multitude of unworldly spirits coming toward him, so that they filled not only the whole house and courtyard in which the dead man had died, but actually there was no place that was apparent in all the streets and ways of the city that was not full of them.

Moreover, they surrounded that miserable soul, although they did not try to console him but to sadden him a good deal saying, "We sing this song of death fitting for this miserable soul, since he is the child of death and food for the inextinguishable fire, the friend of shadows, the enemy of light."

Turning to him they all gnashed him with their teeth, and because of their great anger they tore their cheeks to pieces with their own claws, saying, "Behold, poor soul, the people whom you choose, with whom you will be burning in deepest hell. Nurturer of scandal, lover of discord, why are you not proud? Why do you not adulterate? Why do you not fornicate? Where is your vanity and your vain delights? Where is your immoderate laughter? Where is your courage, by which you insulted so many? Why do you not signal now with your eyes as you used to? Will you not grind with your foot, nor speak with your finger, nor contrive evil with your perverse heart?"

Because of this and similar things the miserable, terrified soul could do nothing else but cry, expecting death without delay from all who were there threatening him. But the all-powerful, pious and merciful Lord, dispensing all good by his secret judgment, who did not wish this sinner's death, met this lonely one to offer him healing after death. The Lord tempered the misery of even this one, as he wished.

III

The Coming of the Angel

The Lord sent his angel to meet Tundale and made him notice and watch from afar the angel's coming like an unremitting, very bright star, hoping to give Tundale some counsel through him. When the angel drew near him, he greeted him by his own name calling and saying, "Hail, Tundale, what are you doing?" When this poor handsome youth – for he had a handsome figure among the sons of humanity – saw the angel and heard him call him by his own name, Tundale cried from fear and joy together, and he broke out in such a voice, saying, "Alas, lord father, the sorrows of hell have surrounded me, the snares of death have taken possession of me."

The angel said to him, "Why do you call me lord and father? You had me with you always and everywhere, and you never judged me worthy of such a name." He answered him, "Lord, where did I ever see you? Where did I hear your most sweet voice?"

The angel answered and said to him, "I followed you ever since your birth, wherever you went, and you never wished to obey my counsels." Extending his hand toward one of the foul spirits who had insulted Tundale with curses greater than the others, he said, "See him. You acquiesced to his counsels, and you entirely neglected my will. But since the Lord always puts mercy before justice, this mercy will not be lacking even for you. Be very happy and secure since you will suffer few of the many things that you would suffer if the mercy of our Redeemer had not come down to you. Therefore you ought to follow me, and whatever I show you keep in your memory because you have to return to your body along this path."

Then Tundale's terrified soul went toward him, beyond the limit, leaving behind his own body, which he formerly stood over. Hearing this and seeing that they were unable to carry Tundale off, the evil ones and the demons who previously threatened the soul, raised their voices to heaven saying, "O how unjust and cruel God is since as he wishes he mortifies them, and as he wishes he revives them – not as he promised: to give back to each one according to his or her merit and work. He frees the souls not free and damns the souls not damned." With these words they rose up against one another and they harmed themselves with whatever blows they could inflict on each other, and they drew back with great indignation and sadness into the rest of the great stench.

Going forward the angel said to Tundale's soul, "Follow me." Tundale answered, "Alas, my lord, if I go forward they will tear me away and hand me over to the eternal fire." The angel said to him, "Do not fear them, for there are more with us than with them. If God is with us, who is against us? Indeed a thousand fall on our left side and ten thousand on our right, so they may not approach you. Nevertheless, you will see and watch the retribution of sins with your own eyes. And you will suffer, just as I said before, a few of the many things that you deserve." With these words they set out.

IV

The First Punishment of Murderers

Together they proceeded a distance, and they had no light except for the splendor of the angel. Finally they came to a very terrible and shadowy valley covered by the fog of death. It was very deep and full of burning coals, with an iron lid, which seemed to be six cubits thick, that was there over the coals that burned with unusual brightness. The stench of this exceeded all the tribulations that the soul had suffered up to this point.

A multitude of most miserable souls descended from above that grate, and they were burned, as broth cooked down in a frying pan is totally liquified, until the heaviest fall through this grate, just as wax usually melts down through cloth, and they were restored again to torment in the fires with burning coals. When he had seen this Tundale's soul was greatly terrified and said to the angel, "Alas, my lord, I ask if you could possibly tell me what evil these souls ever did that they were judged worthy of such torments." To this the angel said, "These are murderers, parricides and fratricides. This is the first punishment of the perpetrators and of those consenting with the perpetrators; and after this they will be led to the greatest punishments that you will see." "And will I ever suffer this?" asked Tundale. The angel said to him, "You deserve it, but indeed you will not suffer. For it is true you are not a patricide or a matricide or fratricide; nevertheless you are a homicide, but it is not charged against you now. From the rest, however, take care so that when you return to your body you do not merit this one more or even greater punishment." He added, "Let us proceed, for the way before us is long."

V

The Punishment of Spies and Traitors

When they had progressed they came to an extraordinarily large mountain of great horrors and vast solitude. The mountain provided a very narrow path here for crossing. A putrid, sulphurous and shadowy fire lay on one side of this path, and on the other side was an icy snow and a horrible wind with hail. On one side and on the other, this mountain was truly prepared for punishing souls; it was full of tortures, so that no one who was cautious about crossing seemed to cross willingly. The same torturers mentioned before even had flaming iron pitch-forks and very sharp and ready tridents, with which they prodded the souls wishing to cross. They threw them into the punishment. Meanwhile, after being miserably enveloped on the sulphurous side for a long time, where they atoned for their sins, they were thrown into the side of snow, prodded with the same instruments. Again from the middle of ice they were thrown back into the flames of fire.

Thoroughly terrified when he had seen these things, the soul said to the angel who went in front of him, "I ask you, lord, while I clearly see the ambush ready for my destruction, how can I walk this way?" The angel answered him: "Do not be afraid, but either follow or precede me." The angel went first and Tundale's soul followed just as before.

VI

The Valley and Punishment of the Proud

As they gradually made their fearful way they came to a very deep valley, very putrid and shaded. The soul was unable to see anything in the darkness, but he could hear the sound of sulphur flaming and of great howling in the depths of endurance. The smoke rose back up fetid from sulphur and bodies and exceeded any punishments that he had seen before. Moreover, a very long platform, which was a thousand feet long and only one foot wide, extended from one mountain to the other like a bridge above the valley. No one except the saved was able to cross this bridge.

He saw many fall from this bridge, but a certain priest was able to cross. He was, moreover, a wandering priest, carrying a palm and wearing a pilgrim's cloak; fearless he crossed first before all others. Then Tundale's soul, seeing and knowing the everlasting ruin below, said to the angel, "Alas, misery to me. Who will free me from the journey of this death?" But, looking at him with a joyful face the angel answered saying, "Do not be afraid. You will indeed be freed from this punishment, but after this you will suffer another."

Going first the angel held him and led him across that bridge. After crossing the narrow way, safe now, the happy soul said to the angel, "I beseech you, lord, if it pleases you, tell me what souls are these that I see tormented in this way?" And the angel said to him, "This place is the most horrible valley of the proud. The putrid and sulphurous mountain is the punishment of the flatterers." And he added, "Let us go until we will come to another that this cannot compare with."

VII

The Greedy and Their Punishment

Then, with the angel preceding, they set out on the long, tortuous and very difficult way. After they had labored much and completed the shadowy journey, Tundale saw an incredibly large and intolerably horrible beast not far from them. In its enormous magnitude this beast exceeded all the mountains that he had ever seen. His eyes really seemed like burning hills. His mouth was open and so wide that it seemed to him it could contain nine thousand armed men. Moreover, in his mouth he had two very unusual parasites with turned heads. One of them had his head against the upper teeth of this beast and his feet down to the lower teeth; the other, just the opposite, had his head down and his feet upwards to the upper teeth. They were almost like columns in his mouth and made his mouth seem as if it were divided into three portals.

Inextinguishable flames also belched forth from his mouth, which was divided into three parts by the three gates, and into this flame the condemned souls were compelled to enter. An incomparable stink also came from his mouth. It was no wonder that both the crying and the howling of the multitude in his stomach were heard through his mouth since there were many thousands of men and women atoning in dire torment inside.

Also in front of his mouth was a multitude of unworldly spirits who forced the souls to enter. But before they entered they attacked them with many diverse strokes and blows. After Tundale's soul watched this horrible and fearful spectacle for a long time, at the same time both destitute before the great terror and in fear for his spirit, he said sobbing to the angel, "Alas, alas, my lord, are these that I see hidden from you. Why do you approach them?" Answering him, the angel said, "We cannot complete our journey in any other way unless we pay attention to this very torment. For none is able to avoid this torment except the elect. This beast is called Acheron, who devours all the greedy. Concerning this beast scripture says, 'He will swallow the river and he will not wonder, and he has courage because the River Jordan flows into his mouth.' These men whom you see placed in

159

his mouth and between his teeth are giants, and they were faithful in their time and in their way of life, but their names are not well known to you. They are called Fergusus and Conallus." To which Tundale's soul said, "Alas, lord, this disturbs me. Since you claimed they were faithful in their way, why does the Lord judge them worthy of such blows?" To this the angel said, "All these that you see here were suited for a greater kind of punishment, and before you return you will be able to see much of these greater punishments."

When he said this, the angel went forward and stood before the beast; and the soul, though unwilling, followed him. When they stood together before the beast the angel disappeared and Tundale's miserable soul remained alone. When they saw him forsaken, the devils approached the miserable soul like rabid dogs; and they dragged him with them into the belly of the beast. Even if he were silent now, the color of his face and change of manners would easily have shown a wise one whatever he or she wished to know about how great or how much torment he then endured.

Since we ought to try to be brief, not all that we hear is worth writing down. Nevertheless, so that we do not seem to neglect this material, we wish to tell a few of these many things for the edification of our readers. For Tundale endured dogs, bears, lions, serpents, the ferocity of other numberless unidentified monstrous animals, the blows of devils, the burning of fire, the harshness of cold, the stench of sulphur, the fog of the eyes, the flowing of burning tears, the fullness of tribulation and the gnashing of teeth. When he had learned these and similar things there, on account of his excessive sorrow and desperation, he was able to blame no other miserable one for his past except himself and to tear his own cheeks. Once the poor one recognized his condition and became afraid to suffer the eternal punishment he deserved, he felt himself outside the beast, not knowing how he was released.

After he laid there weak for a long time, opening his own eyes he saw the angel, the spirit of light, who proceeded before him. Then rejoicing, although greatly afflicted, he said to the angel, "O, my one hope, O comfort given by God not due to me, O light of my eyes and staff of my misery and calamity, what do you wish poor me to forsake? What can I, a wretch, give to the Lord for all that he gave to me? For if he never did me any good except sending you to meet me, what thanks will I pay the worthy one?" The angel answered him, "Just as you said before, so you know it to be: divine mercy is greater than your sin. This one indeed gives back each one according to his or her own work and merit; nevertheless he will judge each one according to his or her end. On account of this, as I said before, it is important for you to be on your guard so that when you regain your strength you may merit this journey." The angel added this saying, "Let us cross to these supplicants who are before us."

VIII

The Punishment of Robbers and Thieves

Rising weakly and trying feebly to maintain his course, the soul wished very much to follow the angel, but he was not able to because he was greatly afflicted. When the angel of the Lord touched him, however, he comforted him; and going ahead with the clear intention of completing the journey, as he said before, he counseled the soul. After they had gone a long way they saw a very full and tempestuous lake. Its water flowed up so high that it did not permit the sky to show. In it there was a great multitude of terrible beasts, who roaring around demanded nothing else except to devour the souls.

Across its width was a very narrow and long bridge, which measured almost two miles in length, for such was the width of the lake. The width of this bridge measured almost as wide as the palm of the hand. This bridge was longer and narrower than the bridge that we mentioned before. Its surface was also pierced with very sharp iron nails, which slashed the feet of all those crossing, so that no one's foot, if he or she touched it a single time, could avoid them. All the beasts also gathered there at the bridge to consume their food: these very souls who were not able to cross. These beasts were also of such magnitude that they well deserved to be compared to great towers. Fire also came out of their mouths so that those who saw it thought the lake boiled.

On this bridge Tundale saw one soul bitterly crying and accusing himself of many crimes. He was burdened with a heavy weight of grain as he tried to cross this bridge. Although he mourned as the soles of his feet were perforated with the iron nails, nevertheless, he feared very much falling into the fiery lake, where he now saw the determination of those beasts.

Seeing the immanent danger, Tundale's soul said to the angel, "Alas, lord, if you will, I wish to know why this soul tries to cross under such a great weight. Which souls in particular might this punishment be for?" He said to him, "This punishment is especially fitting for you and those like you who carried out robberies, whether they were great or small. But those guilty of greater and lesser crimes do not suffer in the same way unless the lesser crime was, perhaps, a regular sacrilege." Then Tundale's soul said, "What do you call a sacrilege?" The angel answered, "Whoever robs either a sacrament or a sacred thing, this act is considered a sacrilege. Whoever is guilty under the covering of religion, unless they convert themselves through penance, are judged guilty of the greatest thing." He added this: "Let us hurry for we must cross this bridge."

But the soul said, "You will be able to cross this bridge through divine power, but in no way, I think, will you be able to lead me with you." The angel said, "I will not cross with you, but you will cross this by yourself, nor will you be able to cross empty-handed, for you must lead a wild cow with you and return it to me again on the other side of the bridge." Complaining, Tundale's soul wept bitterly and said to the angel, "Woe to me. Why did God create me that I should undergo this? Miserable me, how will I be able to lead this across, when I am in such danger myself? Unless divine mercy intervenes, I certainly will not be able to stand." Then the angel said, "Remember that when you were in your body you stole your neighbor's cow." He said to him, "Lord, did I not return the cow, which is the subject of all this, to its rightful owner?" The angel said to him, "You returned it, but only when you were not able to hide it. Because of this you will not suffer the full punishment; for evil willed is less than evil performed, although both are evil before the Lord."

With these words, the angel looked back at the soul and showed him a wild cow. "Here is the cow," he said, "that you are supposed to lead across." Indeed when he saw that he was not able to avoid the punishment due, crying and guilty, Tundale held onto the cow. However little he succeeded, he did try to urge the cow to the bridge. The bellowing beasts came and waited for their food, which they saw set out on the bridge. However, when the soul began to cross, the cow did not wish to go with him. Why delay any longer? When the soul stood, the cow fell, and when the cow stood the soul fell, and so vice versa they stood and they fell until they came to the middle of the bridge. When they arrived there they saw opposite them the one who carried the bundles. I do not mention him in connection with those of whom it is said, "Coming, however, they came not with exultation carrying their burdens," but of those whom scripture warns elsewhere, "Woe to you who now smile since you will cry and weep." For thus weeping and crying they meet each other but neither in mercy and truth, nor in peace and justice, which are themselves prized.

This soul who came with the burdens asked Tundale not to take up the whole bridge himself. From the opposite side, with whatever entreaties he could make, Tundale asked the other one not to block the path, part of which he had already completed with such hard labor. Nevertheless, neither one nor the other was able, not so much to turn back, as even to look back. And so they stood complaining and standing there, staining the bridge with the blood of their soles. After they had stood for a long time and had lamented their guilty crimes, they did not know how, but each knew that the other one had crossed by. Moreover, while Tundale's soul crossed, he saw his angel whom he left behind, who spoke to him with gentle words. He said, "You are coming along well. Do not mind about the cow anymore, since you are no longer obliged to him."

But Tundale showed him his feet and complained that he was not able to go any farther. The angel answered, "You ought to remember how swift your feet were for shedding blood, and such unhappiness was the merit and the grief of your ways, unless the mercy of the Almighty had intervened for you." And when the angel said this, touching him, he healed him, and so Tundale went on. Then the soul said, "Which way do we go?" The angel answered, "A certain frightening torture awaits our coming. His name is Phristinus, and we cannot, in any way, avoid his hospitality. Although his inn is always full of guests, nevertheless this host desires to discover new guests to punish."

IX

The Punishment of Gluttons and Fornicators

After they had gone through a dry and shady place, an open house appeared before them. The house they saw was very large and as a high as a mountain in its great magnitude and as round as an oven where bread is usually baked. A flame also came out of it, which burned up whatever souls it found within a thousand miles. But Tundale's soul, because of a past, similar experience drew away from the torment, since he did not wish to approach more closely in any way. And to the angel who led him he said, "Miserable me, what will I do? See. We approach the gate of death, and what will free me?" The angel answered him saying, "Indeed, you will be free from the flame itself outside; but you will enter this house from where the flame proceeds."

When they approached more closely, they saw executioners with axes and knives and sticks and double needles with pick-axes and bores and very sharp sickles, with spades and delvers and with other instruments. With these they could stand before the gates in the midst of the flames to flail, decapitate, cleave or mutilate the souls. Under their hands this whole multitude of souls endured what we said before. When Tundale's soul saw that this was greater than all the punishments that he saw before, he said to the angel, "I implore you, my lord, if it pleases you, free me from just this punishment, and I will give myself to be delivered over to those other punishments that occur after this." Then the angel said, "This punishment is the greatest of all that you have yet seen, nevertheless you will see all kinds of torments greater than you were able to see or to experience before." He added, "Within this place of punishment certain rabid dogs await your coming." With whatever prayers he could make, trembling and weakened through anxiety, Tundale's entire soul asked if he might avoid this punishment. Nevertheless what the angel wished, the soul would accomplish.

When they saw the soul yielding, the devils surrounded him and reproached him with great clamor; and they chopped him into pieces with those instruments and handed over the disconnected parts to the flames. What can I say about those who were inside this house of Phristinus? For lamenting and sadness, sorrow and groans and gnashing of teeth, he created the lasting exterior of flames, the vast interior of fire. He always had an insatiable desire for food, yet he was not able to satisfy the excess of his gluttony. They were also tortured in their genitals with great pain; but in response their genitals, putrid and corrupt, seemed to gush with worms. And these beasts turned inside the genitals of not only lay men and women but also – which I cannot say without grave sorrow – the fearful beasts twisted under the habits of the clergy, which they entered. So strength could in no way be adequate for enduring the weary torments from all sides.

No sex, no type of person left these punishments unharmed, and – what I fear to say, love compels me to say – the monastic garb of men and women was seen among those tormented; and those who seemed of sacred professions were judged worthy of the greatest pain. When Tundale's soul had endured this and similar incredible pains for a long time, he admitted that he deserved and was bound for such torments. But when it pleased divine majesty, not knowing how, just as we said, he felt himself outside this torment. Nevertheless, he sat in the shadows and the shade of death. When he could no longer sit there, he saw the light, namely the spirit of life, who previously led him.

Tundale's soul, very full of sorrow and bitterness, said to him, "Why, lord, have I, miserable me, suffered so much and such great torment? And what is it that the wise said to us: 'The world is full of the mercy of the Lord'? Where is this mercy and kindness?" Answering, the angel said to him, "Alas, child, how many less intelligent people does this opinion deceive. For, although he may be merciful, God is also just. He renders justice to each one according to his or her merit. He gives great mercy to one judged worthy of punishments.

"Indeed you, for your meager merits, would justly suffer this punishment. But be thankful when you see that he gave this torment to you through his mercy. If God sends everyone out on a journey, why might a man be just? And if he does not fear punishment why would the sinner restrain himself? And what good effect might there be that confessors repent if they do not fear God? Therefore, dispensing well everything good, just as he tempered mercy with justice, God tempered justice with mercy so that neither of them might be without the other. For if he was not restrained from mercifully leading sinners in the body to repentance, they would indeed endure the proscribed, appropriate justice for their faults. Although opportunity is offered for living justly in the body before their just deaths, God mercifully grants them blessed eternity with the angels when they leave the body. In this also his mercy exceeds his justice since he will leave no good work unpaid. In truth he forgives many evil works. Although no one is free from sin except an infant one night old, many are freed from punishment so that the shadow of death does not touch them."

When he had regained his strength, however, Tundale's soul said to the angel concerning this discussion of consolation, "Lord, if it pleases you, since this talk is about justice, why are they led below when they do not deserve to enter the gates of death?" Answering, the angel said, "If it disturbs you that just men, who do not suffer punishment, are led to see these, it is done so that when they have seen the tortures from which they are freed through divine grace, they will burn more ardently in praise and love of their Creator.

"So it is the opposite for the soul of sinners who are judged worthy of eternal punishment. At first they are led to the glory of the saints so that, having first seen these things that they automatically deserved, when they come to their punishments they will regret greatly this glory that they would have been able to gain before, and they will remember it so that their punishment will increase. For no punishment is more serious than to be separated from the companionship of divine majesty and of the holy angels. Therefore that priest, whom you saw first cross the bridge safely, was led to punishment so that, having seen the pains, he might burn more ardently in love of him who called him to glory. For the servant showed himself to be faithful and wise, and he will receive the crown of life that God himself promised to the diligent."

After this he added, "Since we have not yet seen all the evil that will have been shown to you, we should hurry to see what we have not yet seen." Then the soul said, "If we are to reach glory after this I ask that you go before me to the punishment as soon as possible."

X

The Punishment of Fornicators

As the angel led the way they saw a beast very different from all the beasts that they had seen before. It had two feet and two wings, also the longest neck and an iron beak. He even had iron claws, and from his mouth rose inextinguishable flames. This beast sat in a swamp of frozen ice. It devoured whatever souls he was able to find. While they were in his stomach they were reduced to nothing through this punishment. He vomited them into the frozen swamp of ice, and there they renewed their journey to torment.

All of the men and the women who descended into the swamp were actually made pregnant by the beast. In this condition they waited harshly for the time agreed on for their departure. The offspring they conceived stung them in their entrails like vipers, and so their corpses were miserably churned in the fetid waves of the frozen sea of icy death. And when it was time, so that they were ready, they filled the depths crying with howls; and so they gave birth to serpents.

I say not only women, but also men, gave birth to them, not through the part that nature constructed suitable for such a function, but through their arms, just as through their breasts, and they went bursting out through all members. These beasts that were born had burning iron heads and the sharpest beaks, with which they tore the body to pieces wherever they came out. These same beasts had many points in their tails which, like twisted back-hooks, punished those souls from which they emerged. Although the beasts were willing to leave, when they were not able to draw their tails away with them when they exited, they did not stop bending back their burning iron beaks into the body until they consumed it up to the dry bone and the nerves.

So – amid the drowning noise of the ice, the sustained howling of the souls, and the bellowing of beasts crying out together – they arrived at the exit in the sky. So these demons (if there were any spark of piety in them) might be rightly moved to the mercy of sympathy. For these souls were caught in all the different parts and in the fingers of different beasts, who destroyed them to their nerves and bone. The demons also had lively tongues like vipers, which entirely consumed the palate and arteries up to the lungs. The genitals of these men were also like serpents who tried to lacerate the lower parts of the heart and to draw out the entrails.

Then Tundale's soul said, "Tell me what evil these souls performed and for whom this punishment is prepared. It is incomparable to all the pain I think I have ever seen." The angel replied, "I tell you this is greater because these who are considered holier are sentenced to a harsher pain if they err, just as they obtain the greatest glory if, on the contrary, they do not merit this punishment through their guilt." He added, "For this is the punishment of the orders of monks, canons and others in sacred orders who either through their tonsure or their habit are known to lie to God. Their genitals are consumed with different pains since they observed no limits. For they sharpened their tongues just like serpents, and so they suffer these flames. Also their genitals, which were not restrained from the prohibited luxury of sexual relations, are either cut away or they produce ferocious beasts for increasing their pain." And he added, "We have said enough about this. For although this pain is especially for those who are called to be religious and are not; nevertheless those who defile themselves by immoderate luxury also endure this punishment. For that reason you cannot avoid this punishment, since while you were in your body you did not fear to have sexual relations without moderation."

After he said this, the devils came, seized the soul with force and gave it to the beast to devour. Tundale's devoured soul disappeared either into the beast or into the fetid swamp. (Since we described this before, we should not repeat it again.) After he entered the torment of the birth of the vipers, already described, the spirit of piety appeared near him and consoled him saying softly, "I came seeking you, my dearest friend, so that you would not suffer this more fully." Touching him he healed him, and Tundale began to follow him on the rest of the journey.

So the soul did not know when they had advanced a long way in the direction they went, for as we learned before, except for the brightness of the spirit of light, they had no light. Indeed they travelled through terrible places while passing by much. Certainly it was a very narrow way, and it was always descending from the peak of almost the highest mountains into the depths, and the more they descended the less the soul hoped to return to life.

XI

The Pain of Those Who Add Sin to Sin

Tundale said, "I ask, since we have seen so much evil before – so that I would say that what is worse could not be seen or thought of – where then does this path lead so far from these into the depth?" The angel answered him saying, "This way leads to death." And the soul said, "Since this way may be the most narrow and most difficult, and we see no one on it before us, is this what the evangelist spoke of when he said, 'Wide and broad is the way that leads to death and many enter through it'?" "The evangelist did not speak of this one," said the angel, "but about the shameless and illicit life of heathens, for it leads through that to this."

When they had gone farther and labored in another direction they came to a valley, and there they saw many foundry-shops from which they could hear the greatest lamentation. The soul said, "My lord, do you hear what I hear?" He answered, "I hear it and I understand." And Tundale's soul said, "What name does this punishment have?" The angel said, "This torture is called Vulcan. Many run through this engine and are tormented by it as they run." Tundale's soul said, "My lord, do I deserve to suffer this punishment?" He said to him, "You deserve it."

When he had said this the angel went in front of him, and the soul, crying, followed him. As they approached, the torturers ran out to meet them with burning forceps. Without saying anything to the angel, they seized the soul who followed, and holding onto him they threw him into the burning forge, its flames fanned with inflated bellows.

172

Just as iron is usually weighed, these souls were weighed, until the multitude that were burned there was reduced to nothing. When they were so liquified that they appeared to be nothing but water, they were thrown with iron pitchforks. Then placed on a forging stone they were struck with hammers until twenty or thirty or a hundred souls were reduced into one mass. What is worse, they did not perish in this way, for they desired death and they were not able to find it.

The torturers spoke to the conquered saying, "This is enough, isn't it?" And others in another workshop answered, "Throw them to us and let us see if it is enough!" When these threw them, the others seized them with iron pitchforks before they touched the ground; and just as before, these threw them into the flames and they miserably tossed the souls this way and that. There they suffered and burned until their skin and their flesh, their nerves and bones were reduced to the ash and flame of fire.

Finally, after Tundale's soul had been brought through these punishments, his advocate stood by him, and in his usual way he seized him from the middle of the ashes, and he began to say, "How well are you enduring this? Were not the charms of the flesh so sweet to you that for them you would endure all this torment?" Tundale was not able to answer him since after such punishment he did not have the strength to speak.

When the angel of the Lord saw him so excessively afflicted, he spoke to him softly and consoled him saying, "Be comforted, since the Lord is the one who leads toward and away from the depths. Therefore be strong, since although the punishments that you have endured up to now are bad, there are greater punishments from which you will be freed, for such was the will of our Redeemer. For he does not desire the death of the sinner, but he desires that the sinner convert and live." After this he said, "All who you saw above still wait for the judgment of God, but those who are below in the depths are already judged, for you still did not yet come to the deepest of the depths." Embracing him in his usual way, he comforted him and proposed to set off on the rest of the journey.

XII

The Descent into the Depths

When they had travelled and talked together with each other, a sudden horror and cold, an intolerable stench previously inexperienced, a shadow incomparable to those before, and tribulation and anxiety invaded Tundale's soul on all sides at once. All the foundation of the earth's orb itself seemed to tremble, and to the angel who preceded him Tundale was compelled to say, "Alas, my lord, what it is that makes me less able to stand alone? I am disturbed in so many ways that I do not have the strength to speak." Standing, he waited for the angel's response, for he was not able to move because of his very great dread. The angel quickly disappeared from before his eyes, and Tundale was no longer able to see him. Miserable, he saw himself to be far inferior to all the sinners that he saw before. Deprived of his light and his solace, what else could he do but despair completely of the mercy of God? For, as Solomon said, there was no wisdom and knowledge in the midst of the depths into which the soul hastened. Indeed, he had no determination when he lacked God's help.

But the fact was, while he was alone amid so many dangers, he heard the extraordinary cries and howls of the multitudes and the horrible thunder even more, so that, as it was fated, neither could your humble writer understand it nor his tongue tell of it.

XIII

The Deepest Depth

When he looked around to see if he could find in any way where all these came to him from, he saw a four-sided ditch like a cistern. This was a well that emitted a putrid column of smoke and flames. The column extended up to the heavens. In this fire there was the greatest multitude of souls and demons who ascended like ashes with the flames. When they were reduced to nothing in the smoke they fell with the demons into the furnace, down to the depths.

When he saw this great spectacle, Tundale's soul wished to draw back, but he had not the strength to raise his feet from the ground. But while fear urged him to try this often, as he himself wished, he decided he was not able to do it. Filled and inflamed with a great furor, tearing his cheeks with nails, he cried, "Woe is me. Why do I not die? Most miserable me, why did I not wish to believe sacred scriptures? What craziness deceived me?"

Hearing this, the devils who ascended with the flames surrounded him with the instruments with which they seized the souls of the miserable for torment. They encircled him just like bees, and they were inflamed just like fire in thorns, and they spoke with one voice saying,

175

"O miserable soul, worthy of tortures and pains, from where have you come here? Ignorant of the punishments you have not experienced, you will still see torture worthy of your deeds, from which you will not be able to escape; nor will you be able to perish in it, but ever living you will burn in punishment. You will not be able to see or discover light, consolation or refuge; you will no longer be able to hope for mercy or help. You have approached the gates of death, and without delay you will be in the deepest of the deep. Whoever led you here deceived you. He would have freed you, if he could, from our hands, but you will see him no more. Be sorrowful, miserable soul, be sorrowful, cry, complain and howl, for you will mourn with those who mourn, you will weep with those who weep, and forever you will burn with those who burn. There is no one who wishes to, or who can, free you from our hands."

They spoke to one another saying, "Why do we delay any more? Let us drag him off and show him our cruelty. Let us take him to Lucifer for devouring." And so, shaking his shoulders, they threatened him with everlasting death. These spirits were as black as coal, their eyes were like burning fires, their teeth were as white as snow, and they had tails like scorpions, they also had very sharp iron claws, and they had wings like vultures.

While they were tossing him among them – since they had seized him without delay – and while they were wailing and singing the song of death, the spirit of light appeared there. As they fled from the spirits of darkness, the angel consoled Tundale, saying only these words: "Rejoice and be glad, child of light, since you will obtain mercy and not justice. You will certainly see further punishments, but you will suffer no more."

XIV

The Prince of Shadows

"Come therefore," he said, "and I will show you the greatest adversary of the human race." Walking ahead he came to the gates of hell, and he said to Tundale, "Come and see; but realize this, that very little does this light illumine these included here. Nevertheless, you will be able to see them, but they will not be able to see you." Drawing near, Tundale's soul saw the depths of hell, and he would not be able to repeat in any way how many, how great and what inexpressible torments he saw there if he had a hundred heads and in each head a hundred tongues. I do not think it would be useful to omit the few details that he did bring back for us.

He saw the Prince of Shadows, the enemy of humanity, the devil whose size overshadowed every kind of beast that Tundale saw before. Tundale was not able to compare the size of his body to anything, nor would we dare to presume to say what we did not draw from his mouth, but such a story as we did hear we ought not to omit.

This beast was very black, like a raven, with a body of human shape from its feet to its head, except that it had many hands and a tail. This horrible monster had no less than a thousand hands, and each hand was a thousand cubits long and ten cubits wide. Each hand had twenty fingers connected to it; these fingers were one hundred palms long and ten wide; they had very long claws with a thousand points, and they were iron, and in his feet were just as many claws. Moreover, he had a very long and great beak, and his tail was very long and sharp and ready to injure souls with its very sharp points.

This horrible stooping spectacle was seated on a forged iron wicker-work placed over coals inflamed by the inflated bellows of an innumerable number of demons. Such a multitude of souls and demons circled above him that no one can believe how many were there, because the world had produced all these souls from the beginning. This host of humanity was attached through each member and at their joints with very large and flaming iron bonds. Moreover, when this beast was turned into coal and then burned, he turned himself from one side to the other side in very great wrath, and he stretched out all his hands into the multitude of souls and then compressed them when they were all replenished. This thirsty boor pressed out the clusters so that there was no soul able to avoid him who was not either dismembered or deprived of head, feet or hands.

Then by just breathing, he inhaled and exhaled all the souls into different parts of hell. Immediately the pit belched, from which, as we said before, there was a fetid flame. When the dreadful beast drew his breath again he sucked back to him all the souls that he dispersed before, and he devoured those who fell into his mouth with the smoke and sulphur. But whoever fled from his hand he struck down with his tail; and the miserable beast, always striking hard, was struck hard, and the burning tormentor was tormented in the punishment with the souls.

Seeing this Tundale's soul said to the angel of the Lord, "My lord, what is this monster's name?" Answering, the angel said, "This beast whom you see is called Lucifer, and he is the prince of the creatures of God who took part in the pleasures of paradise. He was so perfect that he would throw heaven and earth and even hell into total disorder. Moreover, this multitude of angels are partly ministers of the shadows and of Satan, in truth they are partly Adam's children who did not merit mercy. For these are the ones who did not hope for mercy from God, nor did they believe in God. Indeed they deserved to suffer this without end with this Prince of Shadows, since in their words or their works they do not wish to adhere to the Lord of glory, who returns good without end."

"Are these," Tundale asked, "the ones who are already judged, and do they await many others here who have indeed promised with words to do well but who denied this with their works?" The angel said, "They who either deny Christ completely or who perform works of denial endure this. They therefore are adulterers, murderers, thiefs, bandits, and proud people who do not make worthy penance. Indeed, they suffer first that lesser punishment that you saw before, and now they are led to this punishment from which no one who enters it once is able to exit again. Here also are prelates and princes of the world who desired to be first, not so that they might be useful, but so that they might be first. They suffer without end if they did not consider their power to rule or correct their subjects to be given and granted to them by God and indeed did not exercise the power committed to them as they should have, wherefore scripture says, 'The powerful suffer torture more powerfully.'"

Then the soul said, "Since you say power is given to them by God, why do they suffer on account of that?" The angel said, "Power that is given by God is not bad, but it is bad if it is used badly." And Tundale said, "Why does the all-powerful God not always give power to the good so that they might change their charges and lead them as they ought?" The angel answered, "Occasionally power is offered to the good for driving out the sins of their subjects – although the evil do not deserve to have good rulers – and sometimes on account of this the good ones provided more surely for the health of their souls."

The soul said, "I wish to understand why this monster is called the Prince of Shadows when he can defend no one and he is not able to free himself." The angel said, "He is not called prince on account of his power, but on account of the primacy that he holds in the shadows. For although you saw these many punishments before, they all count for nothing when they are compared to this enormous suffering." Tundale's soul said, "I judge this to be true without a doubt, for it greatly disturbs me to see this lake in this way, and to put up with his stench grieves me more than all the sufferings that I underwent before. If possible, I beg you, do not permit me to be dragged away quickly and tortured as happened to me before. For I see in this torment many associates, acquaintances and friends whom I was glad to have with me as friends on earth. I greatly abhor this alliance of them. For I surely know that, unless divine mercy helps me, I would suffer by my just merits no less than they."

The angel said, "O happy soul, I came to change your place of everlasting rest, since the Lord blesses you. For as you will see, you will suffer no more, unless you continue that way. Up until now you have seen the prisons of the enemies of God, now in this direction you will see the glory of his friends."

XV

The Moderate Pain of the Not-Very-Bad

The soul turned and followed the angel who preceded him, and when they had not travelled far, the stench vanished and light appeared, destroying the shadows. Security quickly returned from fear and flight. Once sadness was left behind and passed over, Tundale's soul was full of joy and happiness. Since he himself was so quickly changed, he wondered and said, "My lord, tell me, I beseech you, what is it that I felt so quickly change me? For I was blind and I see the way, I was sad and I am happy. I passed intolerable stench through the whole way, and now truly I smell no evil odor. I was afraid and very fearful, now I am happy and secure." Answering, the angel said to him, "May you be blessed, so that you do not wonder, for this is the change to the right side of heaven. For we are bound to return into our region by a different path. Therefore bless God and follow me."

When they went on they saw a very high wall, and within the wall on the side they were coming from they saw a great multitude of men and women enduring wind and rain. They were very sad, enduring hunger and thirst; nevertheless they had light and did not smell the stench. The soul asked, "Who are these who linger in a place like this?" The angel responded, "These souls are evil, but not very evil. Indeed they tried to follow honestly, but in good times they were not generous to the poor, as they should have been, and therefore for many years they deserve to suffer this rain; then they will be led to a good place."

XVI

The Field of Joy, The Fountain of Life & The Resting Place of the Not-Very-Good

They went on a little way and came to a gate that was opened out to them. When they entered it they saw a beautiful field, fragrant, planted with flowers, bright and very pleasant, in which there was a multitude of souls that no one was able to count. And there was a multitude of happy men and women; and there was no night, and the sun did not set there, and there was the Fountain of Life.

Indeed, after the great bitterness that he had suffered before Tundale proclaimed the delectable charm of these very beautiful fields in a loud voice and with great devotion saying, "May the name of the Lord, who freed me from the gates of hell in the greatness of his mercy and in part introduced me to the destiny of the saints, be blessed now here and on earth. Now I know the truest word of Holy Scripture to be, 'The eye has not seen, nor the ear heard, nor has it entered into the heart of man what God has prepared for those who love him.'"

And he added, "Of what souls, I ask, is this the resting place, and what name does this fountain have?" The angel answered him: "The not-very-good live here who, freed from the sufferings of hell, did not merit the fellowship of the union of saints. Also this fountain, which you see, is called the Fountain of Life. Whoever tastes its water will live in eternity and will not thirst again."

XVII

King Donachus and King Conchober

After they went on a little they saw some lay people who were well-known to them. Among them were kings Conchober and Donachus. When he saw them, Tundale wondered very much and said, "What is it, lord, that I see? During their lives these two men were very cruel and mutual enemies. Through what merit have they come here and how are they made friends?"

Answering, the angel said, "Before death they repented for their hostility; this is not liable to be blamed on them. For this King Conchober languished a long time and he vowed that if he might live he would become a monk. The other, moreover, was relegated for many years to chains; and whatever he had he gave to the poor, and this justice belongs to him world without end. But you will tell all this to the living." And they went on.

XVIII

King Cormach

When they had gone a little farther, they saw a marvelously decorated house, whose walls and whole structure were made of gold and silver and of all kinds of precious stones. But there were neither windows nor doors, and all who wished to enter entered. The house was so splendid inside but not, I say, as if one sun shone, but as if many shone there. This house was very full and very round and was supported by no columns. The whole vestibule was paved with precious stones and with gold.

While Tundale's soul was being delighted by such features, as he looked around he saw one seat of gold decorated with gems and silk and with all ornaments, and he saw the lord King Cormach sitting on this throne dressed in such garments that neither he nor any other kings on earth could wear in any way. While he stood there a little admiringly, many people came into the house with gifts and one at a time offered their gifts to the king with joy.

While Tundale stood before his lord king for a little – he was his lord while both lived – many priests came and dressed solemnly and calmly with silk chasubles and other very fine ornaments just as for Mass, and the house was decorated everywhere with marvelous regal ornaments. They even put gold and silver chalices and siphons and ivory pyxes upon the altars. Thus was the house decorated, and if there were no greater glory in the reign of God, this would suffice. Therefore all those who came ministered before the king, and they openly genuflected saying, "You who will eat the works of your hands, blessed are you and well you will be."

Then Tundale said to the angel, "I wonder, lord, when all of these ministers approach my lord. Among them I cannot remember one from while he was alive." "They are not," said the angel, "from the household that he had while he was alive. Did you not hear," he said, "how these spoke out, saying, 'Blessed are, and will be, you who eat the labors of your hands'? For all these whom you see are the poor of Christ and those pilgrims to whom this king, while he was alive, gave his goods generously with his own hands for their eternal and unending thanks."

"I wish," said the soul, "to know if this king, my lord, suffered any torment after he left his body and came to rest?" "He suffered," said the angel, "and he suffers and is punished daily." And he added, "We may linger a little and we will see his torment." When they had not waited very long the house was darkened and all its inhabitants immediately grew sad. The king, disturbed and lamenting, rose and left. When Tundale's soul followed him he saw this multitude, which he had seen before inside, raising their hands devoutly to heaven praying to God and saying, "Lord God all-powerful thus you see and know, have mercy on your servant." Looking around, he saw this king in fire up to his navel and from his navel up clothed in a hair shirt. Tundale said to the angel, "How often does this soul suffer this?" The angel replied, "Daily he suffers for three hours and for twenty-one hours he rests." "Lord," said the soul, "why is he judged worthy of these and no other punishments?" The angel answered, "He endures this fire up to his navel, since he defiled the sacrament of legitimate marriage, and from the navel up he suffers a hair shirt since he ordered a comrade to kill near St. Patrick's and is guilty in right judgment. He is blameless of all crimes except for these two."

After this he said, "Let us go further up." And after they had proceeded a little, they saw a very high and very bright wall.

XIX

The Glory of the Married

There was a silver wall, very splendid and adorned. Tundale saw no door in it. Not knowing how divine power led him in, he entered. Looking around he saw the chorus of saints praising God and saying, "Glory to you Lord Father, glory to you, glory to you the Son, glory to you the Holy Ghost." These men and women who sang were dressed in white and very precious robes, and they were very beautiful, without spot or wrinkle. These souls were laughing and joking, always joyful and exultant and always persevering in praise of the holy and eternal Trinity. The white of their garments was as white as snow struck by the radiance of the sun. Harmonious voices produced sounds truly diverse like musical song. Clearness, joy, friendliness, hilarity, beauty, honesty, holiness, eternity, harmony and love was equal for all. What can I say about the scent of this field where they were? For this sweet and delightful odor surpassed all kinds of fragrances and aromas. There was no night; sadness was absent; all burned with delight.

The soul said, "My lord, I beg you, may we possibly remain in this place?" The angel answered, "Although this does seem great to you, it might be well for you to see the greater reward of the saints." The soul then said, "Lord, of what saints are these the rewards?" The angel said, "Of the married, both men and women, who did not mutually befoul their marriage by the stain of illicit adultery and who served the faith of legitimate union. Instead they both ruled their families well and gave their temporal goods to the poor, to pilgrims, and to the churches of Christ. To them the just judge will say at the Last Judgment, 'Come, blessed of my Father, possess the kingdom prepared for you from the beginning of the world. I was hungry and you gave me to eat; I was thirsty and you gave me to drink; I was a stranger and you received me.' Awaiting the blessed hope and the coming of the great glory of God, these are consoled in this resting place. For great is the sacrament of legitimate marriage, and whoever served it well while they were in their bodies will rejoice in this place without end."

The angel added, "We must ascend and see what is above us." And Tundale's soul asked, "Lord, if I discover grace in your eyes, allow me to remain in this place. For I wish to ascend no higher, if it may be your will, but it is most dear to me to remain with these people. I do not seek, nor do I take trouble, nor do I desire to have better."

The angel said, "Although I may not promise that, nevertheless you will see better than this."

After he finished this speech, they did not labor much, for it seemed no work to them, and whomever they passed in all these throngs met Tundale's soul with nodded head and happy face and with immense joy; and they greeted him by calling his name. And they glorified God, who freed him, saying, "Praise to you Lord, King of Eternal Glory, who does not wish the death of sinners, but that they convert and live. According to your mercy this soul is worthy to be delivered from infernal tortures and to join your fellowship of saints."

XX

The Glory of the Martyrs and Virgins

When they had crossed many walls, another wall appeared, much higher than the first. It was of the purest and clearest gold, so that whatever Tundale's soul saw before, it might take more delight in it, in the singular brilliance of the metal, to a greater extent than in all the glory that he had seen before. They crossed this in a way similar to that in which they crossed the first.

Many thrones appeared to them, of gold and gems and constructed of all kinds of most precious stones and enveloped with most precious silk. In them sat the elders, both men and women, dressed with silk and white stoles, with crowns and all ornaments, such as the soul had never seen before nor could ever have known about. The face of each one of these was truly splendid, just as the sun shines in the midday. They had hair like gold, and on their heads they had gold crowns decorated with gems. Their lecterns were not made of inferior metal. On them books were placed written with gold letters; and they sang "Alleluia" to the Lord with a new song and with a sweet melody so that once he heard their voices Tundale's soul was oblivious to all the past.

He therefore stood there where he previously saw the harmonies and the wonderfully delightful thrones. Then the angel said to him, "These are saints who gave their bodies in witness to God, and they washed their stoles in the blood of the Lamb. These are," he said, "the temperate who have paid back their debt of the flesh for a certain time, abandoned the temporal life for the service of God, or suffered martyrdom for Christ's sake, or even those crucified with faults and desires but who lived justly, piously and soberly. They deserve to have the triumphal crown. These are," he said, "holy men and women made friends of God."

XXI

The Glory of Monks and the Virtuous

When the very curious soul looked around he saw a sort of camp and many pavilions, purple and gray, gold and silver, decorated with various wonderful silks. In them he heard strings and organs, drums and cither with organs and cymbals playing and all other kinds of music harmonizing with the sweetest sounds. He said to the angel, "To which souls do these tents and pavilions belong?" And the angel said, "This is the place of the monks and the virtuous who, having promised obedience, excelled. Those who greatly rejoiced to be led rather than to lead remain happy and devout. Relinquishing their own will they submitted to the will of others so that they were truly worthy to say, 'You put others above our heads, we crossed through fire and water and you led us into cold.' While in their bodies they knew the heavenly and not only restrained their tongues from evil but also refrained from good things quietly in love. They deserve to say to the Lord, 'We became dumb and we were humble; and from good things we were silent, and we listened to you with attentive ears.' Souls like these have thrones and pavilions in which they sing the praises of the Redeemer and of all rewards of the generous without stopping."

Tundale's soul said, "If it pleases you, I myself wish to go up and to see more closely those who are inside." The angel replied, "It indeed pleases me that you might see and hear them, but you may not be among them, for these enjoy the presence of the Holy Trinity, and whoever enters among them once will not be separated from the company of the saints, forgetting all that he or she remotely escaped, unless a strong virgin who deserved to join the choirs of angels." Going on they saw inside six other monks who had joined the angels, whose voices sweetly and softly seemed to surpass all musical instruments. Although all the souls whom he saw previously in other places twinkled with a great brightness, nevertheless their splendor and their delectable fragrance and their most sweet song exceeded all the glory that he had seen before. All the instruments produced sounds with no one laboring, but the voices of these souls exceeded all other sweetness; and they spent no labor in spreading their voices. For their lips did not seem to move nor their hands bother to rise to the musical instrument, and yet each resounded a tune at will.

Moreover the firmament, which was above their heads, shone greatly. From it hung chains of the purest gold mixed with silver rods woven with a most beautiful variety. From them goblets and drinking vessels, cymbals and bells, lilies and gold globes hung. Among them a great multitude of angels with gold wings moved, flying and rising lightly amid the floating chains, and they produced the softest and sweetest song for those listening.

XXII

The Defenders and Builders of Churches

When Tundale's soul wished to remain here with these sweet visions, the angel said to him, "Look back." And looking back he saw a great and wide tree with leaves and flowers very green and fertile with all types of fruit. In its leaves lingered many birds of different colors and of different voices, singing and making music. Underneath its branches very many lilies and roses sprang up, and varieties of all herbs and species produced perfumes. Under the same tree there were many men and women in gold and ivory shrines, and without ceasing they praised and blessed the omnipotent God for all his goodness and his gifts, and all of them had gold crowns wonderfully decorated on their heads and held scepters of gold in their hands, and they were dressed with robes like the monks before wore.

The soul turned to the angel and said, "Spirit, what tree is this, and who are those under it? What good did they do when they were alive?" And the angel said, "This tree is a figure of the Holy Church. These who are under it are men and women, builders and defenders of the church, who tried either to build or defend churches. And they gave their goods abundantly to holy churches. They followed the brotherhood and community of those who leave the habit of the world and restrain themselves from the carnal desires that fight against the soul. Sober and just and pious they lived in this world, looking forward to blessed hope which, as you see, did not disappoint them." And the angel said, "Let us go on."

XXIII

The Glory of Virgins &
The Nine Orders of Angels

And when they had proceeded they saw a high wall, unlike the others in beauty and splendor. For it was well built out of all the most precious stones, with different colors, and with metals placed between, so that it seemed to have gold for cement. Moreover its stones were crystal, chrysolite, beryl, jasper, jacinth, emerald, sapphire, onyx, topaz, sardonyx, chrysoprase, amethyst, turquoise, and garnet. With these and similar stones the shining wall roused the feelings of those looking in great love of the Lord. Without doubt Tundale went up to see the wall because "the eye has not seen nor the ear heard, nor has it entered into the human heart, what God has prepared for those who love him."

They themselves saw the nine orders of blessed spirits, namely the angels, archangels, virtues, principalities, powers, dominations, thrones, cherubim and seraphim. Moreover, they heard inexpressible words that a person could neither speak nor be permitted to speak. For the angel said to the soul, "Listen, child, and see, and lend you ear, and forget your people and the house of your father and the king who desires your faith."

What can I say? So much pleasure, so much happiness, so much worthiness is permitted to all. How sublime it is to be among the choirs of angels and saints, to distinguish the praiseworthy numbers of the patriarchs and prophets, to see the army of martyrs clothed in white, to hear the new song of the virgins, to see the glory of the choir of apostles, to deserve the partnership of the confessors, because it surpasses all joy to feel the force of him, the holy and merciful who is the bread of angels and the life of all. Therefore from the place in which they now stood, they saw not only all the glory that they saw before but even the pain of the punished whom we spoke of above. Finally – which greatly amazes us – they were able to see the orb of the earth as if under one beam of the sun. For not anyone could weaken the sight, once it is given by the creator, to see all of creation. In a wonderful way, while they were standing in the same place in which they had been standing before, not turning themselves around, they still saw everything both in front of and behind them. Moreover, not only was it seen but unusual knowledge was given to Tundale so that he also no longer had to ask about anything anymore, since he knew openly and wholly everything that he desired.

XXIV

St. Ruadanus the Confessor

After this was over, Saint Ruadanus the Confessor came to him, greeting him with great joy and embracing him intimately with innermost feelings of charity; and he said,

"The Lord guards your coming and your going here from now and ever more on earth. I am," he said, "your patron Ruadanus, to whom you are rightly indebted by burial." When he had said this, he stood, saying nothing further.

XXV

St. Patrick and the Four Famous Bishops

When he looked around he saw St. Patrick, the apostle of Ireland, with a great crowd of bishops. Among these he saw four bishops whom he knew, namely, Celestine, bishop of Armagh, and Malachy, who succeeded to the bishopric after that man. He went to Rome in the time of Pope Innocent and was made by him legate and archbishop. Whatever he could have, he divided with the poor and holy monks. He was the founder of forty-four congregations of monks, canons, and nuns, for whom he provided all the necessities and kept nothing at all for himself. Tundale also saw there the Christian Bishop of Lyon, a brother in the womb of the aforementioned Malachy, a wondrously temperate man and a willing lover of poverty; and Nemeniah, a priest from the city of Cloyne, a simple and modest man, shining with wisdom and purity above the others. He recognized these four bishops.

Among them there was also a chair marvelously orna-mented, in which no one sat. Therefore Tundale's soul said, "Whose seat is this, and why is it empty?" Malachy answered him, saying, "This seat is for one of our brothers who has not yet left his body; but when he does he shall sit in this seat." But as the soul was taking delight in all these things, the angel of the Lord appeared there. He went before him and gently speaking said the following to him.

XXVI

The Return of Tundale's Soul to his Body

"Do you see all of this?" he asked. Answering, the soul said, "I see, lord, and I beseech you, allow me to remain here." And the angel said, "You ought to return to your body, and all that you saw you ought to keep in your mind for the use of your close friends and relatives." In truth, when Tundale's soul heard that he must return to his body, with a great sorrow and weeping he said, "What great evils did I ever do that I must return to my body, leaving behind so much glory?" The angel said, "None deserve to enter this place except virgins who guarded their bodies from the touch of carnal knowledge, and they burned more for this great glory than they wished to be polluted in the wallowing places of foul desire. In truth, you did not wish to believe in the words of scripture, and therefore you are not able to remain here. Therefore, return to your body, from which you came, and try to abstain from those things that you did before. You will not lack our advice and help either, but they will remain faithful and ready for you."

When the angel said this, the soul was changed. He tried to move himself, and he quickly sensed his body weighing greatly on him. He did not feel any interval or one moment of time to intervene, but in one and the same instant of time he spoke to the angel and felt himself clothed in his body. Then weak in the body, he opened his eyes and sighed; and saying nothing he looked at the priests standing around him. Taking the body of the Lord with thanks, he gave away all that he had to the poor, and wearing the sign of the cross on his clothes, he asked that he be taken under a monastic order. In truth, all that he saw he afterward told; and he warned us to lead a good life, and he preached the word of God, which he did not know before, with great devotion and humility and knowledge. But since we cannot imitate his life, at least we tried to write this for the benefit of our readers.

he Monk of Evesham's Vision

I: Introduction

In those days a monk belonging to the convent of Evesham fell ill, and for fifteen months he was terribly afflicted with bodily pain. Food and drink made him so nauseous that sometimes he would take nothing but the smallest drop of cold water for nine days or more. No physician's skill could cure him, since whatever was offered by anyone to relieve him had the opposite effect. So he lay languishing on his bed, deprived altogether of bodily strength. He could not even move from this spot unless carried by servants.

As the day of our Lord's resurrection drew near, he began to feel easier and walked about his cell leaning on his stick. Finally two nights before the day of the Last Supper, leaning on his stick, he went into the large hall, spurred on by devotion but not knowing whether he was present in his body or in his spirit. Once there, while the assembled monks were making their usual nightly devotions to the Lord, he felt such an influx of divine mercy and heavenly grace that his own holy devotion seemed to exceed measure. From the middle of that night to the sixth hour of the following day he could not restrain himself from crying and praising God.

The monk then sent for two of the brotherhood, called confessors by religious men. They came one after the other, and there with tears and with a completely pure and contrite heart he made to each of them a confession of all his faults, even the smallest of them, whether against the monastic discipline or the commandments of God. He then asked for and obtained absolution, and in devotion and praise to God he passed the whole day.

On the following night he slept a little, and when the bell for matins rang, he rose from his couch and made his way to the church. What happened there the following narrative will tell.

II

The Monk Found Dead

On the morning of the following day, which was the Day of the Preparation, when the brotherhood had risen to primes and were crossing before the chapter-house on their way to the church, they saw this same brother lying prostrate and with bare feet before the abbot's chair, where the brothers generally craved pardon. He had his face close to the ground as if he was asking pardon of someone sitting before him. Astonished at this sight, the brothers ran up and tried to raise him, but they found him breathless and motionless with his eyes turned up and the balls of his eyes and his nose wet with blood.

When they found that he had lost all pulse in his veins for some time, they cried out altogether that he was dead. But finally they discovered that he was breathing, although only slightly. They washed his neck, breast, and hands with cold water. At first they saw his whole body tremble slightly, but he soon became quiet and remained motionless. For a long time they were in doubt how to act, not knowing for sure whether he was dead or had recovered. Finally, after a debate, they carried him into the infirmary and, placing him on a bed, appointed some people to keep a careful watch over him. They next applied plasters to his chest and pricked the soles of his feet with needles but could find no signs of life.

In this manner, then, lying on his bed altogether motionless, he remained for two days, from midnight of the Preparation until midnight of the following Sabbath. But on the great Sabbath, when the monks were about to assemble for midnight Mass, his eyelids began to quiver slightly. After a while a moisture, like tears, began to flow gently over his cheeks, and, as anyone might cry in one's sleep, he seemed to utter frequent sighs; and after a while he seemed to be uttering words in his throat with a deep though scarcely audible sound. Finally, as his breath returned by degrees, he began to call on St. Mary, saying, "O holy Mary! O holy Mary! For what crime am I deprived of a joy so immense?" In this way, often repeating these and other words, he revealed to those standing there that he was deprived of some great joy.

After this, as if waking out of a deep sleep, he shook his head, and weeping bitterly, he began to sob, his tears flowing unceasingly. Then, with his hands clasped and fingers joined together, he raised himself suddenly to a sitting position, and putting his head covered with his hands on his knees, he continued his lamentable moanings unceasingly, as he had begun. After the brethren made many entreaties for him to take something to eat after such long fasting and suffering, he took a small piece of bread and then remained awake in prayer. When he was asked if he expected to escape from his sickness, he answered, "I shall live long enough, because I have entirely recovered from my weakness." On the following night, that is on our Lord's resurrection, when the bell was ringing for matins, he went to church without any help and entered the choir, which he had not done for eleven months. On the next day, when his religious duties were performed, he was judged worthy to be refreshed by participation in Holy Communion.

Afterward this brother eagerly joined in the religious duties of the other monks, and they begged him to tell them for their edification what had happened to him and what he had seen in his sleep. They were convinced by obvious signs and by his words and by his unceasing lamentations when he awoke on the previous day that many things had been shown to him.

After he put them off for some time, they became urgent in their request, and finally with incessant tears and groans, and a choking voice, he told them the circumstances in the following order.

III

His Vision

When I was failing from severe and long bodily illness, as you know, and was blessing God verbally and mentally, and was giving him thanks for condescending to chasten his unworthy servant with his fatherly rod, after I had given up all hope of recovery, as much as I could I began to prepare myself to escape the punishments of the future, since I was on the point of being called from my body. While I was diligently thinking of these things, I fell into a temptation to ask God to condescend to reveal to me in some way the state of the life to come and the condition of souls released from the body after this life. By learning this, I hoped I might more clearly know what I, who I thought was soon about to depart from this life, had to hope for and fear, so that I might gain as much as I could of God's affection while I was wavering in this precarious state.

Desiring to be satisfied in this, then, with incessant supplications I kept invoking at one time our Lord the Savior of the world; at another time the glorious Virgin, his mother; at another I called on all the elect people of God; but it was especially through the intercession of the most pious and holy St. Nicholas the confessor that I hoped to gain the end of my holy prayer. One night near the beginning of the Lent that we have just finished, as I was sleeping a little, a venerable and altogether handsome person appeared there to me, who in the most pleasant words addressed me as follows: "Most beloved son, great is your devotion in prayer, and you have great perseverance in your purpose. Through the clemency of the Redeemer the continuous aim of your prayer will not be fruitless. From now on be calm in your mind, and continue in devout prayer, because without a doubt you will soon reach the object of your petition." When the speaker finished speaking his image vanished and I awoke.

IV

The Monk Before the Cross

Although I was now awake, I still kept this vision steadily in my mind, and after six weeks had passed, on the night of the Last Supper I rose for matins and received discipline at your hands, as you remember. In the middle of it I felt such sweetness of mind extended over me that the next day it felt most pleasant to weep incessantly, as you saw with your own eyes.

On the night after this was the Preparation, and as the hour to get up for matins approached, I sank into a calm sleep. Then I heard the same voice again, but how it was conveyed to my ears, I do not know. "Arise," it said, "go into the oratory, and approach the altar consecrated to the worship of St. Lawrence. Behind that altar you will find the cross that this convent generally worships on the Day of the Preparation. Unless you do this, you can fulfill nothing tomorrow, since a long journey remains for you. Wherefore, adore our Lord's cross in memory of him, and offer the sacrifice of a humble and contrite heart, knowing for sure that the offering of your devotion will be acceptable to the Lord and that you will hereafter rejoice abundantly in its richness."

After this I awoke from my sleep and, it seemed to me, proceeded with the brethren to hear matins. Since it had already begun, in the vestibule of the church I met an old man clothed in white garments. He was the one from whom I had received discipline on the preceding night. I then signaled to him by the usual nod to give me discipline, and so we went to the chapter-house, and after I accomplished my purpose, we returned to the oratory. I then went alone to the altar mentioned to me in my sleep, took off my shoes, and crawling on my knees, headed for the place where I had been told the cross of our Savior would be found.

As had been predicted, I found it there, and soon I became entirely dissolved in tears, and throwing myself on the ground at full length, I worshipped it most devoutly. While I was kneeling before the image and was kissing it on the mouth and eyes, I felt some drops falling gently on my forehead. When I removed my fingers, I discovered from their color that it was blood. I also saw blood flowing from the side of the image on the cross, as it does from the veins of a living man when he is cut for blood-letting. I do not know how many drops I caught in my hand as they fell. With the blood I devoutly anointed my eyes, ears and nostrils. Afterward – if I sinned in this I do not know – in my zeal I swallowed one drop of it, but the rest, which I had caught in my hand, I was determined to keep.

V

The First Place of Punishment

When I had worshipped our Lord's cross, after a time I heard behind me the voice of the venerable man from whom I had received discipline on the preceding night. Then I left my shoes and staff near the altar, and I do not know how I went into the chapter-house. After receiving discipline six times, as I had done before, I received absolution. This same old man was seated in the abbot's chair, and I prostrated myself before him, but he approached me, saying only these words, 'Follow me!'

After he had raised me up, firmly yet gently, he took hold of my right hand, and we remained all the time with our hands linked together. At that same time I was deprived of all sense of body and mind. We then walked on a smooth road, straight towards the east, until we arrived in a large tract of country, dreadful to look at, marshy and deformed with hard thickened mud. In this place there was such a great number of people, or spirits, that no one could count them. They were exposed to various and unmentionable tortures. There was in this place a great crowd of both sexes, of every condition, profession and rank, and all kinds of sinners condemned to torments according to the variety of their professions and the degrees of their offenses. Throughout the broad extent of that plain, beyond the farthest reaches that the eye could see, I saw and heard crowds of wretched beings collected in miserable troops and bound in flocks according to the similarity of their crimes and professions. They were all burning equally, though their cries were different.

Whatever people I saw, and for whatever sins they were punished, I noticed clearly both the nature of their sin and the degree of their punishment. By atoning for their crimes or by the intercession of others, in that place of exile and punishment they might earn admission to the heavenly country. But I saw some endure more severe torments with a calm mind. As if conscious of a reward laid up for them, they thought lightly of the horrible agonies they endured. I saw some leap suddenly from their place of torture and make their way as fast as they could to the farthest reaches of the place, and when they were emerging from the pits, dreadfully burned as they were, the torturers ran to them with forks, torches, and every sort of instrument of torture and returned them back to their punishments again to inflict every kind of cruelty on them.

Nevertheless, though wounded, burned, and pierced to the heart with their lashes, they finally came forth, always going in a regular pattern from the most severe to more tolerable sufferings. For some of the most atrocious there remained a most horrible death, without proceeding to more severe tortures. Each one was treated according to whether they were helped or hindered by their former actions or by the good works of their friends. The kinds of punishment that I saw were endless. Some were roasted before fire; others were fried in pans; red hot nails were driven into some to their bones; others were tortured with a horrid stench in baths of pitch and sulphur mixed with molten lead, brass and other kinds of metal; immense worms with poisonous teeth gnawed some; others were fastened one by one on stakes with fiery thorns. The torturers tore them with their nails, flogged them with dreadful scourges, and lacerated them in dreadful agonies.

In that place I saw many whom I knew and who had been close to me during this life tortured in various ways. Some were bishops, some abbots, some of other stations; some in the ecclesiastical, some in the secular forum, some in the cloister. I saw all of these. The less that they were supported by the privileges of honor in their former lives, the more lenient were the punishments inflicted on them there. Actually, I will now tell what I particularly noticed, which was that all of those whom I knew to have been judges of others or prelates in this life, were tormented more than the rest with a greater degree of severity. It would be too odious for me to say what they each received as their deserts, or what they suffered, no matter how obvious to me all these things were, but God is my witness that if I saw anyone, even if he had slain all of my friends and relatives, condemned to such torture, I would, if it were possible, endure a temporal death a thousand times to snatch him from them, especially since all things that are punishments there exceed all measure of pain, bitterness, and misery.

VI

The Second Place of Punishment

After we had gone beyond this place of punishment, my guide and I passed onward unhurt, as we also did in other places of torment, which I will discuss below. After this then we arrived at another place of torment. Two places were separated by a mountain almost touching the clouds, over the top of which we passed easily and quickly. Under the farther side of this mountain was a very deep and dark valley, girt round on either side by ridges of lofty rocks, over which our sight could not extend. The bottom of the valley itself contained a body of water, whether flowing or stagnant I know not, very wide and dreadful because of its stinking water, which continually sent forth a vapor of intolerable odor. The side of the mountain overhanging one part of the lake sent fire up to the heavens, on the opposite promontory of the same hill there was such an intense cold, caused by snow, hail, and raging storms, that I thought I had never seen anything more torturing than the cold in that place.

The region of this valley and the sides of both mountains, which bore this dreadful appearance of heat and cold, were occupied by a crowd of spirits as numerous as swarming bees. In general their punishment was first to be dipped in the fetid lake; then, breaking away from there, they were devoured by volumes of flame that met them; and finally, in swinging balls of fire, like sparks from a furnace, they were tossed on high and then fell to the bottom of the other bank. They were again restored to the whirlings of the winds, the cold of the snow, and the harshness of the hail. Then, thrown from there, as if flying from the violence of the storms, they were again hurled back into the stench of the lake and the burnings of the raging fire. Some were tortured by the cold, some by the heat, for a long time, and some were kept for a long period in the stench of the lake.

I saw others, like olives in a press, squeezed and jammed together in the middle of the flames so incessantly that it is horrible to describe. The condition for all those who were tortured there then was that in order for them to be purified they were compelled to pass across the whole surface of that lake from its beginning to end. There was, however, a very great and varied distinction among those who were tortured in this place. Some of them were allowed an easy and quick transit, according to their merits and the assistance rendered to them after their death; while those guilty of greater crimes, or less assisted by the Masses of their friends, were punished more severely and for a longer time. But for all of them, the nearer they approached the end of the lake the less severe was the torture still to be endured. Those who were placed at the beginning felt the punishment most severely, although all did not suffer the same, and the lightest torments of that place we saw before.

In this place of punishment I discovered and recognized many more acquaintances than I had seen in the first purgatory, and I even spoke with some. I recognized among them a certain goldsmith whom I knew well during his life. When my guide saw me look at him earnestly, he inquired if I knew him. When he learned that I knew him well, he said, "If you know him, speak to him." The spirit looked at us and recognized us with a gesture of indescribable delight, gave praise to the man, my guide, and with outstretched hands, and frequently bending his whole body, he worshipped him and bowed and thanked him much for the acts of kindness conferred on him. Since he frequently cried out, "Holy Nicholas, have pity on me," I was pleased to recognize the name of my dear protector, St. Nicholas, from whom I hoped to obtain the salvation of both my body and soul.

When I then asked the goldsmith how he had so quickly gone through the cruel torments I had seen him suffering, he answered, "You, my friend and all my acquaintances during my life saw that all the supports of the Christian faith were denied to me, such as confession and Viaticum. You considered me a lost man, not knowing the mercy of my lord, who is with me, namely, St. Nicholas, who did not allow me, his unhappy servant, to suffer the death of everlasting damnation. Now and ever since I was consigned to this place of punishment, when I was suffering under a severe torture, I have been refreshed by the viaticum of his compassion. I now make the most severe atonement for the many frauds that I committed during my lifetime in my art of gold-working, since I am frequently thrown into a heap of burning money and most intolerably scorched. I am often compelled to swallow with gaping mouth those very coins, which consume my insides. Moreover, I am often obliged to count these coins and feel my hands and fingers consumed and burned by them."

I then asked him if people could avoid such a dreadful torture by any remedy. He replied with a sigh, "If they were to write daily with their finger on their foreheads and near their hearts, 'Jesus of Nazareth, king of the Jews,' those of the faith would without a doubt be preserved from harm, and after their death those same places would shine with a bright splendor." These and many other things I heard from him. But let us hurry to describe other things, and let what has been said suffice.

VII

The Third Place of Punishment

Leaving this aptly-named valley of tears that was the second place we visited, my guide and I then arrived at a large plain situated low down in the bosom of the earth, which seemed inaccessible to all except to torturing devils and tortured spirits. The surface of that plain was covered by great and horrible chaos, mixed with a sulphurous smoke and a cloud of intolerable stench with a flame of a pitchy blackness. Rising from all directions, this was diffused in a dreadful way through the whole of that empty space.

The surface of the place was as full of a great number of vipers as courtyards of houses are covered with rushes. Dreadful beyond belief, monstrously large and deformed, with dreadful gaping jaws, exhaling execrable fire from their nostrils, these lacerated the crowds of wretched beings with a voracity they could not escape from. The devils, running in all directions, raging like mad creatures, took the wretched beings and first cut them up piece by piece with their fiery prongs, and then they tore their flesh off to the bone; and finally they threw them into the fire, melted them like metals, and restored them in the shape of burning flame.

God is my witness, I remember little, almost nothing, of the punishments of that place. God knows that in a very brief time I saw those wretched beings destroyed by a hundred or more different kinds of torture, and soon afterwards restored again, and again reduced to almost nothing, and then again renewed. A lost life caused them to be tortured in that place; and because of the different kinds of punishment there was no end to their sufferings. The flame of that fire was so devouring that you would think an ordinary fire or fever was lukewarm in comparison to it. Dead vipers torn in pieces were collected in heaps beneath the wretches, filling everything with an intolerable stench that surpassed all other suffering.

The most loathsome and severe of all remains still to be told, because all who were punished there had been guilty of a wickedness in life that is unmentionable by a Christian, or even by a heathen or pagan. Those therefore were continually attacked by huge fiery monsters, horrible beyond description. Despite their opposition, these committed on them the same damnable crimes that they had been guilty of on earth. Their cries were horrid until they apparently fainted dead, and then they again revived to be exposed to fresh torments.

I tremble while describing it and am confounded by the filthiness of their crime beyond measure. Until that time I had never heard or thought that both sexes could have been corrupted by such filthiness. O shame! There was found such an immense crowd of wretches there most pitiably to be pitied. I neither saw nor recognized many in that place, because I was overcome with horror by the enormity of the torments and obscenity, and by the filthy stench, so that it was offensive to me beyond measure either to stop for a moment or to look at what was being done. Finally in the middle of the dreadful din one of them cried out, "Alas! why did I not repent?" So loud was their grief that you would have thought all the sufferers in the world were lamenting there.

VIII

Punishments of a Lawyer

Although I avoided looking at what was happening there as much as I could, I could not escape seeing a certain clerk, whom I had once known. During his life he was considered a most skillful man among those who are called lawyers and Decretalists. Actually in ecclesiastical revenues he was getting richer than the rest every day. I was astonished at the weight of his sufferings. When I asked whether he was expected to obtain mercy at all, he answered, crying out, "Alas, alas, woe is me, I know that I will not receive mercy this side of Judgment Day; and even then I think it is uncertain, because ever since I have been subjected to these sufferings, my punishment grows worse, dragging me on from bad to worse." I said to him, "Why then did you not confess your sins and repent in the end?" He answered, "Because I hoped to recover, and with the devil beguiling me, I was ashamed to confess such disgraceful crimes, so that I would not seem to be disrespected by those who considered me renowned and noble. Some of my slighter offenses I did confess to the priest, and when he asked me if I knew of any other sins, I asked him to leave me then and promised to let him know if any others should come to my memory. When he had departed and had gone a little way I felt myself dying. When he was fetched back by my servants he found that I was already dead. Therefore none of the thousands of different torments that I daily suffer tortures me as much as remembering my fault, because I am actually compelled to be a slave to the baseness of my former weakness. For besides the greatness of this unspeakable punishment, I am oppressed with intolerable shame when I appear as one to be denounced for such great offenses."

At the moment when he was speaking to me, I saw him tortured in numberless ways, and in the middle of them he was reduced to nothing and dissolved like melted lead by the force of heat. I also asked St. Nicholas, who stood by me, if such torments could be alleviated by any kind of remedy. He answered, "When the Day of Judgment arrives, then the will of Christ will be accomplished, because he alone knows the hearts of all, and then he will grant a just retribution to all." Afterwards when I had returned to the body, that priest, to whom the lawyer had confessed only his light offenses, came to me and called on God to witness in the presence of many what I had said was true, since only he knew these things. Of the punishments of many that I saw, I will avoid mentioning more because I am afraid that if I said any more about them I would create a loathing in my readers. Let these few punishments chosen from the many suffice.

IX

The Eternal Glory of the Blessed

Having partly described what we saw of the punishment places of the wretched, it now remains for us to describe the consolations of those at rest and of the eternal glory of the blessed, which we saw with our own eyes.

After we walked a long time amid the different kinds of punishments, which I have mentioned above, and saw the various sufferings of the wretched, as we made our way toward the inner regions, little by little the light began to appear more pleasant.

Here was the fragrance of a sweet odor, there the richness of a plain flourishing with many kinds of flowers affording us incredible pleasure. On this plain we found endless thousands of people or spirits who, after passing through their punishments, were enjoying the happy rest of the blessed. Those whom we found in the first part of this plain had white garments, but they were not shining, and although there did not appear any blackness or stain on them, they shone with an inferior degree of whiteness.

Among these I saw several whom I had formerly known. I recognized there a certain abbess who had just come from the places of punishment. She was clothed in unstained garments, though not very bright. I also saw and recognized there a certain prior who, after being freed from all punishment, was rejoicing in happy peace with the spirits of the just, in sure hope of the divine vision with which he was about to be rewarded. In that same place too I saw a priest who, blessed by the grace of preaching united to the example of a good life, had reclaimed from deadly sin not only people in the parishes where he had the pastoral care, but also those who were farther from him. Through the Lord's cooperation an inexpressible glory rested on him and on many others through him.

X

The Second Place of Glory

As we proceeded from there to the interior of this region of sweetness, the clearness of the light and the sweetness of the odor smiled on us even more. All in this place were inhabitants of the Upper Jerusalem, who had passed through all their punishments very easily, since they had been less ensnared by the vices of the world.

The tongue cannot reveal nor human weakness worthily describe what we saw as we went on. For who could worthily explain it in words? In the middle of endless thousands of blessed spirits who stood round, as if present at the sacred solemnity of our Lord's passion, the pious Redeemer of the human race himself appeared. It was as if he were hanging on the cross with his whole body bloody from scourgings, insulted by spitting, crowned with thorns, with nails driven into him, pierced with the lance; while streams of blood flowed over his hands and feet, and blood and water dropped from his holy side! Near him stood his mother, not anxious and sorrowful now, but rejoicing and looking with a most calm countenance on such an indescribable sight.

Indeed, can anyone imagine how eagerly all ran together to this spectacle, what devotion there was among those who saw it, what a meeting of worshippers there was, how many were their signs of thanks for such great kindness? As I thought more profoundly on these things I did not know whether it was grief or devotion that distracted my unhappy mind, but astonishment and admiration deprived me of my sense. But what devotion is it that the devil should be conquered by this reproach, and hell be defeated and robbed of its weapons and spoils, the lost one be recovered, and the prey of devils be snatched from their infernal prison-house and placed in heaven among the choir of angels? Many things that I saw and heard there I fear to tell, because they might appear unusual and incredible to many.

At length, after I looked at this blessed vision awhile, the vision itself suddenly disappeared, and in the hallowed place where the glory of such a mystery had existed, they all returned with delight, each to his appointed place. Full of admiration, I followed my guide to the inner regions into the abodes of the blessed. Here was the brightness of those assembled, here the fragrance of sweet smell, here the harmony of those singing praise to God.

XI

The Third Place of Glory

After going on for some distance, and while the pleasantness of the places before us increased, I saw what appeared to be a wall of crystal that was so high that no one could look over it and so long that there appeared to be no end. When we approached it, I saw it glittered with a most noble shining brightness from within. I also saw the entrance to it open, but marked with the protecting sign of the cross. The crowds of those nearby who were very anxious to enter, approached there. The cross in the middle of the gate now raised itself up, opened an entrance to those who approached; and afterward, falling again, it denied entrance to those who wished to enter.

I cannot describe how joyfully those who were admitted went in, or how reverently those who remained shut out waited for the next raising of the cross. Here my guide stopped with me some time, but as we finally went forward the cross was raised and the entrance was opened for us to enter. My companion entered without hindrance; and I was following when suddenly the cross descended on our hands and was about to prevent me from following my guide. When I saw this I was in great alarm but heard these words proceed from him, "Fear not, just put your trust in the Lord and enter in safety."

Then my confidence returned, and when the cross granted an entrance I went in.

But let no one ask me how glittering was the inconceivable brightness or how strong was the light that filled all those places. I am not able to express this in words, not even to recollect it in my mind. That soft and glittering splendor so dazzled my eyes that I could think of nothing compared with it that I had ever seen before. That brightness, inconceivable as it was, did not blind the eyesight, but rather sharpened it; and as I looked on it, nothing else met my sight except the light and the wall of crystal mentioned before.

From the bottom to the top of it there were arranged steps of a wonderful beauty, by which the crowds ascended as soon as they were let in the door. There was no toil for those who went up, no difficulty, and no delay in ascending, because the step above was always easier to ascend than the one below had been. When I directed my eyes up, I saw, sitting on a throne of glory, our Lord and Savior in human form and, as it seemed to me, the spirits of five or seven hundred blessed beings who had lately ascended by the road mentioned before to the place of the throne. They were coming around him in a circle and were worshipping him with signs of thanksgiving. But it was evident to me that the place that I saw was not the heaven of heavens, where the Lord of Lords will appear in Sion, as if he were in his majesty. But from there, after all difficulty and delay is removed, spirits ascend to the heaven that is blessed by the presence of the eternal deity. In this vision, however, I conceived in my mind so much delight and joy, so much happiness and exultation, that whatever can be explained by human ingenuity would fail to express the delight of my heart that I felt there.

XII

The Monk Returns

After I had seen and heard these and numberless other things, St. Nicholas briefly spoke to me and said, "My son, you now have what you wished, as far as it was possible for you. In part you saw the conditions of the life to come, the dangers of sinners, the punishment of the wicked, the repose of the purified, the joys of those who at length reach the court of heaven, and the mysteries of our Lord's suffering. You must now return to your mortal struggles; but, if you persevere in the fear of God, you will receive the things that you have seen with your own eyes, and much greater than these, if you try with an immaculate body and innocent heart to await the day of your last calling."

While he was thus speaking to me, I suddenly heard a note of wondrous sweetness, as if all the bells of the world, or everything musical, were all sounding together. In this sound there was a wonderful sweetness and a various mixture of melody, and I do not know whether I admired it most for its greatness or its sweetness.

While I was anxiously listening to such an unusual sound, I lost my recollection. As soon as it ceased I found myself deprived of the company of my guide. The strength of my body was returning, and sight was restored to my eyes. The pain of my former sickness was destroyed, and I was altogether freed from my weakness. I sat among you strong and healthy, although anxious and sorrowful. Once restored to myself, as soon as I heard from the brothers that the feast of Easter was approaching, I knew that the music that I had heard was a sign that even among the inhabitants of heaven the mystery of the salvation of the human race is observed with joy and festivity just as it was wrought on earth by him who created the world and the heavens out of nothing, Jesus Christ, our Lord, to whom, with the Father and the Holy Spirit, be all honor and glory, world without end. Amen!

hurkill's Vision

There was a certain man of simple habits who was as hospitable as his humble means would allow. He lived in a town called Tunsted in the diocese of London. After the hour of evening prayer, on the eve of the day of the apostles St. Simon and St. Jude, he was busy draining his field, which he had sown that day. When he raised his eyes, he saw a man hastening toward him from a distance. After he looked at him, he began the Lord's prayer. When the stranger stepped up to him he asked him to finish his prayer and then speak to him. So, as soon as his prayer was ended, they exchanged greetings.

Then the man who had come to him asked where in the neighborhood he might find suitable lodging for the night. But when this man praised the great hospitality of his neighbors, the other found fault with the hospitality of some of those named. The laborer then understood that the stranger was acquainted with his neighbors and eagerly asked him to accept a lodging with him. The stranger said to him, "Your wife has already received two poor women to lodge with her, and I too will turn to your house for tonight so that I can lead you to your lord, namely Saint James, to whom you have even now devoutly prayed; for I am Julian the Entertainer and have been sent on your behalf to show you by divine means certain things that are hidden from men

219

and women in the flesh. Proceed to your house and try to prepare yourself for a journey." After his words, this man disappeared from the spot.

But Thurkill, for that was the laborer's name, hurried home, washed his head and feet, and found the two women as guests there, just as St. Julian had foretold. Afterwards he threw himself on a bed that he had prepared in his house apart from his wife for the sake of continence, and slept outside the room. As soon as all the members of the household were asleep, St. Julian woke the man and said, "Here I am, as I promised. It is time for us to be going. Let your body rest on the bed. It is only your spirit that is to go with me. So that your body does not appear to be dead, I will inspire the breath of life into you." In this way they both left the house, St. Julian leading the way, and Thurkill following.

After they had travelled to the middle of the world, as the man's guide said it was, towards the east, they entered a church of wonderful structure. Its roof was supported only by three pillars. The church itself was large and spacious, but without partitions, arched all around like a monk's cloister. On the northern side there was a wall not more than six feet high, which was joined to the church and rested on the three pillars. In the middle of the church there was a large baptistry. A large flame rose from it that did not burn yet unceasingly illuminated the whole church and the places around it like a noon-day sun. This brightness proceeded, as he was told by St. Julian, from the tithes of the just.

When they entered the hall, St. James met them, wearing a priest's miter. Seeing the pilgrim for whom he had sent, he ordered St. Julian and St. Domninus, who were the guardians of the place, to show his pilgrim the places of punishment for the wicked as well as the mansions of the just; and after speaking thus, he moved on.

Then St. Julian informed his companion that this church was the place that received the souls of all those who had recently died, so that they might be assigned the abodes and places of condemnation as well as of salvation by the atonements of purgatory that were destined for them by God. Through the intercession of the glorious virgin Mary that place was mercifully designed so that as soon as they left their bodies, all the spirits who were born again in Christ might be assembled there free from the attacks of devils and receive judgment according to their works. Thurkill said that in this church, which was called the Congregation of Spirits, he saw many spirits of the just, white all over and with the faces of youth.

After being taken beyond the northern wall, he saw a great number of spirits standing near the wall, marked with black and white spots. Some had a greater show of white than black, and others the reverse; but those who were whiter remained nearer to the wall, and those who were farthest off had no whiteness about them and appeared deformed in every part.

Near the wall was the entrance to the pit of hell, which incessantly exhaled the smoke of a most foul stench through the surrounding caverns and into the faces of those who stood by. This smoke came from tithes unjustly retained, and crops unjustly tithed; and the stink inflicted incomparable agony on those who were guilty of this crime. Thurkill, after twice smelling this same stink, was so oppressed by it that he was compelled to cough twice. Those who stood around his body declared that his body coughed twice at the same moment. St. Julian then said to him, "It appears that you have not duly tithed your crop, and therefore you have smelled this stench." He pleaded poverty as an excuse, but the saint told him that his field would produce a more abundant crop if he paid his tithes justly. The holy man also told him to confess this crime in the church openly to all and to seek absolution from the priest.

On the eastern side of this church between two walls was a very large purgatorial fire. One of these walls rose on the north side, and the other on the south. They were separated by a large space that extended a long way in width on the eastern side to a very large lake, in which were immersed the souls of those who were passing through the purgatorial fire. The water of the lake was incomparably salty and cold, as was afterwards proved to the man. Over this lake was a large bridge planted all over with thorns and stakes. Every one was obliged to pass over this bridge before he or she could arrive at the Mount of Joy. On this mountain was built a large church of wonderful structure. It appeared to Thurkill large enough to contain all the inhabitants of the world.

Blessed Julian conducted him altogether unhurt through the fire to the lake; and the two then walked together on the road that led from the church through the middle of the flames. No wood supplied the fuel for this fire, but the sort of flame seen in a fiercely-heated oven rose and was diffused over the whole space. It consumed the black and spotted spirits for either a shorter or a longer period, according to the degree of their crimes.

The spirits who had escaped the fire descended into that cold salty lake at the command of Blessed Nicholas, who presided over that purgatory. Some of these were immersed over the head, some up to the neck, some to the chest and arms, others up to the navel, some up to the knees, and others scarcely up to the hollow of their feet.

After the lake, there remained the crossing of the bridge on the western side in front of the church. Some of the spirits passed over this bridge very tediously and slowly, others more easily and faster, and some passed over quickly, at will, experiencing no delay or trouble in crossing. Some went through the lake so slowly that they stayed in it many years. There were those who were not assisted by any special Masses, or who in their life-time had not tried to redeem their sins by works of charity toward the poor. When they reached that bridge and wanted to cross over to their destined place of rest, they walked painfully with naked feet amid the sharp stakes and thorns that were set on the bridge. When they were no longer able to endure the extreme agony of the pain, they placed their hands on the stakes to support themselves from falling, and their hands were pierced straight through. In the violence of their pain and suffering, they rolled on their bellies and all parts of their bodies on the stakes, until by degrees they grovelled along, dreadfully bloody and pierced all over, to the farther end of the bridge. But when they reached the hall of the church, they gained a happy entrance and remembered little of their vehement tortures.

After Thurkill saw all these things, he and St. Julian returned through the middle of the flame to the church of St. Mary. There they stopped with the white spirits who had lately arrived. These spirits were sprinkled with holy water by St. James and St. Domninus so that they might become whiter. Here at the very first daylight of the Sabbath, St. Michael the Archangel and the apostles Peter and Paul came to assign the places ordained by God to the spirits assembled inside and outside the church according to their deserts. St. Michael gave all the white spirits a safe passage through the middle of the flames of purgatory and through the other places of punishment to the entrance of the large church that was built on the Mount of Joy, which had a door on the western side always open. The spirits stained with black and white spots, who were lying outside the hall on the northern side, were brought by St. Peter through a door on the eastern side into the purgatorial fire, without any discussion of their works, so that they might be cleansed by that raging flame of the stains of their sins.

Blessed Paul too sat inside the church at the end of the northern wall. Outside the wall, opposite the apostle, sat the devil with his followers. A flame-vomiting aperture, which was the mouth of the pit of hell, burst out close to the feet of the devil. On the wall between the apostle and the devil was fixed a scale hanging on an equal balance. The middle part of it hung outside in front of the devil. The apostle had two weights, a greater and a lesser one, shining like gold; and the devil also had two, sooty and dark.

The black spirits approached one after the other from all directions with great fear and trembling to try the weight of their good or evil deeds in the scale. The weights estimated the deeds of each of the spirits according to the good or evil they had done. When the balance inclined toward the apostle, he took that spirit and brought it through the eastern door, which was joined to the church, into the purifying fire to expiate its offences. When the balance inclined and shifted its weight toward the devil, he and his followers at once hurried the spirit away to eternal torment, wailing and cursing its father and mother for having begotten it. With huge grins they cast it into the deep and fiery furnace, which was at the feet of the devil who was weighing. The weighing of good and evil in this way is often mentioned in the writings of the holy fathers.

On the Sabbath day near evening, while St. Domninus and St. Julian were in the church, a certain devil came there from the north, riding a black horse with furious speed and urging him to run through the many turnings of the place amid great noise and laughter. Many of the evil spirits went out to meet it, dancing about and grinning at one another over the prey that was brought to them. St. Domninus then commanded the devil who was riding to come directly to him and tell him whose spirit it was that he had brought. The devil dissembled for a long time because of the great delight that he experienced over the wretched spirit. The saint immediately snatched up a whip and beat the devil severely. The devil then followed the saint to the northern wall where the scale of the spirits stood.

The saint then asked the devil whose spirit it was that he was tormenting by riding like that. He replied that it was one of the nobles of the kingdom of England, who had died on the preceding night without confession and without partaking of the body of the Lord. Among the other faults that he committed, his principal crime was his cruelty toward his own people. He had brought many of them to extreme want chiefly at the instigation of his wife, who always incited him to deeds of cruelty. He said, "I have transformed him into a horse, since we are allowed to turn the condemned spirits into whatever form we please. I should have already descended with him into hell and should be consigning him to eternal punishment, but Sunday night is here, when it is our duty to stop our theatrical sports and inflict more severe tortures on the wretched spirits."

After he had spoken these words, he directed his look on Thurkill and said to the saint, "Who is that rustic standing with you?" The saint answered, "Do you not know him?" The demon then said, "I saw him at the church of Tidstude in Essex on the feast of its dedication." The saint then asked, "In what dress did you enter the church?" He replied, "In the dress of a woman, but when I advanced to the font, intending to enter the chancel, the deacon met me with the sprinkler of holy water. Sprinkling me with it, he put me to flight so precipitately, that I uttered a cry and leaped from the church as far as a field two furlongs distant." This man and several other parishioners as well bore witness to this same circumstance, declaring that they heard that cry but were entirely ignorant of its cause.

After this St. Domninus said to the devil, "We want to go with you to see your sports." The devil answered, "If you want to go with me, do not bring this laborer with you. On his return among his fellow mortals he would reveal our acts and secret kinds of punishment to the living and would reclaim many from serving us." The saint said to him, "Hurry and go on, St. Julian and I will follow you." The demon went on in advance and the saints followed him, bringing the man with them by stealth.

They proceeded to a northern region, as if they were going up a mountain. After descending the mountain, there was a very large and dark-looking house surrounded by old walls, and in it there were a great many rows filled all around with innumerable heated iron seats. These seats were constructed with iron hoops glowing white with heat. They had nails driven into every part of them, above and below, right and left. In them there sat people of different status and sex. They were pierced all over their bodies by the glowing nails and were bound on all sides with fiery hoops. There was such a number of seats and such a multitude of people sitting in them that no tongue would be able to count them.

All around these courts were black iron walls, and near these walls were other seats, in which the devils sat in a circle, as if at a pleasant spectacle, grinning at each other over the tortures of the wretched beings and recounting to them their former crimes. Near the entrance to this detestable scene, on the downward slope of the mountains, as we have said, there was a wall five feet high, from which whatever was done in that place of punishment could be seen plainly. Near this wall these saints stood outside looking at what the wretched beings inside were enduring. The man lying concealed between them plainly saw all that was going on inside.

When the servants of hell were all seated at this shameful arena, the chief of that wicked troop said to his followers, "Let the proud man be violently dragged from his seat, and let him sport before us." He was dragged from his seat and clothed in a black garment. In the presence of the devils who applauded him in turn he then imitated all the gestures of a man proud beyond measure. He stretched his neck, elevated his face, cast up his eyes with the brows arched, imperiously thundered out lofty words, shrugged his shoulders, and scarcely could he bear his arms for pride. His eyes glowed; he assumed a threatening look, rising on tiptoe; he stood with crossed legs, expanded his chest, stretched his neck, glowed in his face, showed signs of anger in his fiery eyes, and striking his nose with his finger, gave expression of great threats. Swelling with such inward pride, he provided a ready subject of laughter to the inhuman spirits.

While he was boasting about his dress and putting on his close-fitting gloves, his garments suddenly were turned to fire, which consumed the entire body of the wretched being. Finally, the devils, glowing with anger, tore the wretch limb from limb with prongs and fiery iron hooks. One of them put fat with pitch and other greasy substances in a glowing pan and fried each limb in that boiling grease as it was torn away. Each time the devil sprinkled them with the grease, the limbs hissed like cold water poured on boiling blood. After his limbs were fried, they were joined together again, and that proud man returned to his former shape.

Next the hammerers of hell approached the wretched man, with hammers and three red hot iron bars nailed together in triple order. They applied two bars to the back of his body, on the right and left, and cruelly drove the hot nails into him with their hammers. These two bars, beginning at his feet, were brought up his legs and thighs to his shoulders and were then bent around his neck. The third bar, beginning at his middle, passed up his belly, and reached the top of his head. After this wretch had been tortured for a length of time in the manner described above, he was mercilessly thrust back into his former seat. When he was placed there, he was tormented in all parts by the burning nails and by having his five fingers stretched. After he was taken from this place of punishment, he was put back in the dwelling that he had made for himself while he was living, to await further tortures.

A priest was next dragged violently from his fiery seat into the arena and placed before these inhuman goblins by the servants of sin, who cut his throat in the middle, pulled out his tongue, and cut it off at the root. When he could have done so, this priest did not repay the people entrusted to his care for the temporal goods that he had taken from them by holy exhortation or by an example of good works. He had not given them the support of prayers or of Masses. Afterwards, as we described for the proud man, they tore him limb from limb and then restored him again entirely and placed him in a chair of torture.

After him a certain soldier was brought, who had spent his life in slaying harmless people, in tournaments, and in robberies. He sat on a black horse armed with all his weapons of war. When the horse was urged on by the spur, he breathed a pitchy flame with stench and smoke to torture his rider. The horse's saddle was pierced all over with long fiery nails. His armour and helmet, his shield and boots were covered with flames and severely burdened the rider by their weight and at the same time consumed him to his very marrow with no less torture. After he had urged his horse to headlong speed, in imitation of his former habit in war, he shook his spear against the devils who met him and derided him. He was dismounted by them and torn piecemeal. His limbs were fried in the execrable liquid mentioned before, and after they were fried they were joined together again in the same way as those who had come before and were fastened by three bars. Once restored he was violently thrust back into his own seat.

After the soldier, a man well-skilled in worldly law was dragged into the middle with great torture that he had brought on himself by a long course of evil living and by accepting presents for perverting judgments. This man was well known throughout the English territories among the higher ranks, but he had ended his life miserably in the same year in which this vision was seen. He died suddenly without executing any will, and all the wealth that he had amassed by his rapacious greediness was entirely alienated from him and spent by strangers.

He used to sit in the king's exchequer, where he often received presents from both of the litigating parties. He was also dragged to the arena, and in the presence of the wicked spirits he was compelled by the insulting goblins to imitate the actions of his former life. Turning himself now to the right and now to the left, he was teaching one party how to establish a cause and another how to reply to it. While he did this, he did not refrain from accepting presents, but received money at one time from one party, at another time from the other. Then he would count it and put it in his pockets.

After the demons had watched this wretched man's gestures for some time, the money suddenly became hot and burned the wretch in a pitiable manner. He was forced to put the burning pieces of money in his mouth and afterwards to swallow them. After swallowing them, two demons came to him with an iron cart-wheel, studded all around with spikes and nails. They placed it on the sinner's back and whirled it round, tearing away his whole back in its quick and burning revolutions. They compelled him to vomit in still greater torture the money that he had swallowed with great agony. After he had vomited them up, the demon ordered him to collect them again, so that he might be fed again in the same way with the money. Afterward, the servants of hell became enraged and exhausted on him all the tortures that were mentioned above.

This man's wife was sitting in one of the fiery spiked seats. She was excommunicated in several churches because of a ring that she had put in her casket and declared to have been stolen. She was prevented by sudden death from ever being absolved from this decree.

An adulterer was now brought into the sight of the furious demons together with an adulteress, united together in foul contact. In the presence of all they repeated their disgraceful love-making and immodest gestures to their own confusion and amid the cursing of the demons. Then, as if smitten with frenzy, they began to tear one another, changing the outward love that they seemed to entertain toward one another before into cruelty and hatred. Their limbs were torn to pieces by the furious crowd all around them, and they suffered the same punishments as those who had preceded them. All the fornicators who were also present were tormented in the same way, and the intensity of their sufferings was so great that the pen of this writer is not adequate to portray them.

Among the other wretched beings, two from the company of slanderers were brought into the middle. With continual distortions they gaped with their mouths open to their ears, and turning their faces toward each other, they gazed with grim eyes. The ends of a kind of burning spear were put in their mouths, and they ate and gnawed at it with distorted mouths, until they quickly reached the middle of the spear, drawing close to each other. In this way they tore at each other and stained their whole faces with blood.

Among others, thieves, incendiaries, and violators of religious places were brought out. The servants of hell placed them on wheels of red hot iron set with spikes and nails. From their excessive heat a constant shower of sparks of fire were emitted. The wretches were whirled around on these and endured horrific tortures.

Then there came to the spot a tradesman with false scales and weights and also those who stretch new cloths in their shops to such a length and width that the threads are broken and a hole appears. Afterwards, cunningly stitching up the holes, they sell these same cloths in poorly-lit places. These were cruelly torn from their seats and compelled to repeat the motions of their former sins to their disgrace and to increase their punishments. Afterward they were tortured by devils in the way we have related for those before them.

Besides this the man saw four courts near the entrance of the lower hell. The first contained innumerable furnaces and large wide cauldrons filled to the brim with burning pitch and other melted substances. In each of these the spirits were heaped together, boiling fiercely. From the violence of the boiling, their heads, like the heads of black fish, were at one time forced up out of the liquid and at other times forced down. The second court contained similar cauldrons, but these were filled with snow and cold ice, in which the spirits were tortured by the dreadful cold in intolerable agony. The cauldrons in the third court were filled with boiling sulphureous water and other things, which emitted a stench mixed with a foul smoke. Here the spirits who died in the foulness of their lusts were particularly tormented.

The fourth court contained cauldrons full of very black salt water, its bitter saltiness would immediately take the bark off any kind of wood thrown into it. Boiling incessantly in these caldrons was a multitude of sinners, murderers, thieves, robbers, sorceresses, and rich folk who oppressed their fellow men and women by unjust exactions. The servants of iniquity, standing all around them, pressed them together inside so that they could not escape from the heat of the molten liquid. Those who had been boiling for seven days in this burning grease were plunged on the eighth day into the dreadful cold that was in the second court. On the other hand, those who had been tortured in the cold were put into boiling liquid. In the same way those who had been boiling in the salt water were tortured in the stench. The devils observed these changes continually every eight days.

After they had seen these things, when the morning of the Lord's day was just beginning to appear, these saints and the man they were conducting proceeded to the Mount of Joy through the purifying fire and the lake and over the spiked bridge, until they arrived at a hall on the western side of the temple, which was situated on the mount. There was a handsome and large gate always open, through which the spirits who were made entirely white were brought by St. Michael. In this hall were assembled all the purified spirits praying with all the eagerness of expectation for a happy admission to the place.

In the southern quarter outside the temple the man saw an infinite number of spirits, all with their faces turned to the church. They were praying for the assistance of their friends who were alive, by which means they might deserve to gain admission to that church. The more special the assistance they received, the nearer they approached the church. In this place Thurkill recognized many of his friends, as well as all those of whom he had a passing acquaintance in life. St. Michael informed the man about the spirits and about how many Masses each spirit needed to be set free and permitted to enter the temple. The spirits who were waiting for admission suffered no punishment, except that they were waiting for special assistance from their friends. Nevertheless, all the spirits who stood there approached nearer the entrance of that church every day by the general assistance of the whole church.

This man was brought into the temple by St. Michael. There he saw in white apparel many of both sexes whom he had seen in life. They were climbing up to the temple and enjoying great happiness. The further the spirits climbed up the steps of the temple, the more white and shining they became. In that great church he saw many very beautiful mansions. In them dwelt the spirits of the just, whiter than snow. Their faces and crowns glittered like golden light. At certain hours of each day they heard songs from heaven, as if all kinds of music were sounding in harmonious melody. This soothed and refreshed all the inhabitants of the temple by its agreeable softness, as if they were being served all kinds of dainty meats. But the spirits who stood in the halls outside did not hear anything of this heavenly song. Several saints had abodes of their own in this place where they received with joy those who served them especially, next to the Lord, in everything. Afterwards they presented these souls before the sight of God.

After this they turned to the eastern part of the temple and came to a most pleasant place that was beautiful in the variety of its herbs and flowers and filled with the sweet smell of herbs and trees. There the man saw a very clear spring that sent forth four streams of different colored water. Over this fountain there was a beautiful tree of wonderful size and immense height that abounded in all kinds of fruits and the sweet smell of spices.

Under this tree near the fountain a large and handsome man rested. He was clothed from his feet to his breast in a garment of various colors and of wonderfully beautiful texture. This man seemed to be smiling in one eye and weeping from the other. "This," said St. Michael, "is the first parent of the human race, Adam. By the smiling eye he indicates the joy that he feels in the glorification of his children who are to be saved. By the weeping eye, he expresses the sorrow he feels for the punishment and just judgment of God on his children who are to be condemned. The garment that covers him, not quite entirely, is the robe of immortality and the garment of glory. He was deprived of it for his first transgression. From the time of Abel, his just son, he began to regain this garment and continues to do so through the whole succession of his righteous children. Just as the chosen ones shine in their different virtues, this garment is dyed with various colors. When the number of his elect children is completed, Adam will be entirely clothed in the robe of immortality and glory. In this way the world will come to an end."

After proceeding a little way from this place they came to a most beautiful gate adorned with jewels and precious stones. The wall around it shone as if it were made of gold. As soon as they entered the gate, a kind of golden temple appeared, much more magnificent than the former in all its beauty, in its pleasant sweetness, and in the splendor of its glittering light. The places they had seen before did not appear at all pleasant in comparison with that place. After they had gone into this temple, Thurkill beheld a kind of chapel on one side filled with wonderful ornaments. In it there sat three virgins shining in indescribable beauty. The archangel informed him that these were St. Catherine, St. Margaret and St. Osith.

While Thurkill was admiring and contemplating their beauty, St. Michael said to St. Julian, "Restore this man directly to his body, for unless he is quickly taken back, the cold water that the bystanders are throwing in his face will suffocate him." Right after these words were spoken, not knowing how, the man was brought back to his body and sat up in bed.

He had been lying senseless on his bed – as if oppressed with a heavy sleep – for two days and nights, that is, from Friday evening until the following Sunday evening. As soon as morning came he hastened to the church and, after Mass, the priest with other parishioners who had seen him lifeless a short time before asked him to inform them about what had been revealed to him. In his great simplicity, however, he hesitated to relate his vision, until on the following night St. Julian appeared to him and gave him orders to reveal everything that he had seen, because he said he had been taken from his body for the purpose of making public all he had heard. In obedience to the commands of the saint, on All Saints' Day, and at times afterwards, he related his vision plainly and openly in English, and all who heard him wondered at the man's unusual gift of speech, since formerly he had appeared clownish and unable to speak because of his great simplicity. By his continual narration of the vision he had seen he moved many to tears and bitter lamentations.

*   *
*

NOTES

And Primary Sources

ST. PETER'S APOCALYPSE

This work dates from the mid-second century. There is no pure and complete text. There is, however, an early but incomplete Greek version known as the Akhmim Fragment. Our text is based on the James translation (see below) of the Ethiopic version. This version has some extraneous material at the end, which has been edited to agree with what James proposes as a sensible text of the vision.

St. Peter's Apocalypse is one of the Christian apocryphal books. It and *St. Paul's Apocalypse* and the *Apocalypse of the Virgin* form the group of otherworld visions among the Christian apocrypha. *St. Paul's Apocalypse* is presented here, but the *Apocalypse of the Virgin* is omitted since it follows Paul's very closely.

St. Peter's Apocalypse is an account of Peter's vision of the apocalypse at the time of the Transfiguration of Christ before the Apostles. In addition to seeing Jesus and Moses and Elias in their heavenly glory, Peter and the disciples see a vision of the otherworld.

The vision is revealed in response to the Apostles' request that Christ show them signs by which they will know that the last days are at hand.

Unlike later visions, Peter has no guide, unless Christ himself might be considered one. Peter is strictly a witness to, and not a participant in, the punishments that are

237

revealed to him on the palm of Christ's hand. Peter's soul does not depart from his body and travel into the other-world. There is a full range of sins from idolatry to usury and a full range of punishments, mainly involving fire and attacking beasts.

Peter sees prophets and other Hebrew leaders, but this work has none of the more informal flavor of later visions where people meet former acquaintances.

This work is significant in the tradition because it is the first vision of heaven and hell in the Christian tradition after the biblical Book of Revelation of John.

Primary Sources

James, Montague Rhodes. *The Apocryphal New Testa-ment.* Oxford: Clarendon, 1924; reprint, 1955 (pp. 504-21).

"The Apocalypse of Peter." Translated by Andrew Rutherfurd. *The Ante-Nicene Fathers.* Edited by Allan Menzies. Vol. 9. 5th ed. New York: Charles Scribner & Sons, 1912 (pp. 141-47).

ST. PAUL'S APOCALYPSE

This work dates from the late fourth century. Our text is based on the James translation (see below) from the Latin. This vision was a popular work with versions in almost every European language and in Syriac, Coptic and Ethiopic.

The vision begins with the discovery of a sealed lead box under Paul's house in Tarsus in 388 CE. The box contains the story of Paul being taken up bodily into heaven. An unusual feature of this vision is the opening in which Paul witnesses the sun, moon and stars, sea, waters, and earth, all asking the Lord to let them destroy, in one way or another, the inhabitants of the earth because they

238

are so dreadful. The repetitive style is reminiscent of a litany.

Paul is introduced to the guardian angels who recount the deeds of their charges before God. Then Paul is taken up in the spirit to the Place of the Righteous where he sees the Firmaments and the Powers and the evil and good angels. Paul is also shown what happens when both evil and good souls departs from the body and how their angels present them before God.

This vision presents a fairly detailed description of three heavens with the third being a city, similar to the apocalyptic heavenly Jerusalem, with walls, twelve gates, and four rivers. In heaven Paul meets many Hebrew prophets and has a conversation with Enoch, which he is not allowed to reveal.

In his vision of hell Paul sees the usual range of sinners, and, in addition, unworthy priests, bishops, deacons and lectors. The punishments in hell generally include immersion in a river of fire up to various parts of the body, but there are also worms and dragons that devour the sinners, and vile pits into which the sinners are thrown. St. Paul witnesses these scenes but does not suffer any pains. This vision results in the Lord granting the souls, at the request of Paul, Michael and the angels, a day without torments. Such interest in the relief of sinners becomes an increasingly important feature of visions of heaven and hell.

Paul's vision presents the first instance of the judgment of individual souls at their death. It is also worth noting that the church and the levels of the hierarchy in the church have developed to a point where different classes of male clerics are mentioned in connection with their specific roles and not fulfilling them properly.

Primary Sources
Brandes, Herman, ed. *Visio Sancti Pauli; ein Beiträg zur Visionsliteratur mit einen deutschen und zwei*

lateinischen Texten. Gesellschaft für deutsche
Philologie. Festschrift 5. Halle: M. Niemeyer, 1885.
Hennecke, Edgar and Wilhelm Schneemelcher, eds. *New
Testament Apocrypha.* Translated by R. McL. Wilson.
2 vols. Philadelphia: Westminster Press, 1965 (2: 790-
95).
James, Montague Rhodes. *The Apocryphal New Testa-
ment.* Oxford: Clarendon, 1924; reprint, 1955 (pp.
525-55).
Silverstein, Theodore. *Visio Sancti Pauli: The History of
the Apocalypse in Latin together with nine texts.*
London and Toronto: Christophers, 1935.

THREE VISIONS FROM GREGORY THE GREAT

These short visions are from Book IV, Chapter 36 of
Gregory's *Dialogs,* which were written in 593-594 in
Latin. Our text is based on the edition by Gardner (see
below).

These visions appear amid a discussion of the nature of
heaven and hell, and each of them illustrates a different
way in which one might be affected by a vision of the
otherworld. The first visionary, Peter, dies and sees
many torments. He is just about to be cast into them when
an angel sends him back to earth. He converts and leads a
good life.

The second visionary, Stephen, sees "many things" in
the dungeon of hell, but the judge had wanted another
Stephen, so this Stephen gets sent back to earth. His
repentance is rather weak, as we learn from what the next
visionary saw.

This was a soldier who left his body and saw in the
otherworld the steward of the pope's family bound by a
weight of iron because he was a sadist. He also saw the
above-mentioned Stephen on a bridge being pulled up
because of his charity and down because of his impurity.

The soldier wakes without knowing what happens to Stephen.

None of these visionaries suffers during his vision; which is generally sent as a warning. Since these are not fully developed visions, but mere glimpses, we have neither a full range of sins covered nor a full range of punishments. Nor is the geography of the otherworld very well-defined. Only the soldier attempts some description of the topography of the otherworld. None of these visionaries is accompanied by a guide, although we do find here, for the first time in our collection, the visionary meeting near contemporaries in the otherworld. This is also the first example in which the visionaries are average people; neither saints with special authority, nor the religious men who became very popular as visionaries in the later Middle Ages.

Gregory concludes that visions are sometimes for the benefit of those who see them and sometimes for those who learn of them. Sometimes those who see these tortures amend their lives and avoid hell. Others, who do not, are tortured all the more.

Primary Sources

Gregory the Great. *Dialogi*. Edited by Umberto Moricca. Rome: Tip. del Senato, 1924.

Gregory the Great. *Dialogues*. Translated by Odo John Zimmerman. New York: Fathers of the Church, 1959.

Gregory the Great. *The Dialogues of Saint Gregory*. Edited by Edmund G. Gardner. London, Philip Lee Warner, 1911 (pp. 223-26).

FURSEUS' VISION

This vision apparently occurred in 633 CE, since it is included under that date in Bede's *Historia Ecclesiastica Gentis Anglorum,* which was written in 731 in England in

241

Latin. The text here is based on the translation published by Dent (see below).

Like many later visions this one has its origins in Ireland, which is where Furseus comes from. The vision, in this case a series of visions, actually occurs while he is in the province of the East Saxons. Furseus is a holy man who is occupied with preaching the Gospels. Of his three visions, the most significant is the third in which he sees combat among the evil spirits, is accused of evil by devils, is led up high by the three angels and sees the four fires that will kindle and consume the world – falsehood, covetousness, discord, and iniquity. The three angels act as guides, but they are not very clearly drawn.

This is the earliest example of the punishment of a visionary. A devil throws the soul of a sinner at Furseus because he once received a garment from this sinner. Furseus' shoulder and jaw are burned. When Furseus returns to life he bears the mark of this burn.

Although after his vision he exhorts all to practice virtue, he tells his tale only to those most likely to profit from it. Physically affected by his vision, he wears only a thin garment and sweats even during East Anglian winters.

Primary Sources

AS, January 16, 36b-41b.

Bede, The Venerable. *The Ecclesiastical History of England.* London: Dent, 1916 (pp. 132-37).

Krusch, B., ed. *Vita virtutesque Fursei Abbatis Latiniacensis.* MGH, Scriptores M., 4: 423-51.

DRYTHELM'S VISION

This vision is included under the date 699 CE in the *Chronicle* of Roger of Wendover, and according to Vincent of Beauvais' (d. 1264) *Vision of an English Man* it occurred in 941. Bede, however, lists it under 696 CE in his *Historia Ecclesiastica Gentis Anglorum,* which was written in 731 in England in Latin. The text here is based on the translation published by Dent (see below).

Drythelm is a good man who becomes sick and appears to die, but his soul is led to the otherworld by an anonymous guide with a shining countenance, wearing a bright garment. A limited number of sins are treated here, although both fire and ice are used as punishment. Drythelm is attacked at one point by devils, but he is rescued by his guide. One of the more remarkable features of this vision is Drythelm's visit to the mouth of hell where he sees globes of fire, containing souls of the dead, rising and falling. Between heaven and hell there is a place where souls not worthy of being immediately admitted to heaven await a favorable judgment. This region is an early precursor of purgatory.

Drythelm returns to earth to live a good a life and to show others how to do the same. He divides his wealth among his family and the poor and enters a monastery. His vision is the first in this collection to make a point of the efficacy of the prayers, alms, fasting and masses of the living for the dead, since it is through these that those souls not quite worthy of heaven are eventually advanced to heaven.

The *Vision of the Monk of Melrose* by Helinand de Froidmont in *Chronicon* (PL 212, cols. 1059-60) is based on *Drythelm's Vision.*

Primary Sources
Bede, The Venerable. *The Ecclesiastical History of England.* London: Dent, 1916 (pp. 241-50).
Otloh of Emmeran. *Liber visionum.* PL 146, col. 380 ff.
Roger of Wendover. *Chronica, sive Flores historiarum.* Edited by Henry O. Coxe. 3 vols. London: English Historical Society, 1841; reprint, Vaduz: Kraus, 1964 (1: 190-95).

Roger of Wendover. *Chronicle/Flowers of History.*
Edited by J.A. Gilles. 2 vols. Bohn: London, 1849 (1:
120-24).

WETTI'S VISION

This vision dates from 824. It was written in prose by
Heito in the same year and then re-composed in verse by
Walahfrid Stabo in 827. This is a translation of Heito's
prose work.

Wetti, a monk in the monastery at Reichenau, falls ill
on October 30, 824. He tells his vision on November 3
and dies the following day, November 4.

During a first brief vision Wetti speaks with an angel.
When this vision ends he asks his brothers to read to him
from the *Dialogs* of Gregory the Great. After the reading
he rests himself, and lying as if dead his soul is led by the
angel on a tour of the otherworld. On this journey he sees
many who are known to him.

This vision is particularly interested in the sins of the
clergy and in sins of a sexual nature. Wetti claims that
while the angel, his guide, mentions most sins once,
"again and again the angel introduced a discussion of the
sin of sodomy...five times and more [he said] that it
should be avoided." At one point, right after mentioning
"sodomy" he mentions "the plague," – a unique connection in this genre. One can hardly help wondering with
the modern consciousness of the transmission of AIDS
whether there was some connection in the mind of the
author between certain forms of sexual activity and the
spread of disease and particularly the plague.

A particularly interesting point of this vision is the
author's efforts at verifying its truth by mentioning facts
that would not have been known to Wetti but were
revealed to him in his vision and then confirmed indepen-

dently – device later used to excellent dramatic effect by Dante.

The vision particularly calls the rich and the powerful to task for abusing their power by amassing great fortunes through extortion and plunder.

This vision strongly encourages aiding the souls of the dead with Masses, prayers, alms, etc. as the duty of the clergy and other Christians.

Wetti spends a considerable time while in the areas of the blessed seeking intercessors among the virgins, martyrs and saints to help him on his course toward heaven. He is apparently accused of giving bad example to his followers, and although not physically punished, he does undergo some psychological punishment as he tries to gain assurance that he will be able to obtain forgiveness.

His obligation after his vision is to have it copied down and disseminated so that others can learn from what he has seen. Apparently there have been other cases when a monk has been shown some of these very same things, but the visions and their messages fell into oblivion and only a few remembered them. Most important apparently is Wetti's message for the reform of religious houses for both men and women in Gaul and western Germany. Such elements point to this vision's ties with the Lotharingian monastic reform movement connected with St. Benedict of Aniane in the early 9th century and with Louis the Pious at Aachen.

Primary Sources
Dümmler, Ernst, ed. *Vision of Wetti.* MGH, Poetae M.E., 2: 267-334. (Heito and Strabo versions.)
Traill, David A. *Walahfrid Strabo's Visio Wettini: Text, Translation and Commentary.* Bern and Frankfurt/M: Lang, 1974. (Strabo version.)
Visio Guetini. PL 105, cols. 771-80. (Heito version.)

ST. BRENDAN'S VOYAGE

Although Brendan lived c. 486-578, the account of his voyage is from an early tenth-century narrative based on an eighth-century legend. The work is entitled *Navagatio Brendani*. Our English translation is based on the one found in *Brendaniana* (see below).

This story differs considerably from the other works included in this volume, because it is not strictly a vision. The legend is based on what apparently are the true voyages of this saint who travelled as far as the Hebrides, Shetlands, Faroes and Iceland; he may have travelled to the Azores, and some even think as far as Mexico. Brendan's soul does not leave his body, and he takes his journey to the otherworld in the company of seventeen companions who join him in his boat and set off in search of the Land of Promise of the Saints.

This type of work is called an *imram*; and the influence on this genre is so fundamental to the visions of the otherworld that it had to be included here. Another *imram* of importance, which has not been included, however, is the *Voyage of Bran the Blessed*.

In this work there is a great deal of attention paid to the physical hardships endured by Brendan and his companions during their six-year search for the Land of Promise of the Saints. One particular recurrent topic in this work is food: how it is obtained and prepared, and how often the travellers are required to fast because of short supplies of food. These are all details that point to the origins of this story among actual seafarers.

Brendan spends six years journeying, and during this time the Lord shows him the marvels of the ocean, which are described for us along with the wonders of the monastic and hermetic life styles that Brendan encounters on various islands.

He touches on the outskirts of hell, sees the forge of Vulcan and meets Judas Iscariot, who is enjoying a brief respite from his horrendous suffering. But all that Brendan sees, occurs on the surface of the earth. Here he meets devils and saints and blessed souls enjoying eternal bliss in the Land of Promise of the Saints. He is told that this Land will be revealed when the "days of tribulation come upon the people of Christ."

It is important to note that, in imitation of the very physical dimension of this and other voyages, the line between vision and experience becomes blurred in many of the later visions of the otherworld. For instance, although Tundale clearly leaves his body behind when he "goes on" his vision, he nevertheless experiences the torments of hell as if his body were present along with his soul.

Primary Sources
Moran, Patrick F., ed. *Acta Sancti Brendani.* Dublin: William Bernard Kelly, 1872 (pp. 85-131).
O'Donoghue, Denis, ed. and trans. *Brendaniana: St. Brendan the Voyager in Story and Legend.* Dublin: Browne & Nolan, 1893 (pp. 111-75).
O'Meara, John, trans. *The Voyage of Brendan: Journey to the Promised Land.* Atlantic Highlands, NJ: Humanities Press, 1976.
Selmer, C., ed. *Navagatio Sancti Brendani Abbatis.* Publications in Medieval Studies 16. Notre Dame, IN: University of Notre Dame Press, 1959.

CHARLES THE FAT'S VISION

This vision apparently occurred in 885. It is recorded in the *Gesta regis angelorum* of William of Malmesbury who lived c. 1095-1143, and is based on Hariulf's *Chronicle*, Book III, Chap. 21. Our translation is based on the Sharpe edition of William of Malmesbury.

This is a very interesting and unusual vision since its purpose is highly political. The visionary is Charles I, King of Swabia and Holy Roman Emperor. While Charles is resting on his bed a guide comes and leads him through his vision. The guide holds a ball of thread of great brightness made of light – a feature unique to this vision. The guide ties it around Charles' finger, and it not only casts light for their journey, but protects Charles from devils, and provides a way by which the guide can lead Charles along. Charles is not punished during his vision.

Other major features of this work are very different from the other visions that we encounter here. First of all the visionary is a noble and a very powerful one. His vision, unlike the others, has a political agenda, which is not entirely unrelated to the important religious and ethical principle of nonviolence. In the infernal regions Charles meets only acquaintances like the bishops, vassals, princes and counselors of his father and uncles, as well as his father, uncle and cousin. All are being or have been punished for either counseling for, or partaking in, war.

This vision is tied closely to actual political events too, because Charles announces that he has learned in his vision that he will be succeeded by his cousin and that he should give him the throne without opposition. In fact, his rule does end when his cousin Arnulf gains power after Charles makes a pact with the Vikings, offering them Normandy in return for their sparing Paris. Again, such prophesy after the fact is a device used by Dante with disarming effect.

The geography is not very clearly distinguished; everything appears to take place on one plain through which Charles passes from those undergoing the worst punishments to those who have already passed beyond punishment. This vision encourages the living to aid the dead through Masses, prayers, psalms, alms and vigils, invoking the aid provided to the dead by the saints, particularly here St. Peter and St. Remigius.

Primary Sources

Hariulf. *Chronicon Centilense ou Chronique de l'Abbeye de Saint-Riquier.* Edited by Ernest Prarond. Translated by the Marquis Le Ver. Mémoires de la Société d'émulation d'Abbeville. Abbeville: Fourdrinier, 1899.

Hariulf. *Chronique de l'Abbaye de Saint-Riquier.* Edited by Ferdinand Lot. Paris: Picard, 1894.

William of Malmesbury. *History of the Kings of England.* Edited by John Sharpe. London: Longman, Hurst, Rees, Orme: 1815 (pp. 117-21).

ST. PATRICK'S PURGATORY

There are many different accounts of visits to St. Patrick's Purgatory, dating from when it was founded in c. 445 until 1497, when it was temporarily closed by Pope Alexander VI. Probably the fullest version, more in the spirit of the other visions included here, is the vision of the Knight Owen, written in 1153 (according to Hugh of Sawtry, who wrote his version in either 1186-90 or 1208-1215) or 1154. Our version of the text is based on the translation found in the Gilles edition of Roger of Wendover's *Chronicle.*

Most of the works concerning St. Patrick's Purgatory are connected with a particular site in Ireland, Lough Derg, which was a popular pilgrimage site. The origins of the site are explained at the beginning of Owen's vision. Many who entered the little cave at Lough Derg, northeast of Limerick, and spent an evening or three there, told of visiting the Purgatory. But some of the works describing a visit to this site, like that of Antonio Mannini in 1411, involve only a detailed description of the paperwork, interviews and permissions involved in gaining admission.

Owen's vision, however, does describe his experience of the purgatory itself. His visit occurs just at the time when the concept of purgatory is becoming set as a doctrine in the Christian church. One of the important characteristics of this work, which distinguishes it from most of the other visions included here is the presumption of the actual physical and corporeal nature of the experience of the knight Owen whom we follow through the Purgatory. As in *St. Brendan's Voyage,* there is no separation from the body, and all that he experiences he is assumed to experience corporally. Although other visions, like Tundale's, approach the otherworld with the same attention to physical and corporeal details, in other cases the soul of the visionary is actually separated from the body.

A similarity might be pointed out between this work and *Charles the Fat's Vision.* In both cases the question of war plays a significant part. In Charles' vision the punishments he sees are related strictly to participation in and condoning of war. In this work the motivation for the penance undertaken by Owen is his own participation, as a knight of King Stephen, in a life of plunder and violence. He enters the Purgatory to begin the purgation that will continue when he returns from the Purgatory, and even in the afterlife, unless he has managed to cleanse himself completely.

Shortly after Owen descends into St. Patrick's Purgatory, he enters a hall enclosed by pillars where he meets fifteen men. Although he is not guided by these, he is advised by one of them to say the name of "Jesus" whenever things are going awry, and he is warned not to accept any offers to return back to the cave before completing the journey through the Purgatory. The otherworld begins with a series of plains where souls are tortured. Owen is treated badly by the demons he meets in purgatory, but he always remembers to invoke the name of Jesus, and he also refuses the numerous offers to lead him back to the entrance.

In addition to the plains of tortured, there is also a wheel of red-hot nails, a house of boiling cauldrons, a mountain swept by a whirlwind, a stinking and cold river, a pit that some demons claim is the mouth of hell, and a narrow and slippery bridge. These trials are not associated with individual sins but are general punishments.

Finally Owen arrives at an antechamber to heaven, which is described in terms of walls and gates of precious stones and metals, music, and wonderful vegetation. He is shown the gate of heaven and then refreshed with celestial food. Despite his own misgivings about his ability to reform, he is sent back to the entrance past all the demons who can no longer hurt him.

Owen meets no acquaintance on his journey through purgatory. As a result of his experience he repents further of his evil life, makes a pilgrimage to the Holy Land, and finally devotes the rest of his life to helping a monastic community in Ireland. His companion in establishing this community, Gilbert, writes down the story.

Primary Sources

Delehaye, Hippolytus, ed. "La Pèlerinage de Laurent de Paszthou au Purgatoire de S. Patrice." *Analecta Bollandiana* 27 (1908): 35-60.

Frati, Ludovico, ed. "Il Purgatorio di S. Patrizio secondo Stefano di Bourbon e Umberto di Roma." *Giornale Storico della Letteratura Italiana* 8 (1886): 140-79.

—. "Tradizioni Storiche del Purgatorio di San Patrizio." *Giornale storico della Letteratura Italiana* 17 (1891): 46-79.

Jeanroy, A., and A. Vignaux. *Voyage au purgatoire de S. Patrice; Visions de Tindal et de S. Paul; textes languedociens du quinzième siècle.* Bibliothèque méridonale, ser. 1, vol. 8. Toulouse: E. Privat, 1903; reprint, New York, 1971.

Krapp, G.P. *The Legend of Saint Patrick's Purgatory, Its Later Literary History.* Baltimore: John Murphy, 1900.

Leslie, Shane, ed. *Saint Patrick's Purgatory: A Record from History and Literature.* London: Burns, Oates & Washbourne, 1932.

Mall, E., ed. "Zur Geschichte der Legende vom Purgatorium des heil Patricius." *Romanische Forschungen* 6 (1881): 139-97.

Messingham, Thomas, ed. *Tractatus de purgatorio sancti Patricii.* PL 180, cols. 973-1004.

Mörner, Marianne, ed. *Le Purgatoire de Saint Patrice par Berol.* Lund: P. Lindstedd, 1917.

Roger of Wendover. *Chronica, sive Flores historiarum.* Edited by Henry O. Coxe. 3 vols. London: English Historical Society, 1841 (2: 256-71).

Roger of Wendover. *Chronicle/Flowers of History.* Edited by J.A. Gilles. 2 vols. London: Bohn, 1849 (1: 510-22).

van der Zanden, C.M., ed. *Étude sur le purgatoire de Saint Patrice, accompagnée du texte latin d'Utrecht et du texte anglo-normand de Cambridge.* Amsterdam: H.J. Paris, 1927.

Vincent of Beauvais. *Bibliotheca mundi seu Speculi maioris.* Vol. 4 *(Speculum historiale)*: 789. Douay: B. Belleri, 1624.

Warnke, K., ed. *Das Buch vom Espurgatoire S. Patrice der Marie de France und seine Quelle.* Halle/Saale: M. Niemeyer, 1938.

TUNDALE'S VISION

Tundale's Vision was written in 1149 by an Irish monk who had travelled to Regensburg in Bavaria. This work was enormously popular in the Middle Ages and was translated into at least thirteen different languages. The translation presented here is from the Latin edition by Wagner listed below.

Tundale was an Irish knight, and more than any other visionary here was almost surely on the road to hell. Most of our other visionaries have been good laymen or religious with, perhaps, one or two faults. Tundale, is however, a true sinner.

Tundale is struck dead, but a little warmth on his left side prevents his friends from burying him. In the meantime his soul is met by his own guardian angel who leads Tundale on a tour of hell and heaven.

Tundale, like the knight Owen, is severely punished as he journeys through a hell that is strictly divided into punishments for particular sins. These are mentioned in sequence, beginning with murder. This description of hell is the most fully and consistently developed one before the *Inferno* of Dante. In hell many of the usual features are present, like pits of fire, mountains of fire and ice, valleys of fire, narrow bridges, furnaces and ovens, a horrible beast who tortures fornicators, the forge of Vulcan and finally the pit of hell. There is also a beast belching flames and consuming the souls of the damned. All the souls tortured in the upper regions of hell, that is, not in the pit of hell, are not yet finally judged, so the greater part of this hell of Tundale actually serves as a place of purgation, although not actually called a purgatory. As in Dante's later *Comedy* Lucifer is given a full and careful description. After hell, Tundale then proceeds on a gradually rising path visiting better and still better souls in fields and pavilions, then over walls of precious stones and metals and finally through gates.

Throughout this vision the angel guide and Tundale maintain an important discussion on the nature of divine mercy and justice, a running dialog that prefigures that between Dante and Virgil. This replaces the discussion in many of the other visions of holier men, which are generally about the need for Masses, prayers and alms for the dead. Here we are concerned with the salvation of this individual soul, who has come so close to perdition, rather than with the extra things that the living can do for those already dead.

As in the *Divine Comedy,* Tundale meets many whom he recognizes. Particularly, as he approaches heaven, he meets some important people who were known to him in life, such as various kings and bishops.

Primary Sources

Friedel, V.-H. and Kuno Meyer, ed. *La Vision de Tondale, textes français, anglo-normand et irlandais.* Paris: H. Champion, 1907.

Gardiner, Eileen, ed. "An Edition of the Middle English 'Vision of Tundale.'" Ph.D. Dissertation: Fordham University, 1980.

Mearns, Rodney, ed. *The Vision of Tundale, edited from B.L. MS Cotton Caligula A II.* Middle English Texts 18. Heidelberg: Carl Winter, 1985.

Palmer, Nigel F., ed. *Visio Tnugdali: The German and Dutch Translations and Their Circulation in the Later Middle Ages.* Munich and Zurich: Artemis, 1982.

Turnbull, W.B.D.D., ed. *The Visions of Tundale.* Edinburgh: Thomas G. Stevenson, 1843.

Vincent of Beauvais. *Bibliotheca mundi seu Speculi maioris.* Vol. 4 *(Speculum historiale):* 1127-33. Douay: B. Belleri, 1624.

Wagner, Albrecht, ed. *Visio Tnugdali lateinisch und altdeutsch.* Erlangen: Andreas Deichert, 1882.

THE MONK OF EVESHAM'S VISION

This vision is dated 1196. The work was written in 1197 by Adam, the brother of Edmund our monk, who is never

mentioned by name. Our text is based on the translation
in the Gilles edition of Roger of Wendover's *Chronicle*

A very sick monk, who believes he is about to die, is
the visionary in this work set in England about ten miles
southwest of Stratford-on-Avon. Here there was a rich
Benedictine abbey dating from the eighth century. The
monk asks to be shown the afterlife beforehand. On the
night before Good Friday his fellow-monks find him and
think he is dead. He begins to revive at midnight before
Easter, and afterward he is persuaded to tell of his vision.

The monk is guided by St. Nicholas, who has little to
say. The vision strongly promotes the idea of praying or
offering Masses for the dead to help them through their
own punishments.

The places of punishment include two plains and a hot
and cold mountain above a stinking body of water. The
sins and punishments are not matched for the reader
although sinners are punished according to their sins.
The work does mention that those punished most severely
are those most honored in life. Particularly singled out
are judges and prelates, but the worst of all punishments
are reserved for a certain sexual sin. The visionary says
that this sin is so awful he will not even mention it, and he
claims that he never knew of its existence before this
vision.

The visionary also singles out for attention a particular
lawyer who robbed his clients, neglected to repent before
dying, and now despairs of the mercy of God. The monk
meets some here whom he knows, including a goldsmith,
who has been granted assistance by St. Nicholas, although
those he knew on earth denied that he would obtain heaven. The monk is asked to pray for him after he returns.

The monk next sees the three places of glory,
including the Heavenly Jerusalem, and a vision of Christ
on the cross, before returning to life.

The visionary is not punished during his vision, but he
is asked to tell his vision when he returns and to request

the prayers of the living for the dead. The idea of working one's way through punishment toward reward is very prominent here, and there is no sense that any of the souls the monk meets are eternally damned.

Primary Sources

Arber, Edward, ed. *The Revelation to the Monk of Evesham.* Westminster: A. Constable, 1895, 1901.

Huber, Michael, ed. "Visio monachi de Eynsham." *Romanische Forschungen* 16 (1904): 641-733.

Paget, Valerian, trans. *Visio monachi de Eynsham.* New York: McBride, 1909.

Roger of Wendover. *Chronica, sive Flores historiarum.* Edited by Henry O. Coxe. 3 vols. London: English Historical Society, 1841 (3: 97-117).

Roger of Wendover. *Chronicle/Flowers of History.* Edited by J.A. Gilles. 2 vols. London: Bohn, 1849 (2: 148-64).

Salter, H.E., ed. *Visio monachi de Eynsham.* In *Eynsham Cartulary.* 2 vols. (Oxford Historical Society Publications, vols. 49 and 51.) Oxford: Oxford Historical Society, 1908 (2: 257-371).

Thurston, H., ed. "Visio monachi de Eynsham." *Analecta Bollandiana* 22: 225-319.

THURKILL'S VISION

This vision is dated October 1206 (All Souls' Week) by both authors, Ralph of Coggeshall and Roger of Wendover. Or text is based on the translation in Gilles's edition of Roger of Wendover's *Chronicle*.

Thurkill is a humble laborer in Essex, England. He is visited one evening by St. Julian, who takes him on an otherworld journey, leaving his body behind. Thurkill has only been guilty of not tithing correctly – for which his punishment is a whiff of the stench of a certain fire.

Unlike that of Tundale, for example, this vision is not particularly meant to save Thurkill's soul but to make him a witness on earth to the torments and rewards of the otherworld. Some of the devils actually reinforce this point by saying that they don't want Thurkill to see what goes on in their realm, because he will then warn those on earth and the devils will lose their followers.

The physical structure of the otherworld is particularly interesting in this vision, because heaven is constructed like a huge church and called the Congregation of the Saints where all are assembled after they die to wait for their assignments. During his vision Thurkill also meets St. James and St. Domninus. He sees St. Nicholas, Michael the Archangel, Peter and Paul and a devil riding one of the recently deceased nobles of England like a horse.

On the way to the mount of joy there is a purgatorial fire, a cold and salty lake, and a bridge with thorns and stakes. St. Nicholas presides over purgatory and, as in the *Monk of Evesham's Vision,* is responsible for helping the souls toward salvation. This is the only vision in this collection using scales to weigh souls to determine whether they merit reward or punishment. St. Paul and a devil weigh the souls, and each takes charge of those who tip the scale toward their side. The scale is such a popular image in medieval visual representations of the Last Judgment that it is interesting that it does not occur in more of these visions.

The place of punishment is quite unusual compared to what we have seen before. It is described as a theater. Those to be punished are arranged around on seats, which themselves inflict pain. The devils view a spectacle that involves the sinners re-enacting their sins and then being tortured fiercely by demons before being finally returned to their seats. The sinners who are singled out for punishment include a proud man, a priest who took goods from his people and did not perform his duties, a soldier who killed and robbed, a lawyer who took bribes, adulterers and adulteresses, slanderers, thieves, incendiaries and violators of religious places, and bad merchants.

Adam, who has not appeared in any other visions here, appears briefly in this vision as a symbol of the slowly evolving history of salvation.

When Thurkill returns to earth he is reluctant to tell the story of his vision until he is warned in another vision that the reason he was given the first vision was so that people would learn from it.

Primary Sources

Roger of Wendover. *Chronica, sive Flores historiarum.* Edited by Henry O. Coxe. 3 vols. London: English Historical Society, 1841 (3: 190-209).

Roger of Wendover. *Chronicle/Flowers of History.* Edited by J.A. Gilles. 2 vols. London: Bohn, 1849 (2: 221-35).

Schmidt, Paul Gerhard, ed. *Visio Thurkilli relatore, ut videtur, Radulpho de Coggesghall.* Leipzig: B.G. Teubner, 1978.

Ward, H.L.D., ed. "The Vision of Thurkill, Probably by Ralph of Coggeshall, Printed from a MS. in the British Museum." *The Journal of the British Archeological Association* 31 (1875): 420-59.

OTHER VISIONS

THE VISION OF ADAMNAN.
Adamnán of Iona d. 704. Written in Celtic. Part II of Vision dates from early tenth century; Part I from eleventh century.

Windisch, Ernst, ed. "Fis Adamnán." *Irische Texte*
1(1880): 165-96.
Boswell, C.S. *An Irish Precursor of Dante.* London: D.
Nutt, 1908; reprint, New York: 1972.

THE VISION OF ALBERIC
Alberic of Settefrati b. c. 1100; vision at 10; monk at
Monte Cassino under Gerard (1111-23); vision told to
Guido who is the first to write it down; under Abbot
Senioretto Peter the Deacon helps Alberic to rewrite his
vision (1127-37).
Bibliotheca Casinensis 5, 1 (1894): 191-206.
Cancellieri, Francesco, ed. and trans. *Osservazioni
intorno alla questione promossa dal Vannozzi del
Mazzochi dal Botari especialmente dal P. Abate D.
Giuseppe Giustino di Costanzo sopra l'originalità della
Divina Commedia di Dante, appoggiata alla storia della
Visione del Monaco Casinese Alberic.* Rome: Presso F.
Bourlie, 1814.
Inguanez, Mauro, ed. "La Visione di Alberico."
Introduction by Antonio Mirra. *Miscellanea Cassinense*
11 (1931-2): 33-103.
Peter the Deacon. *Chronica monasterii Casinensis.*
Edited by W. Wattenbach. MGH, Scriptores G., 7: 793-
94.

THE VISION OF ANSELLUS SCHOLASTICUS
Ansellus of Rheims, written in verse by order of Odo of
Fleury, late tenth century.

THE VISION OF SAINT ANSGAR
St. Ansgar of Bremen, 801-865, written by Rimbertus
(and others) in the late ninth century.
Dahlmann, C.F., ed. *Vita Sancti Anskarii a Rimberto et
alio discipulo Anskarii conscripta.* MGH, Scriptores G.,
2: 690-92.

THE VISION OF BALDARIUS
Written in Latin by Valerio of Bierzo (fl. 675-95).
Valerio of Bierzo. *Sancti Valerii Abbatis opuscula.* PL 87, cols. 435-36.

THE VISION OF BARONTUS
Dates from end of eighth century.
De SS. Baronto et Desiderio ememetis. AS 3, March 16, pp. 567-74.
Visio Baronti Monachi Longoretensis. MGH, Scriptores M., 5: 368-94.

THE VISION OF BERNOLDUS.
Attributed to Hincmar of Rheims (806-882).
PL 125, cols. 1115-19.
MGH, Poetae C., 2: 268 ff.

THE VISION OF BONELLUS
Written in Latin by Valerio of Bierzo (fl. 675-95).
Valerio of Bierzo. *Sancti Valerii Abbatis opuscula.* PL 87, cols. 433-35.

THE VISION OF THE BOY WILLIAM
Dated 1146 according to its author, Vincent of Beauvais (d. 1264).
Vincent of Beauvais. *Bibliotheca mundi seu Speculi maioris.* Vol. 4 *(Speculum historiale)*: 1146. Douay: B. Belleri, 1624.

THE VOYAGE OF BRAN
See ST. BRENDAN'S VOYAGE above for the place of the *imram* in the otherworld vision tradition.
Meyer, Kuno , ed. and trans. *The Voyage of Bran Son of Febal to the Land of the Living.* With an essay on "The Irish Vision of the Happy Otherworld and the Celtic Doctrine of Rebirth" by Alfred Nutt. 2 vols. London: D. Nutt, 1895, 1897.

Notes

THE VISION OF AN ENGLISH MAN
Written by Vincent of Beauvais (d. 1264), and dated by
him 941. See THE VISION OF DRYTHELM.
Vincent of Beauvais. *Bibliotheca mundi seu Speculi
maioris.* Vol. 4 *(Speculum historiale)*: 941. Douay: B.
Belleri, 1624.

THE VISION OF AN ENGLISH NOVICE
Written by Vincent of Beauvais (d. 1264).
Vincent of Beauvais. *Bibliotheca mundi seu Speculi
maioris.* Vol. 2 *(Speculum morale)*: 739. Douay: B.
Belleri, 1624.

THE VISION OF AN ENGLISH PRIEST
Written by Prudentius of Troyes (835-61).
Prudentius of Troyes. *Annales Bertiniani.* MGH,
Scriptores G., 1: 433.

THE VISION OF GOTTSCHALK
Dated 1190.
Leibniz, G.W., ed. In *Scriptores Rerum Brunsvicensium.*
1 (1707): 870-75.
Usener, R., ed. In *Quellensammlung für schleswig-
holsteinisch-lauenburgische Geschichte* 4 (1875): 75 ff.

THE VISION OF GUNTHELM
Dated 1161 by Helinand.
Constable, Gilles, ed. "The Vision of a Cistercian
Novice." *Studia Anselmiana* 40 (1956): 96-98.
Constable, Gilles, ed. "The Vision of Gunthelm and
Other Visions Attributed to Peter the Venerable."
Revue Bénédictine 66 (1956): 105-113.
Helinand de Froidmont. *Chronicon.* PL 212, cols. 1060-
63.
Vincent of Beauvais. *Bibliotheca mundi seu Speculi
maioris.* Vol. 4 *(Speculum historiale)*: 1187. Douay: B.
Belleri, 1624. "Vision of a Cistercian Novice."

THE VISION OF HERIGER
Eleventh-century poetic satire of otherworld visions.

THE VISION OF LAISRÉN
Early tenth century.
Meyer, Kuno, ed. and trans. In *Otia Merseiana* 1 (1899): 113-19.

THE VISION OF LAZARUS
Fifteenth-century work.
Voigt, Max. *Beiträge zur Geschichte der Visionen- literatur im Mittelalter.* Leipzig: Mayer & Müller, 1924; reprint, New York, 1967 (pp. 8-13).

THE VISION OF LEOFRIC
Leofric, Earl of Mercia, d. 1057; vision dates from late eleventh century.
Napier, A.S., ed. "An Old English Vision of Leofric, Earl of Mercia." *Transactions of the Philological Society* 1907-1910, ii (1909): 180-87.

THE VISION OF LOUIS OF FRANCE
Voigt, Max. *Beiträge zur Geschichte der Visionen- literatur im Mittelalter.* Leipzig: Mayer & Müller, 1924; reprint, New York, 1967 (pp. 226-45).

THE VISION OF MAXIMUS
Written in Latin by Valerio of Bierzo (fl. 675-95).
Valerio of Bierzo. *Sancti Valerii Abbatis opuscula.* PL 87, cols. 431-33.

THE VISION OF THE MONK OF MELROSE
Dated 1160, see DRYTHELM'S VISION above.
Helinand de Froidmont. *Chronicon.* PL 212, cols. 1059- 60.

THE VISIONS OF A MONK OF SAVIGNY
Edited by E.P. Sauvage. In *Analecta Bollandiana* 2 (1883): 505-8.

THE VISION OF THE MONK OF WENLOCK
From a letter (716 CE) from St. Boniface to Abbess Eadburga.

THE VISION OF OLAV ASTESON
Dated early thirteenth century.

THE VISION OF ORM
Orm d. 1126; vision in November 1125; written by Sigar of Newbald c. 1126.
Farmer, H., ed. In *Analecta Bollandiana* 75 (1957): 72-82.

THE VISION OF A POOR WOMAN
Early ninth century.
Wattenbach, Wilhelm and Wilhelm Levinson, ed. *Visio cuiusdam pauperculae muleris.* Deutschlands Geschichtsquellen im Mittelalter, 5 vols., 1: 260-61; reprint, by Heinz Lowe in *DGQM Vorzeit und Karolinger* 3: 317-18. Weimar, 1957.

THE VISION OF RADUIN
835 CE.
Holder-Egger, O., ed. In *Neues Archiv des Gesellschaft für ältere deutsche Geschichtekunde* 11 (1886): 262-63.

THE VISION OF ROTCHARIUS
Early ninth century.
Wettenbach, W., ed. In *Anzeiger für Kunde der deutschen Vorzeit,* Neue Folge, 22 (1875): 72-74.

THE VISION OF SALVIUS
Written in Latin in 590 by Gregory of Tours.

Gregory of Tours. *Historiae Francorum libri decem.* Edited by Rudolf Buchner. Berlin: Rutten & Loening, 1957 (2: 89-94).
Gregory of Tours. *History of the Franks.* Translated by O.M. Dalton. 2 vols. Oxford: Clarendon, 1927.

THE VISION OF SUNNIULF
Written in Latin in 575 by Gregory of Tours.
Gregory of Tours. *Historiae Francorum libri decem.* Edited by Rudolf Buchner. Berlin: Rutten & Loening, 1957 (1: 240).
Gregory of Tours. *History of the Franks.* Translated by O.M. Dalton. 2 vols. Oxford: Clarendon, 1927.

APOCALYPSE OF THE VIRGIN
See ST. PAUL'S APOCALYPSE.

THE VISION OF WALKELIN
Marjorie Chibnall, ed. and trans. *The Ecclesiastical History of Odericus Vitalis.* Oxford: Clarendon Press, 1973 (4: 236-50).

THE VISION OF WILLIAM STAUNTON
Dated 1406; see ST. PATRICK'S PURGATORY above.
Krapp, G.P. *The Legend of Saint Patrick's Purgatory, Its Later Literary History.* Baltimore: John Murphy, 1900 (pp. 54-77).

GLOSSARY

ABEL: Second son of Adam and Eve, slain by his brother Cain; prefigures Christ in his sacrifice.

ABRAHAM: Hebrew figure; patriarch of the Jews, father of ISAAC and Ishmael.

ACHERON: One of the five rivers in Hades, the river of woe across which Charon ferried the dead. In *Tundale's Vision* this name is applied to a beast, possibly intending Charon.

ACHEROUSIA: Acherusa in Greek; a lake, as in the *Apocalypse of Moses,* where Adam is washed.

ADAM: The first man, created by God in the Book of Genesis.

ADFERT-BRENDAN: Site of Brendan's monastery in the west of Ireland, northwest of Tralee.

ALDFRITH: King of the Northumbrians, 685-704, a patron of literature and responsible for the flourishing of scholarship in that northern province.

ALL SAINTS' DAY: Feast, which is celebrated on November 1, commemorating all of the Christian saints.

AMOS: Minor Hebrew prophet of the 8th century BCE.

ANCHORITE: A hermit who withdraws into an isolated region to lead a more spiritual life.

ANNAS: The priest who turns Jesus over to Caiphas, his son-in-law, who in turn hands him over to Pilate.

ANTIPHON: Verse or sentence from Scripture that serves to introduce, often to express, the thought of the psalm that followed. The antiphon is repeated after the psalm.

ARMAGH: A city in northern Ireland, which was considered Ireland's religious center; from 1152 it was one of the four metropolitan sees of Ireland.

ASSUMPTION: The feast commemorating the raising of the Virgin Mary's soul into heaven after her death; celebrated August 15.

BAPTISM: The sacrament of the Christian churches by which one enters the community.

BARINTHUS: Abbot of Drumcellen; religious confident and kinsman of St. Brendan; d. 548 or 552 CE.

BOOK OF JUDGES: The seventh book of the Hebrew Bible.

CAIPHAS: The high-priest who hands Jesus over to Pilate.

CASHEL: Town in Tipperary county, Ireland; a religious center of Ireland.

CELESTINE: Bishop of Armagh in Ireland.

CHARLES THE FAT: Charles III, Frankish king and emperor, youngest son of Louis the German. King of Swabia and Italy, crowned emperor in 881, king of east Franks 882, and west Franks 884, thereby reuniting most of the Carolingian Empire. Called "incompetent and weak, perhaps epileptic as well." Fought unsuccessful campaigns against the Saracens in Italy and in 886 bought off the Vikings who were attacking Paris. This last act led the East Franks to repudiate his authority (887) and swear allegiance to Arnulf, his nephew. Charles died in 888.

CLOYNE: Bishopric in southwest Ireland.

CNOBHERESBURG: Burgh Castle near Yarmouth.

COMMUNION: See EUCHARIST.

COMPLINE: The last liturgical hour of the day, at nightfall.

CORK: Town on south coast of Ireland; site of 6th century monastery.

CORMACH: Cormac Mac Cuilennáin, bishop of Cashel and from 902 king of Munster; d. 908.

CYNEGIUS: Maternus Cynegius, consul of Rome with Theodosius Augustus II, 388 CE.

DAVID: One of the greatest figures of Hebrew history and literature; king of Judah and Israel, 1013?-973 BCE.

DAY OF RESURRECTION: Also known as the Last Judgment, when the bodies of all men and women rise from the dead, are reunited with their souls and judged by God for eternity; the Last Day.

DAY OF THE PREPARATION: The day before the Sabbath or other festival in Jewish observance. Here especially the day before the Passover or Holy Thursday's Last Supper. A moveable feast.

DELILAH: Hebrew Bible figure; Philistine woman who lured SAMSON into capture by the Philistines.

DIALOGS OF GREGORY: Written in 593-594 CE by Pope Gregory the Great; there are four books mainly devoted to the holy men of Italy and their miracles, especially St. Benedict. The last book seeks to prove the immortality of the soul and the doctrine of purgatory.

DIONYSIUS: Probably St. Denis of Paris, bishop and martyr, d. 258 CE. Popularly regarded as the patron saint of France.

DIVINE OFFICE: The psalms, hymns, scriptural readings, as well as excerpts from patristic and hagiographic literature read by people in religious orders at specific times of the day and night.

EASTER: The feast commemorating the resurrection of Christ's body and soul on the Sunday after his death on the preceding Friday. A moveable feast.

ELIAS: Hebrew prophet of the 9th century BCE.

ELYSIUM: Isles of the Blest, Blessed Isles, heaven, paradise.

ENOCH: The seventh patriarch after creation; the apocalyptic Book of Enoch (c. 110 BCE) is attributed to him; this work is a vision of heaven and hell that was well-known in early Christianity.

EOGHAN: Son of KING NIAL.

EPIPHANY: The feast celebrating the visit of the three kings or wise men to Bethlehem shortly after the birth of Jesus. January 6.

ESSEX: County in southeast England.

EUCHARIST: Also known as Communion or Viaticum, a sacrament in which the participants receive the body and blood of Christ in the form of bread and often wine.

EUPHRATES: River in southwest Asia; birthplace of Babylonian, Assyrian and Chaldean civilizations; long believed in Judeo-Christian tradition to be one of the rivers of paradise.

EVESHAM: Borough in west-central England.

EZEKIEL: One of the major Hebrew prophets; fl. 6th century BCE.

GEON: Or Gihon; one of the four rivers of paradise; identified with the Nile.

GOLIAH: The Philistine giant of Goth killed by David with a sling.

GOMORRAH: City in the plain of Jordan, ancient Palestine, notorious for its wickedness and destroyed with SODOM; site unknown, possibly under Dead Sea.

HEROD: Our text refers to the Herod responsible for the slaughter of the Innocents, referred to in the Gospel of Matthew merely as King Herod; probably Herod the Great, king of Judea 37-34 BCE.

HILARY OF ANIANE: Probably St. Hilary of Poitiers, bishop and theologian; b. c. 315 CE, d. c. 367.

HOLY LAND: The area of the Middle East comprising Palestine and Israel.

HOLY SCRIPTURES: The Bible, encompassing the Old Testament or Hebrew Bible and the New Testament.

HOUSE OF ISRAEL: The descendents of JACOB; his twelve sons became the leaders of the twelve tribes of Israel.

ISAAC: Hebrew figure; son of ABRAHAM and Sarah, father of JACOB and Esau.

ISAIAH: One of the major Hebrew figures, a prophet, c. 740-701 BCE.

JACOB: Hebrew figure; grandson of ABRAHAM and son of ISAAC.

JASCONIUS: Sea monster associated with Fraken of northern mythology and Midgardsworm of Germanic mythology.

JEREMIAH: Major Hebrew prophet, 650-585 BCE.

JERUSALEM: City of Israel, capital of Judea; holy city of Jews, Christians and Muslims; also called City of David.

JOB: Hebrew patriarch; renowned for his afflictions and patience.

JONAH: According to the Hebrew Bible, a Hebrew prophet who disobeyed God's command and was swallowed by a large fish in whose belly he remained for three days.

JORDAN RIVER: In southwest Asia; rises in Syria and flows south to the northern end of the Dead Sea.

JUDAS: Iscariot, one of the original twelve apostles; he betrayed Jesus and afterward committed suicide.

KING NIAL: D. 405; king of Ireland who fought against rulers in Ireland, Britain and Gaul.

KING STEPHEN: Stephen of Boulogne, king of England 1135-54.

LAKE ARCHERUSA: See ACHEROUSIA.

LAND OF PROMISE: Found in *St. Paul's Apocalypse* and in *St. Brendan's Voyage;* originally, as predicted in Revelations, a part of the afterworld where Christ will reign with the saints for a thousand years before the final establishment of the Kingdom.

LAST JUDGMENT: The judgment of each individual man and woman by God at the end of the world to determine whether he or she will enter heaven or hell.

LAST SUPPER: The Passover meal celebrated by Christ with his Apostles and possibly others on the Thursday preceding Good Friday, the day of his crucifixion. A moveable feast.

LENT: A forty-day period extending from Ash Wednesday to the eve of Easter Sunday during which

Christians were required to observe regulations concerning fasting and abstinence.

LEVIATHAN: Frequently mentioned in Hebrew poetry, meaning a enormous aquatic animal, real or imaginary; also the enemy of God, Satan.

LONDON: City in southeast England on the Thames river, the major city of England.

LOT: Figure from the Hebrew Bible; ABRAHAM's nephew who escaped the destruction of SODOM, although his wife was turned into a pillar of salt.

LOTHAIRE: Lothair I, Holy Roman emperor 840-55, son of Louis the Pious, uncle of Charles the Fat.

LOUIS: Father of Charles the Fat, known as Louis the German, king of the East Franks 843-76, son of Louis the Pious.

LOUIS: Son of Lothaire, Holy Roman emperor 850-75.

LOW SUNDAY: The first Sunday after Easter. A moveable feast.

LUCIFER: Latin for "light bearer," name of the leader of the fallen angels. See also SATAN.

LYONS: City on the middle Rhône, a major Roman capital, which became a bishop's seat in the 2nd century CE.

MALACHY: D. 1148; Archbishop of Armagh (1132); served as papal legate for Ireland and was responsible for introducing Roman liturgy to the island; in 1139 visited Clairvaux and St. Bernard.

MARTIN: Probably St. Martin of Tours, bishop, b. 315 CE, d. 397.

MASS: The Eucharistic rite of the Christian church. See also EUCHARIST.

MATINS: The divine office recited during the morning hours; practice varies as to the hour - anywhere between midnight and dawn.

MELROSE: City of southeast Scotland, the site of a Cistercian abbey.

MICAH: Minor Hebrew prophet of 8th century BCE.

MICHAEL: The Archangel, mentioned in the Hebrew Bible and the *Apocrypha.*

MOSES: Hebrew prophet and lawgiver who led the Israelites from Egypt (c. 1200 BCE?).

MOUNT OF JOY: Probably derived from *Mons gaudii* in Jerusalem. There is also a *Mons gaudii* at Compostella where the Church of the Holy Cross is built.

MOUNT OF OLIVES: A ridge that runs north/south on the east side of the city of Jerusalem, above the Garden of Gethsemane.

MOUNT SINAI: In the southern Sinai peninsula; thought to be the same as the biblical Mt. Herob, where Moses received the tablets of the Ten Commandments from God.

MUNSTER: Large Irish province; one of the traditional "Fifths" of Ireland; included all southwest Ireland.

NEMENIAH: Bishop of Cloyne in southwest Ireland, d. 1149.

NEW COMMANDMENT: The rite of the EUCHARIST.

NONES: The liturgical hour occurring at the ninth hour of the day. Originally at 3 PM, but later shifted earlier, hence our noon. Also the ninth day of the month.

NORICI: From Noricum, an ancient country and Roman province south of the Danube and extending from Austria to Bavaria.

ORKNEYS: Some 90 islands off the north coast of Scotland, claimed in 875 for Norway.

PENTECOST: The feast commemorating the descent of the Holy Spirit on the disciples of Christ on the Sunday fifty days after Easter. A moveable feast.

PHISON: Or Pison; one of the four rivers of paradise; associated with either the Indus or Ganges, or sometimes the Danube.

PILATE: Pontius Pilate; procurator of Judea under the Emperor Tiberius in first half of 1st century CE; in this capacity he tried and condemned Jesus Christ.

POPE INNOCENT II: One of the most important medieval popes; reigned from 1130-43 during the schism that was resolved by the Second Lateran Council.

PURIFICATION OF THE BLESSED VIRGIN: The feast commemorating the symbolic purification of Mary forty days after the birth of Jesus, as required by the law of Moses. February 2.

SAMSON: One of the Hebrew judges, of prodigious strength, who performed heroic deeds against the Philistines but was finally captured by them through the machinations of his paramour, DELILAH.

SATAN: In Judeo-Christian tradition, as well as in Islam, the supreme embodiment of evil. He is called the devil, Lucifer, the prince of angels whom God drove out of heaven because of his pride.

SEPULCHER OF OUR LORD: In Jerusalem, in Church of the Holy Sepulcher; burial place of Christ from Good Friday until his resurrection on Easter Sunday; the most important pilgrimage site in the Christian church.

SEXT: The liturgical hour occurring at the ninth hour of the day; afternoon.

SIGEBERT: King of East Anglia, d. 635.

SION: East part of the city of Jerusalem; site of the Temple and the center of Jewish spiritual life; a metaphor for heaven. Mount Zion.

SODOM: City in the plain of Jordan, ancient Palestine, notorious for its wickedness and destroyed with GOMORRAH; site unknown, possibly under the Dead Sea.

SOLOMON: King of Israel c. 973-933 BCE; son of DAVID and Bathsheba; builder of Solomon's Temple; renowned for his wisdom and mystical poetry.

ST. AILBE: Died c. 526. Irish preacher who was an effective missionary. He may have received a grant of the Aran Islands from King Aengus of Munster for ST. ENDA. Reputed to be first bishop of Emly and the author of a monastic rule.

ST. BRENDAN: C. 486-578; Irish abbot, founder of monastery of Clonfert in Galway c. 560.

ST. CATHERINE: D. c. 310 CE; venerated in the East since the 10th century; unreliable legend has her born in Alexandria, Egypt of a patrician family. She converts to Christianity after a vision and is responsible for numerous conversions that enrage the Emperor Maxentius. He eventually has her beheaded after a failed attempt to put her to death on the famous "Catherine Wheel." Patroness of philosophers, maidens and preachers.

ST. DOMNINUS: Probably St. Dominic, who died in 1109 and gave his name to the town of Santo Domingo de la Calzada near Compostella.

ST. ENDA: Died c. 530. Considered the co-founder with St. Francis of Clonard of monasticism in Ireland. A warrior who became a monk, went on pilgrimage to Rome and returned to Ireland to build churches, most notably the monastery of Killeaney on Aran Island.

ST. JAMES: Either the disciple of Jesus (d. 42 CE), who is the same as Santiago de Compostela; or James the Apostle (d. 62), son of Alpheus and the head of the primitive church in Jerusalem.

ST. JUDE: Also known as Thaddeus and one of the original twelve apostles; martyred with St. Simon in Persia.

ST. JULIAN: The Hospitaler; apparently fictitious saint who is the patron of hotel-keepers, travellers and boat people; a noble who unwittingly slew his parents and to atone for his sin became an innkeeper for travellers.

ST. LAWRENCE: D. 258 CE; martyr in Rome who was grilled during the Emperor Valerian's persecution of the Christians; his death led to widespread conversion and devotion in Rome.

ST. MARGARET: An untrustworthy legend surrounds this immensely popular saint who apparently converted to Christianity and was martyred, inspiring the conversion of many; the story of her imprisonment and torture would fit very well among these scenes of hell.

ST. MARY: The virgin mother of Jesus; born without original sin and assumed into heaven at her death.

ST. NICHOLAS: Of Bari, d. c. 350 CE; a great legend has grown up around this figure who is associated with Christmas as Santa Claus; he is the patron of children and associated with goldsmiths.

ST. OSITH: Queen of the East Saxons in the 7th century, wife of Sighere; she founded a convent at Chich.

ST. PATRICK: C. 385-c. 461; patron saint of Ireland who was responsible for the spreading Christianity throughout that country.

ST. PAUL: D. 67 CE; apostle of the Gentiles; beheaded in Rome at Tre Fontane.

ST. PETER: D. 64 CE; leader of the apostles and first pope; crucified upside down at Rome near the site of the present-day Vatican.

ST. REMIGIUS: C. 437-530 CE; also known as Remi; born at Laon, son of Count Emilius and St. Celina; converted Clovis, pagan king of Gaul, and his followers in 496; known as the Apostle of the Franks.

ST. RUADANUS: D. c. 584 CE; disciple of St. Finian of Clonard; founding abbot of Lothra Monastery in Tipperary; considered one of the twelve apostles of Ireland.

ST. SEBASTIAN: D. c. 288 CE; his life is surrounded by untrustworthy legend; he was, however, a martyr who was buried on the Appian way outside Rome; patron of archers, athletes and soldiers, protector against plague.

ST. SIMON: D. c. 107 CE; apparently a first cousin of Christ; successor to James as bishop of Jerusalem; crucified when he was well over 100 during the persecution under Trajan.

ST. VALENTINE: D. c. 269 CE; a priest and physician in Rome where he was beheaded under Claudius the Goth and buried on the Flaminian Way on February 14.

SWABIA: Duchy located east of the upper Rhine in southwestern Germany.

TARSUS: Town in what is now southeast Turkey, birthplace of St. Paul.

TARTARUS: the lowest regions of hell, where the most wicked of humanity are punished.

TATIROKOS: Tartaruchus, keeper of hell.

TEMLAKOS: A care-taking angel.

TERCE: The liturgical hour occurring at the third hour of the day; morning.

THEODOSIUS AUGUSTUS THE YOUNGER: Theodosius Augustus II, Consul of Rome with Maternus Cynegius in 388 CE.

TIDSTUDE: Found in Roger of Wedover's *Chronicle* as a corruption of Stidstede, in Essex, three miles northeast of Braintree.

TIGRIS: River in southeast Turkey and Iraq; long believed in Judeo-Christian tradition to be one of the rivers of paradise.

TUNSTED: A corruption of TIDSTUDE, see above.

TWEED: River in southeast Scotland and northeast England.

UPPER JERUSALEM: The Heavenly Jerusalem; a metaphor for heaven.

URIEL: An angel who served as a guide to ENOCH.

VESPERS: The last divine office of the day before compline, occurs between afternoon and an hour before sunset.

VIATICUM: See EUCHARIST.

VULCAN: The Roman name for the god of fire and metalworking; he established a forge in the heart of Mount Aetna.

ABBREVIATIONS

AS - *Acta Sanctorum.* Antwerp: Meusium, 1643-1931.
MGH, Poetae C. - *Monumenta Germaniae historiae: Poetae latini aevi Carolini.* Weimar: H. Böhlaus Nachfolger, 1880-1951.
MGH, Poetae M.E. - *Monumenta Germaniae historiae: Poetae latini medii aevi.* Leipzig: K.W. Hiersemann, 1937-39.
MGH, Scriptores G. - *Monumenta Germaniae historiae: Scriptores rerum Germanicarum.* Hanover: Gesellschaft für ältere deutsche Geschichtskunde, 1826 - .
MGH, Scriptores M.- *Monumenta Germaniae historiae: Scriptores rerum Merovingicarum.* Hanover: Gesellschaft für ältere deutsche Geschichtskunde, 1884-1920.
PL - *Patrologiae cursus completus.* J.P. Migne, editor. Series prima (Latina). Vols. 1-221. Paris: J.P. Migne, 1844-65.

BIBLIOGRAPHY
Secondary Sources

Amat, Jacqueline. *Songes et visions: L'au-delà dans la littérature latine tardive*. Paris: Études Augustiniennes, 1985.

Bar, F. *Les routes de l'autre monde: Descentes aux infers et voyages dans l'au delà*. Paris: Presses universitaires de France, 1946.

Becker, Ernest J. *A Contribution to the Comparative Study of the Medieval Visions of Heaven and Hell*. Baltimore, MD: J. Murphy, 1899.

Boswell, Charles Stuart. *An Irish Precursor of Dante: A Study of the Vision of Heaven and Hell Ascribed to the Eighth Century Irish Saint Adamnán*. London: David Nutt, 1908.

Chiffoleau, Jacques. *La compatabilité de l'au delà: Les hommes, la morte et la religion dans la région de Avignon. (1320-1480)*. Rome: École Française de Rome, 1980.

Ciccarese, Maria Pia. *Visioni dell'Aldilà in Occidente*. Florence: Nardini Editore, 1987.

Dana, H.W.L. *Medieval Visions of the Other World*. Cambridge, MA: Harvard University Dissertation, 1910.

D'Ancona, Alessandro. *I precursori di Dante*. Florence: G. Sansoni, 1974.

Delepierre, Octave. *L'Enfer: Essai philosophique et historique sur les légendes de la vie future*. London: Truebner, 1876.

Fritzsche, C. "Die lateinischen Visionen des Mittelalters bis zur Mitte des 12. Jahrhunderts" in *Romanische Forschungen* 2 (1886): 247-79; 3 (1887): 337-69.

Himmelfarb, Martha. *Tours of Hell: An Apocalyptic Form in Jewish and Christian Literature.* Philadelphia: University of Pennsylvania Press, 1983.

Le Goff, Jacques. *The Birth of Purgatory.* Translated by Arthur Goldhammer. Chicago: Chicago University Press, 1984.

McDannell, Colleen and Bernhard Lang. *Heaven: A History.* New Haven, CT and London: Yale University Press, 1988.

Os, Arnold Barel van. *Religious Visions and the Development of Eschatological Elements in Medieval English Religious Literature.* Amsterdam: H. J. Paris, 1932.

Owen, D. R. R. *The Vision of Hell: Infernal Journeys in Medieval French Literature.* New York: Barnes & Noble, 1971.

Patch, Howard Rollin. *The Other World According to Descriptions in Medieval Literature.* Cambridge, MA: Harvard University Press, 1950.

Russell, Jeffrey Burton. *Lucifer: The Devil in the Middle Ages.* Ithaca, NY: Cornell University Press, 1984.

Seymour, St. John Drelincourt. *Irish Visions of the Otherworld: A Contribution to the Study of Medieval Visions.* New York: Macmillan, 1930.

Tabor, James D. *Things Unutterable: Paul's Ascent to Paradise.* Lanham MD: University Press of America, 1986.

Wright, Thomas. *St. Patrick's Purgatory: An Essay in the Legends of Purgatory, Hell and Paradise.* London: John Russell Smith, 1844.

Zaleski, Carol. *Otherworld Journeys: Accounts of Near-Death Experience in Medieval and Modern Times.* New York and Oxford: Oxford University Press, 1987.

INDEX

Aachen 245
Abel 234, 265
abortion 6-7, 41
Abraham 11, 32, 265, 268
Acheron 159-60, 265
Acherousia 10, 265
Adam 178, 234, 258, 265
Adamnán, Vision of 258
Adfert-Brendan 81, 265
adultery xvii, 15, 39, 40,
  179, 230-31, 258; see
  also fornication,
  promiscuity, and sexual
  sins
Alberic, Vision of 259
Aldfrith, king 62, 265
Alexander VI, pope 249
Alien xviii
Aliens, The xviii
All Saints' Day 235, 265
Amos 32, 265
Anania 69
anchorite 265; see also
  Island of Anchorites
Angels, Nine Orders of
  191-92
Anna, king 52
Annas 119, 265
*Ansellus Scholasticus,
  Vision of* 259
anvils 115
Apostles 66, 192, 237
Archangels 21, 24, 191
Armagh 149, 193, 266,
  270
Assumption 118, 266

avarice 71, 75; see also
  greed, rich people, and
  usury
Baldarius, Vision of 260
bandits 179; see also
  robbery and theft
Barontus, Vision of 260
Baptism 10, 53, 144, 266
Barinthus 81-84, 85, 266
Bavaria xiv, 252
Bede, The Venerable
  (*Ecclesiastical History of
  England*) xxviii (n.5),
  241-44; see also *Furseus'
  Vision* and *Drythelm's
  Vision*
bellows 115, 172, 178
Bernoldus, Vision of 260
blasphemy 6
Bonellus, Vision of 260
Book of Enoch, see Enoch
Book of Judges 75, 266
Book of Revelation, see
  Revelations
Bosch xxvii
Boy William, Vision of the
  260
*Bran the Blessed, Voyage
  of* 246, 260
bridge 48-49, 142-43, 157-
  58, 162-64, 168, 222-23,
  232, 251, 253, 257
brimstone 40, 41, 130-31,
  140, 142
Britain 57
Britons 149
Bruegel xxvii
Caiphas 119
Calvino, Italo (*Invisible
  Cities*) xi
Cashel 149
cauldron 104, 116, 119,
  141, 231-32
Celestine, bishop 193, 266
charity xvii, 42, 50

279

Charles the Fat's Vision
xvi, 129-33, 247-49, 250,
266, 270
Cherubim 21, 191
Christ, Crucifixion of 45;
false 1-2; Resurrection of
90, 94, 104, 197, 199;
Second Coming of 1;
Transfiguration of 11, 237
Christmas 101, 105, 112,
118
churches, defenders and
builders of xix, 190-91
*Cistercian Novice, Vision of
a* 261
City of Christ 30-35
clergy, punishment of xvii,
38, 59, 68-70, 72, 130,
167, 170-71, 179, 205,
228, 239, 257; reward of
49, 72, 143-44, 188-90,
213
Cloyne 193, 266, 271
Cnobheresburg 52, 266
Communion 110, 137,
151, 199, 266; see also
Eucharist and Viaticum
Conallus 160
Conchober 182-83
concubines 75
concupiscence 53-54; see
also sexual sins,
fornication, and adultery
Congregation of the Saints
221, 257
Constantinople 47
Cork 150, 266
Cormach, king 183-85,
266
covetousness 53, 242
cruelty, punishment for 40,
49, 225
Cuningham 57
Cynegius 13, 266, 275

Dante *(Divine Comedy)* xi,
xiii, xxvi-xxvii, 245, 248,
253, 254
David 34-35, 106, 267,
268, 269, 272
Day of Judgment 3-10, 24,
26, 61, 89, 212; see also
Last Judgment, Day of
Resurrection, and
Resurrection of the Dead
Day of Resurrection 20,
22, 267
Day of the Preparation 198,
202, 267
Delilah 75, 267, 272
Dialogs, see Gregory the
Great
Dionysius 73, 267
discord 53
disobedience 8, 9
dispair 37
Divine Comedy, see Dante
Divine Office 82, 88, 94,
99, 100, 115, 267
dogs 41, 87, 160, 166
Donachus 182-83
Drythelm's Vision 57-63,
242-44
Eadburga, abbess 263
East Anglia 51, 55, 242
Easter 90, 93-96, 104-5,
112, 118, 120, 123, 217,
267, 272
elders 21, 45
Elias 2, 11-12, 27, 237,
267
Elysium xviii, 10, 267
England 149, 225
English Man, Vision of an
242, 261
*English Novice, Vision of
an* 261
English Priest, Vision of an
261
Enoch xii, 2, 27, 239, 267

entertainers of strangers 33, 42
envy 33
Eoghan 81, 267
Epiphany 101, 118, 268
Essex 225, 268
Ethelwald 63
Eucharist xiv, 43, 268; see also Viaticum and Communion
Euphrates 31, 268
Evasa 47
Evesham 197, 268
extortion 71
Ezekiel 32, 268
Ezraël 6, 7, 9, 10
false witness 7
falsehood 53, 242
famine 68
fasting 31, 40, 85, 243, 246
Fergusus 160
fig tree, parable of 2
Finnbur Ua Alta 81
flowers xii, xviii, 10, 11, 48, 60-61, 82, 92, 109, 143, 146, 182, 190, 213, 234
forges xviii, 115-16, 172-73, 246
fornication xvii, 6, 7, 14-15, 23, 26, 30, 36, 38, 44, 165-67, 169-71, 253; see also sexual sins, adultery, and promiscuity
Fountain of Life 181-82
four beasts 45
Franks 129, 133, 266
fruit xviii, 2, 4, 11, 15, 24, 29-31, 40, 44, 82, 110-12, 125-26, 143, 190, 234
furnaces xviii, 8, 60, 116, 131, 175, 224, 231, 253
Furseus' Vision xx, xxi-xxii, 51-55, 241-42

gates in otherworld 12, 21, 26-34, 137, 143, 159, 165, 168, 176-77, 181, 182, 206, 215, 232, 234-35, 251-53
Gaul 76, 245
Gauls 149
gems xix, 82, 183, 187-88, 191, 234-35; see also precious stones and jewels
Geon 31, 268
Germany 76
Geroldus 77
Gervais, abbot of Louth 147
Gilbert 147
gluttony 75, 165-67
gold, in heaven 19, 26, 30, 34, 49, 72, 143-45, 183-84, 187-88, 190-91, 224, 235
Goliah 106, 268
Gomorrah 40, 268, 272
Gottschalk, Vision of 261
Gospel xxiii, 1, 10, 51, 242, 268
greed 158-61
Gregory of Tours *(History of the Franks)* xxviii (n.5), 263-64
Gregory the Great, *(Dialogs)* 47-50, 67, 240-41, 244, 267
Gunthelm, Vision of 261
hail 58, 108, 157, 206
hammers xviii, 115, 173, 228
Hariulf *(Chronicle)* xxviii (n.5), 247, 249
heathens 40
Heavenly Jerusalem xviii-xix; see also Upper Jerusalem and Jerusalem
Heito 244-45

Helinand de Froidmont
  (Chronicle) xxviii (n.5),
  243, 261, 262
Hemgils 62
herbs 11, 102, 107, 108,
  112, 143, 190, 234
Heriger, Vision of 262
Herod, king 32, 119, 268
Hincmar of Rheims 260
Hibernia 149
Hilary of Aniane 73, 268
Holy Ghost 86, 185
Holy Land 147, 251, 268
Holy Saturday 103, 124
Holy Trinity 100, 189
Homer xii
hooks, as instruments of
  torture 37, 139-40, 143,
  170, 227
horses, in otherworld 71,
  224-25, 228-29
House of Israel 2, 268
Hugh of Sawtry 249
humility 31
ice 40, 63, 157, 169-70,
  232, 253
idle talk 36
idolatry 5, 8
imram 246
incendaries 231
iniquity 53
Innocent, pope 193, 272
Innocents, the 32, 268
Invisible Cities, see
  Calvino, Italo
Ireland xiv, 51, 62, 135,
  136, 147, 149, 193, 249,
  251, 270, 271
Isaac 11, 32, 265, 268
Isaiah 32, 268
Island of Anchorites 101,
  108
Island of Delights 83, 126
Island of St. Ailbe 96-101,
  105, 112
Isle of the Strong Men 110

Island of the Three Choirs
  of Saints, see Island of the
  Anchorites
Italy 70
Jacob 11-12, 32, 268, 269
Jasconius 92, 96, 104,
  124, 269
Jeremiah 32, 269
Jerusalem xxiii, 13, 34, 94,
  109, 239, 269, 271, 272;
  see also Upper Jerusalem
jewels 34, 234; see also
  gems and precious stones
Job 32, 269
Jonah 106, 269
Jordan, river 159, 269
Judas 117-20, 246, 269
justice 167-68, 253
Lake Archerusa 30, 269
Land of Promise xxii, 28,
  82, 83, 85, 94, 105, 125-
  26, 246-47, 269
Laisrén, Vision of 262
Lamb, the Immaculate 90,
  104, 110
Last Judgment 1-10, 69,
  186, 257, 269; see also
  Day of Judgment, Day of
  Resurrection, and
  Resurrection of the Dead
Last Letters from Hav, see
  Morris, Jan
Last Supper 90, 96, 102,
  103, 104, 197, 201, 269
lawyers, punishment of
  211-12, 229-30, 255, 258
Lazarus, Vision of 262
Le Guin, Ursula xxvii
Lent 102, 201, 269
Leofric, Vision of 262
Lessing, Doris xxvii
Leviathan 118, 270
Limerick 249
Lindisfarne 63
London 219, 270
Lord's Prayer 219

Lot 32, 270
Lothaire 132-33, 270
Lough Derg 249
Louis, king 132-33, 266,
  270
Louis of France, Vision of
  262
Louis the Pious 245
Louth 147
Lucifer xvii, 93, 176, 177-
  80, 253, 270; see also
  Satan
Lyons 193, 270
Mandeville's Travels xi
Malachy 193-94, 270
Mannini, Antonio 249
married, reward of xix, 29,
  185-87
martyrs xix, 2-3, 73, 77,
  187-88, 192, 245
Mary 43, 105, 118, 199,
  221, 223, 274
Mass 91, 95, 99, 104, 113,
  114, 124, 137, 184, 199,
  235, 270; for the dead
  xxi, 61, 132, 145, 207,
  223, 233, 243, 245, 248,
  254, 255
Maximus, Vision of 262
meadow 48, 143
Melrose 57, 270
mercy 24, 167-68, 253
Mernoc 81, 84
Micah 32, 270
Michael the Archangel 21,
  30, 32, 33, 44, 45, 223,
  232-34, 239, 257, 271
monastic reform 75-76,
  245
Monk of Evesham's Vision
  xix, xxiii, 197-218, 254-
  56
*Monk of Melrose, Vision of
  the* 243, 262
*Monk of Savigny, Vision of
  a* 263

*Monk of Wenlock, Vision
  of the* 263
Morris, Jan *(Last Letters
  from Hav)* xi
Moses 11-12, 237, 273
Mount of Joy 222, 223,
  232
Mount of Olives 1, 271
Mount Sinai 101, 271
mountains 11, 12, 68-70,
  85, 117-18, 130, 141,
  145, 156-59, 165, 171,
  206, 222, 226
mouth of hell xvi, xvii, 42-
  44, 141-42, 145, 251,
  253
Munster 81, 271
murder xvii, 6, 14, 15, 25,
  155-56, 179
music xii, xviii, 186, 188-
  90, 217, 233, 251
mysticism xix-xx, xxiii,
  xxix (n.11)
Nemeniah 193, 271
New Commandment 84,
  98, 271
Nial, king 81, 267, 269
Norici 129, 271
Northumbrians 57
Odericus Vitalis 264
Odo of Fleury 259
Olav Asteson, Vision of
  263
original sin 144
Orkneys 149, 271
Orm, Vision of 263
Otloh of Emmeran *(Book of
  Visions)* 243
ovens 141, 165, 222
Paradise of Birds 91, 104,
  124
Patriarchs 61, 192
Paul the Spiritual 120-23
penitential literature xiii,
  xvi, xvii, xxviii (n.3)

Pentecost 89, 91, 95, 104, 105, 118, 124, 271
perjury 15
persecutors of the righteous, punishment of 7
Peter the Deacon 259
Phison 31, 271
Phristinus 165
Pilate 119, 271
pilgrimage 101, 105, 109, 126, 147, 158, 251
pilgrims 42, 69, 184, 186, 220
plague 48, 68, 77
plunder 135
Poor Woman, Vision of a 263
powerful, punishment of xvii, 71-72, 179-80, 205, 229-230; see also clergy
precious stones xix, 126, 132, 143, 183, 187, 191, 235, 251, 253
pride 31-32, 33, 46, 76, 131, 157-58, 179, 227-28
Principalities 23
promiscuity xvii, 9, 40; see also sexual sins, fornication, and adultery
prophets 32, 66, 192
Prudentius of Troyes 261
psalms 34, 35, 63, 67, 68, 109, 110, 145
Purification of the Blessed Virgin 105, 118, 272
Raduin, Vision of 263
Ralph of Coggeshall 256
Regensburg xiv, 252
Reichenau 244
Resurrection of the Dead 1; see also Last Judgment, Day of Resurrection, and Day of Judgment
Revelations xiii, xviii-xix, 238

rich people xvii, 8, 39; see also powerful, usury, and greed
Rimbertus 259
rivers, in otherworld xii, 5, 9, 28, 29, 30-41, 48-49, 57, 63, 68, 82-83, 125-26, 130-31, 141-43, 159, 251
robbery 71, 162-65; see also theft and bandits
Robinson Crusoe xi
Roger of Wendover *(Chronicle)* xxviii (n.5), 242, 243-44, 249, 255, 256, 258
Rome 70, 193
Romans, empire of the 129, 132, 133
Rothcarius, Vision of 263
sacrilege 162-63, 231, 258
Saffira 69
Salvius, Vision of 263
Samson 75, 272
Satan xvii, 11, 88, 177-80, 272; see also Lucifer
scales 224, 231, 257
Scandinavians 149
Scots 149
Scriptures 12, 34, 41, 175, 179, 268
Sepulcher of Our Lord 147, 272
Seraphim 191
Seven Seals 42
sexual sins, punishment of xvii, 50, 68, 71, 210, 255
Sigar of Newbald 263
Sigebert, king 51, 52, 272
silk 183, 184, 187, 188
Sion 52, 94, 109, 110, 216, 272
slander 7, 33, 37, 231, 258
snow 40, 43, 156-57, 206, 232
Sodom 40, 268, 272

sodomy xvii, 40, 74, 76, 244
soldiers, punishment of 228-29, 257; see also war
Solomon 174, 272
sorcery 9, 15, 39
Spain 47
Spaniards 149
spies, punishment of 156-57
St. Ailbe 96, 98, 272
St. Ansgar, Vision of 259
St. Benedict of Aniane 245
St. Boniface 263
St. Brendan 265, 273
St. Brendan's Seat 85
St. Brendan's Voyage xv, xxii, 81-127, 246-47, 250
St. Catherine 235, 273
St. Domninus 220, 223-26, 257, 273
St. Enda 85, 273
St. James 219, 220, 223, 257, 273
St. Jude 219, 273
St. Julian 219-35, 256, 273
St. Lawrence 202, 273
St. Margaret 235, 273
St. Martin 73, 270
St. Nicholas 201-17, 222, 255, 257, 274
St. Osith 235, 274
St. Patrick 98, 122, 135-36, 185, 193, 274
St. Patrick's Purgatory xv, xvi, xx, xxii, 135-48, 249-52, 264
St. Paul xv, xxiv, 13-46, 223-24, 257, 274
St. Paul's Apocalypse xxiv, 13-46, 237, 238-40
St. Peter xv, 1-12, 132-33, 223-24, 249, 257, 274; feast of 113
St. Peter's Apocalypse xv, 1-12, 237-38

St. Remigius 132-33, 249, 274
St. Ruadanus 192-93, 274
St. Sebastian 73, 274
St. Simon 219, 274
St. Valentine 73, 274
Stephen, king 135, 147, 250, 269
Stone Mountain 81
Stratford-on-Avon 255
sulphur 130, 141, 156-58, 160, 178, 205, 209, 232
Sunniulf, Vision of 264
Swabia 129, 248, 275
Tarsus xxiv, 13, 238, 275
Tartaruchus 24, 26, 275; see also Tatirokos
Tartarus 41, 275
Tatirokos 10; see also Tartaruchus
Temlakos 7, 277
Theodosius Augustus the Younger 13, 266, 275
theft 15, 71, 162-65, 179, 231, 258
Thurkill's Vision xx-xxi, xxiv, 219-36, 256-58
Tidstude 225, 275
Tigris 31, 275
tithing 220, 221-22, 256
tradesmen 46, 231, 258
traitors, punishment of 156-57
Tundale's Vision xiv-xvi, xviii, xx, xxii, xxiv, xxvi, 149-95, 247, 250, 252-54
Tunsted 219, 275
Tweed 57, 275
uncharitable, punishment of 8, 42
Upper Jerusalem 213, 255, 275; see also Jerusalem
Uriel 4, 5, 9, 275
usury 8, 39
Valerio of Bierzo 260, 262

vegetables 82, 102, 112, 251
Viaticum 79, 89, 208, 275; see also Communion and Eucharist
Vincent of Beauvais xxviii (n.5), 242, 252, 254, 260, 261
violators of religious places, see sacrilege
violence 26, 135
Virgil 253
Virgin, Apocalypse of 237, 264
virgins xix, 29, 74, 78, 187-89, 191-92, 245
virtuous, rewards of the 188-90
Vulcan 115-16, 172-73, 246, 253, 275
Walafrid of Strabo 244-45
Walkelin, Vision of 264
walls, in otherworld xix, 30, 33, 39, 60, 143, 181, 183, 185, 187, 191, 215-16, 220-27, 235, 253
war, punishment of those counseling for xvii, 130-32, 248, 250
Wetti's Vision xvii, xxi, xxiv, 65-79, 244-45
wheels, as instruments of torture 9, 140, 230-31
whirlwind 141, 251
whoremongers 39
William of Malmesbury *(History of the Kings of England)* xxviii (n.5), 247, 249
William Staunton, Vision of 264
wind, as instrument of torture 45, 69, 118, 142, 157, 181, 206
witchcraft 15
Zachariah 32

* * *

*This Book Was Completed on January 29, 1989
at Italica Press, New York, New York and Was
Set in Times Roman. It Was Printed on
50 lb Glatfelter Natural Paper with
a Smyth-Sewn Binding by
McNaughton & Gunn,
Ann Arbor, MI
U. S. A.*
* *
*